EARTH AND OTHER ETHICS

Other titles by Christopher D. Stone:

Should Trees Have Standing?–Towards Legal Rights for Natural Objects
Where the Law Ends: The Social Control of Corporate Behavior
Law, Language and Ethics

EARTH
AND OTHER
ETHICS

The Case for Moral Pluralism

CHRISTOPHER D. STONE

HARPER & ROW, PUBLISHERS, New York
Cambridge, Philadelphia, San Francisco, Washington
1817   London, Mexico City, São Paulo, Singapore, Sydney

For my father

FIRST EDITION

Designer: Sidney Feinberg

Copy editor: Rick Hermann

Indexer: Olive Holmes for Edindex

Library of Congress Cataloging-in-Publication Data
Stone, Christopher D.
    Earth and other ethics.

    Bibliography: p.
    Includes index.
    1. Natural resources—Law and legislation. 2. Law and ethics.   I. Title.
K3478.S76   1987   346.04'4   86-46103
ISBN 0-06-015731-3   342.644

87 88 89 90 91 HC 10 9 8 7 6 5 4 3 2 1

Contents

Acknowledgments

In 1982 Laura Fried, Editor-in-Chief of Boston University's *Bostonia* magazine, organizing a colloquium on Humanity and Nature, prevailed upon me to return to a theme I had sketched ten years previously in a book called *Should Trees Have Standing?* For some years previous I had put aside the thesis of *Trees;* that thesis, and the reasons for my returning to it now, are set forth in chapter 1. Here I shall say only that in recording those to whom I feel gratefully obliged, Ms. Fried should make an early appearance.

The first short stab at the current work, essentially the substance of my B.U. Symposium lecture, appeared in the July–August 1983 issue of *Bostonia.* As the paper expanded toward its present book form, several groups provided me with the opportunity to deliver it, or parts of it: The American Society of Landscape Architects, in New Hope, Pennsylvania; the Wissenschaftzentrum (Science Center), Berlin; McGill Law School, Montreal; the University of Iowa, as the 1985 Ida Beam Lecture; and the University of Toronto, as part of its 1985–86 Legal Theory Faculty Workshop series. Each setting provided so many thoughtful critics (and good hosts) that I can scarcely reconstruct a fair inventory and am left, in the large, to thanking institutions. A partial list of those who ought to be singled out (although none would wish to share culpability for more than a slice of the manuscript) would include Layman Allen, Richard Craswell, Charles Kennel, Rod Macdonald, Edwin Smith, Matt Spitzer, and Richard Warner.

For editing—a man who makes his living lecturing develops tendencies not always welcome on the printed page, such as windy interjections set off with dashes, like this—I am grateful to Marc Stern of the *U.S.C. Law Review;* Kim King, my research assistant; and my live-in literary stylist (who deserves thanks for much beyond), my wife Ann Stone.

Esther L. Robertson, my secretary through most of the production period, shepherded the manuscript through innumerable drafts and metamorphoses with her characteristic—that is to say, unexcelled—skill, patience, and loyalty. Word processing and supplemental secretarial services were provided by Raquel Andrade, Stacie Dimon, Ann Farthing, Linda Otten, Madeline H. Paige, and Barbara A. Yost, under the direction of Shirly M. Kennedy.

Finally, there is special pleasure in acknowledging my continuous debt to the U.S.C. Law Library for the services provided by Albert M. Brecht's outstanding staff. Pauline Aranas, Paul George, Peggy Maupin, John Hasko (now Assistant Law Librarian at Cornell), Nancy Young, Fannie Fishlyn, Mark Miner, and Will Vinet all contributed, with imperturbable comradely good spirits, countless hours hunting down and chasing up the elusive resources and references of which the following pages are spun.

I

THE EVALUATIVE FRAMEWORKS

A Personal Preface

IT HAS BEEN over a dozen years since I wrote "Should Trees Have Standing?–Towards Legal Rights for Natural Objects."[1] The history of that little essay best explains how I came to undertake the book that follows. In 1969 the U.S. Forest Service had granted Walt Disney Enterprises a permit to construct a $35 million resort complex in Mineral King Valley, located in California's Sierra Nevada Mountains. The Sierra Club, seeking to block the development, won a temporary restraining order in the U.S. district court, but then lost on appeal for want of standing. Perhaps there were legal grounds on which the Disney plan could be assailed. But these were not grounds the Sierra Club could raise, not having shown *itself* to be adversely affected. "The right to sue," the appeals court declared, "does not inure to one who does not possess it, simply because there is no one else willing and able to assert it."[2]

It occurred to me that if standing were the barrier, why not designate Mineral King, the wilderness area, as the plaintiff "adversely affected," let the Sierra Club be characterized as the attorney or guardian for the area, and get on with the merits? Indeed, that seemed a more straightforward way to get at the real issue, which was not what all that gouging of roadbeds would do to the Club or its members, but what it would do to the valley. Why not come right out and say—and try to deal with—*that?*

By the time I started writing *Trees,* the lawsuit, *Sierra Club* v.

Morton, was already pending review by the U.S. Supreme Court. There was no possibility of getting an article in print in time for the lawyers to work the idea into their briefs. Nonetheless, with the comradely connivance of the *U.S.C. Law Review* staff, my hastily drawn essay was wedged into a special symposium issue on Law and Technology, then nearly in press. I had no assurance that the symposium would be published while the Court still had *Morton* under consideration. But I knew that the manuscript would fall into the hands of Mr. Justice Douglas, a sympathetic environmentalist, who had agreed to review the symposium in order to write its foreword.

The Supreme Court upheld the circuit court, the four-man majority affirming that "[t]he 'injury in fact' test requires more than an injury to a cognizable interest. It requires that the party seeking review be himself among the injured."[3] But Justice Douglas opened his dissent with warm endorsement for the new theory he had just then had a chance to browse:

> The critical question of "standing" would be simplified and also put neatly in focus if we . . . allowed environmental issues to be litigated . . . in the name of the inanimate object about to be despoiled, defaced, or invaded. . . . Contemporary public concern for protecting nature's ecological equilibrium should lead to the conferral of standing upon environmental objects to sue for their own preservation. See Stone, *Should Trees Have Standing?* . . . This suit would therefore be more properly labeled as *Mineral King* v. *Morton.*

Justices Blackmun and Brennan favored a liberal interpretation of some earlier cases as a basis for upholding the Sierra Club's right to sue. But in the alternative they would have permitted the Club to replead in a way that incorporated the "imaginative expansion" of standing for which Douglas had been willing to speak.

Boosted by Douglas's endorsement, the media got onto *Trees* overnight. It is not unusual for judges to cite law review articles. But there was something, if not prophetic, at least amiably zany, about a law professor who "speaks for the trees"—and gets a few justices to listen.

Writing in the *Journal of the American Bar Association* one practicing
lawyer took to verse for rejoinder:

> If Justice Douglas has his way—
> O come not that dreadful day—
> We'll be sued by lakes and hills
> Seeking a redress of ills.
> Great mountain peaks of name prestigious
> Will suddenly become litigious.
> Our brooks will babble in the courts,
> Seeking damages for torts.
> How can I rest beneath a tree
> If it may soon be suing me?
> Or enjoy the playful porpoise
> While it's seeking habeas corpus?
> Every beast within his paws
> Will clutch an order to show cause.
> The courts, besieged on every hand,
> Will crowd with suits by chunks of land.
> Ah! But vengeance will be sweet
> Since this must be a two-way street.
> I'll promptly sue my neighbor's tree
> for shedding all its leaves on me.*

*John Naff, *Journ. Am. Bar Assn.* 58 (1972): 820. The style—a reluctance to confront
us natural-object advocates head-on, prose to prose—spread. In disposing of a 1983 suit by
a tree owner to recover from a negligent driver for injuries to the tree, the Oakland, Michigan,
County Appeals Court affirmed dismissal with the following opinion in its entirety:

> We thought that we would never see
> A suit to compensate a tree.
> A suit whose claim in tort is prest
> Upon a mangled tree's behest.
> A tree whose battered trunk was prest
> Against a Chevy's crumpled chest.
> A tree that may forever bear
> A lasting need for tender care.
> Flora lovers though we three
> We must uphold the court's decree.

—Fisher v. Lowe, No. 60732 (Mich. Crt.App.), *Journ. Am. Bar Assn.* 69:(1983): 436.

On the tide of such attention, the article was brought out in book form utterly without reediting—essentially photocopied, in fact—and sold briskly. Most reactions were favorable. The *Berkeley Monthly*, for one, took me as a sign of better times to come. Others were critical, either of my ideas, or of nearly unrecognizable mutations which the writers proceeded to connect, at their convenience I thought, with my name. I might have expected that I would be considered a Born Again Pantheist, but I did not expect the intimations of one reviewer, who wrote that my agenda was transparently communistic. (The gist, as I recall, was that if we couldn't own *things*—and, after all, what else was there?—the whole institution of ownership was done for.) My name—and little chatty, uncritical versions of the idea—began to embellish the sorts of journals that carry pictures. A revised mass-market paperback edition was issued by Avon Books, unsentineled by scholarly footnotes. At the faculty club, my own standing took on the slight sully that public notoriety brings an academic.

I had not been an environmental lawyer or teacher—I still am not —and the focus of my concern soon settled back to other things. But the movement in which *Trees* played a modest role roiled on. Several complaints were filed in the name of nonhumans—including a polluted river (the Byram, which divides part of New York from southern Connecticut), a marsh (No Bottom), a brook (Brown), a beach (Makena), a national monument threatened by strip mining (Death Valley), a town commons that lay in the path of a highway project (Billerica), a species of endangered Hawaiian bird (the palilla), and an unnamed tree.* In New York, a lady acting as "next friend and guardian for all

*Ezer v. Fuchsloch, 99 Cal.App.3d 849, 160 Cal. Rptr. 486 (1979). Strictly speaking, the tree was not a party plaintiff. The action was by landowners for injunctive relief against a neighbor based on a land-use covenant recorded by their predecessors providing that no shrub, tree, or other landscaping would obstruct any lot's view. The trial court granted a mandatory injunction requiring both defendants to trim their pine trees to afford their neighbors a view of the ocean. On appeal, the defendants argued that the trial court failed to consider the rights of the pine trees to exist untrimmed independent of the interhuman rights created by the restrictive covenant. Judge Jefferson, rejecting the argument, quoted back to the defendants a passage I had written in *Trees:* "[T]o say that the environment should have rights is not to say that it should have every right we can imagine, or even the same body of rights that human beings have. Nor is it to say that everything in the environment should livestock now and hereafter awaiting slaughter," sued to challenge as "inhumane" and unconstitutional an exemption to the Humane Slaughter Act in favor of the Orthodox Jewish ritual which prescribes that cattle be conscious when knifed, shackled, and hoisted. In Hawaii, a young laboratory assistant "liberated" two dolphins from the university's tanks into the Pacific Ocean so that they could "exercise their freedom of choice" whether to return to captivity. Tried for first-degree theft, he argued that the dolphins were legal "persons," a defense that won him considerable public sympathy until marine biologists were quoted to the effect that, forced to fend for themselves in the ocean, the raised-in-captivity dolphins were as good as dead. He wound up with a six-month jail term plus five years probation.[4]

What principle have these cases established? It is hard to say. Thus far, none of the lawyers bringing suit in the name of a nonhuman has been emboldened to bring it in the name of the nonhuman *alone*. That is to say, a river or valley may be denominated the lead plaintiff, so that the case bears in the official law reports a title such as *Byram River* v. *Village of Port Chester*. But because of the joinder of conventional plaintiffs, ordinarily natural persons and associations, to reinforce the claims on the object's behalf, the courts have not been forced to decide how they would deal with a suit were it to be brought in the name of an object by itself.

There are reasons why the law has remained so inconclusive. Throughout the seventies, as the social climate grew more sympathetic to the environment (even in the face of the "energy crisis"), several developments reduced the value of *Trees'* "standing" thesis as a strategy for environmental litigation. To begin with, the courts gradually liberalized the traditional standing requirements. That is, they stretched conventional notions of when a human was being "harmed" to provide environmental lawyers with an alternate and, in most situations, equally satisfactory route to the courthouse door. In the Mineral King contro-

have the same rights as every other thing in the environment" (99 Cal. App.3d at 864). As California law now stands, whatever rights a tree might have, it may have to put up with a little trimming every now and then.

versy the Sierra Club simply redrafted its complaint to accentuate how the development would infringe its "associational interests" as well as prove detrimental to some individual Club members. It was a pithy amendment, but the trial court bought it.[5]

There is no better illustration of the changing climate than the seal litigation. In 1976 several animal welfare groups sued to restrain the Secretary of Commerce from issuing permits for the importation of South African sealskins. They asserted that the permits would result in the taking of South African fur seals in an inhumane manner, permitted in South Africa, but in violation of the U.S. Marine Mammal Protection Act. To meet the standing requirement, the groups claimed an interest in the maintenance of a safe, healthful environment for marine mammals, to which group interests they added allegations of injury to the recreational, aesthetic, scientific, and educational interests of individual group members. The U.S. district court dismissed the action on the basis of *Sierra Club* v. *Morton,* noting that like the Sierra Club, the groups before it, "however great their interests," were not "on any different footing from any other concerned citizen." In fact, in some respects their claim was considerably weaker than that of the Sierra Club in *Morton.* At least Mineral King was in the United States, easily accessible to the Sierra Club membership. In the seal case, South Africa was not only remote, but, as the district court pointed out, the area of the Cape that the seals inhabited was accessible only with the special permission of the South African government, a permission not likely to be granted to American seal-watchers.

Hence, considering how the U.S. Supreme Court had disposed of *Morton* in 1971, the district court felt itself bound to reject jurisdiction. But by the time the seal case reached appeal, it was 1977, and the U.S. court of appeals said that it had to consider the allegations "in the wake of rapidly developing case law." The reviewing court impressed an expansive interpretation upon the post-*Morton* law, gave a friendly reading to the facts (one of the groups' members had filed an affidavit expressing a plan to go to South Africa in the future), and proceeded to invalidate the permits on the grounds that South Africa was allowing nursing seals to be clubbed and skinned. (What an irony, that a decade before Soweto erupted the U.S. courts had shown themselves ready to interpose in South Africa's mistreatment of its *seals.*)[6]

More recently, the American Cetacean Society, portraying itself as a whale interest group, challenged the United States' failure to sanction Japan for butchering whales in violation of international conservation treaties. The government pointed out (not without merit) that a suit on behalf of whales was a doubtful mechanism for plunging the judicial system into the imbroglios of international relations. In an editorial titled "Do Whales Have Standing?" the *Wall Street Journal* concluded hopefully not. The U.S. Supreme Court, although holding for the government on the substantive issue, ruled that the pro-whale groups were "sufficiently aggrieved" (because "harvesting" interfered with their interest in whale watching) to have standing.[7]

While the courts have been busy liberalizing standing through such sympathetic interpretations of existing rules, legislatures have been enacting special new laws expressly worded to secure the same effect. Much of the last decade's environmental legislation includes explicit provision for "citizen's suits" in which the party initiating judicial review of an environment-threatening action can dispense with the formality of alleging personal harm. Other legislation has fortified the government's right to sue private environment-despoilers through a revival and expansion of the ancient public trust doctrine, which endows the government with a protective interest over beaches, dunes, and other public areas.

Certainly, none of these strategies will suffice to secure review of all environment-threatening actions. Most of the "liberal" devices require that there be a federal or state statute which can be construed as touching the controversy, and which the despoiler is violating. Often no such provision will be available. An animal rights group recently attempted to challenge the navy's proposed slaughter of the goats on Catalina Island where the military has a weapons installation. The suit was rejected by the federal appeals court in California with the comment that the group's standing to bring the action was "extremely questionable." In such circumstances, where it is unpersuasive to base standing on harm to human plaintiffs—even in a liberally extended sense of "harm"—and no special "citizen's suit" statute is available, a suit in the animal's or object's own name, applying *Trees'* thesis, might remain the only feasible alternative. But it is fair to say that today, in general, the environment's own standing has become more of a matter of theoretical and spiritual interest than a real practical constraint on the bringing of environmental litigation.

Standing, on the other hand, does nothing but get you through the courthouse door; it does not mean the case on behalf of the environment is won, or can even be argued intelligibly. As we saw, the courts may allow whale watchers, because of the harms they suffer, to initiate the interpretation of an international whaling convention. There is, in that sense, standing to seek review of government action affecting the whales. But as long as the judges, in analyzing the treaty, remain within the bounds of conventional international and U.S. legal principles, with no accounting for invasion of the whales' interests, the "harvesting" will continue. An argument truly on behalf of the whales has as its starting point not the sanctity of treaties and regard for "political questions," but respect for whales.

But how does one do that: respect a whale, or pay heed to a hillside? In its general form, the problem is this. Suppose that someone is authorized to argue the case truly and frankly "for the environment." At that point, we face the other facet of *Trees:* deciding how to evaluate and deal with damage *to the environment.* That issue remains as problematical as, and perhaps even more practically pressing than, ever. Several federal statutes invite suits, ordinarily by the state or other "public trustee," to recover for "damages to the natural resources" from spills of oil and other hazardous substances.[8] These laws have transferred onto the public agenda questions that were once considered purely "academic." Will a public trustee be entitled to recover for natural resource "damages" that entail no demonstrable injury to humans? Indeed, in what sense can we label as "damages" alterations in the environment that no human even finds objectionable? In cases of toxic spill, will the measure of damages be limited to the loss of human benefit, for example, the lost commercial value of the fish killed? Or will it be appropriate, as *Trees* proposed, to make the defendant pay the costs of restoring the area (making the environment "whole") even if the costs of restoration exceed the area's consumption and use value? If the particular injury is irreversible and irreparable at any price, may the trustee divert damages recovered to general, human-benefiting revenue purposes (to build highways, and so on), or will he have to apply them to the next-closest feasible use "for the environment?"

In enacting CERCLA* in 1980, Congress foisted off on the president the task of resolving such quandaries, with a mandate to bring back the answers by December 1982. But the statutory deadline has come and gone without—as of the time of this writing—promulgation of the executive guidelines. Part of the delay must be attributed to the political delicacy of the subject matter. But even were the regulations being fashioned in the most supportive administration, there are underlying philosophical difficulties. Is there a coherent notion of *damages to the environment,* independent of damages persons suffer on account of *changes in the environment?* And is it morally defensible to subordinate our own human benefit to achieve some philosophical ideal of what nature (which itself couldn't care less) should look like?

Because the concept of *environmental damage* has yet to be given an adequate definition of treatment, the damages aspect of the original *Trees* thesis now seems particularly ripe for reexamination. I might, on that basis alone, be tempted to say something further in this area, particularly as I now enjoy the luxury of less breathless circumstances than I worked under originally. The present work is not, however, simply a renewed and updated plea for the environment, a sequel in that sense to *Trees.* My interest in the environment carries forward. But it appears here as one element of a more comprehensive inquiry into the reach of law and morals generally. Environmental objects such as whales and trees and mountains are not the only unconventional entities edg-

*The gratefully accepted acronym for the Comprehensive Environmental Response, Compensation, and Liability Act of 1980.

ing into public debate. Issues regarding the moral and legal status of "things" other than individual normal persons crop up all the time. In New York recently, parents of a severely deformed and retarded newborn infant, "Baby Jane Doe," decided against life-prolonging surgery. A New York attorney responded with an effort to sue on its behalf as guardian. Can a defective newborn have "rights" assertable against its parents? Can a fetus have rights? A robot? Can we have obligations to the unborn? The furor over President Reagan's trip to lay a wreath at Kolmeshoehe Cemetery in Bitburg, where forty-nine Nazi SS members lie buried, rekindled old controversies about collective and group responsibility. What does it mean not for an individual, but for a *people* or a *nation*—or, for that matter, a *corporation*—to be (in morals) "to blame" or (in law) "guilty"?

The best evidence of the increasing significance of these unconventional "things" are the several bodies of literature one finds growing up around them. There is an animal rights literature, a fetus (including abortion) literature, a future-generations literature, an environmental literature, a cultural literature, and so on. Writers in one area venture an occasional glance at the others to draw an *ad hoc* comparison or contrast. But there has been almost no effort to gather the common problems together under a general framework. Hence, the present work begins by considering as a matter of general theory the following question: On what basis, and in what manner, might a nonhuman, a *thing*, be accorded legal or moral standing or considerateness?

Once begun, such an inquiry bores to the very bedrock of law and morals. Orthodox legal and moral theories provide nonhumans only a limited accounting, one that generally makes the claim on behalf of the thing directly dependent upon human interests. This is particularly so when we turn to things like rivers that (unlike whales) have no interests or preferences of their own. Hence, the more expansively one seeks to make a moral-legal accounting, the more critically we have to probe orthodox legal and moral philosophy. Before I am finished this time, my inclination to speak for unconventional entities shall have led me to offer the outlines of an unconventional view of normative thought generally.

Put briefly, the position that emerges is this. The conventional approach to ethics is to put forward a single coherent body of principles, such as utilitarianism's greatest good of the greatest number, and to demonstrate how it guides us through all moral dilemmas more satisfactorily than does its rivals. This conventional view of the ethicist's mission, which I call Moral Monism, has far-reaching implications for moral discourse. First, it is very much either-or. The writer typically proposes that there is a single key: life, or the capacity to feel pain, or the powers of reason, or something else. Those things that possess the key property count morally—all equally, and all in the same way. Those things that lack it are utterly irrelevant, except as resources for the benefit of those things that do count. Moreover, Monism implies that in arguing for, say, the preservation of a species, we have to appeal to the same principles that we would invoke in determining the punishment of terrorists or the obligations to one's kin.

These ambitions of Monism, to unify all ethics within a solitary framework capable of yielding the One Right Answer to all our quandaries, strike me as unattainable. First, the Monist's mission collides with the fact that morality involves not one, but several distinguishable *activities*—choosing courses of conduct, praising and blaming actors, and evaluating institutions, to mention three. Second, there is the variety of *things* whose considerateness commands some intuitive appeal: normal persons in a common moral community, persons remote in time and space, embryos and fetuses, nations and nightingales, beautiful things and sacred things. Trying to force into a single framework all these diverse moral activities as they touch on all these diverse entities seems fruitless. Worse, it imposes strictures on thought that stifle the emergence of more valid approaches. The alternative conception I will propound—what I call Moral Pluralism—invites us to conceive moral activities as partitioned into several distinct frameworks, each governed by distinct principles and logical texture. We do not try to force the analysis of good character into the same framework as for good acts; nor are our obligations to the spatially and temporally remote subject to exactly the same rules that relate us to our kin, on the one hand, or to species, on the other. The frameworks for each of these analyses are distinguishable in their respective capacities to produce a single right (or wrong) answer, and in the strictness of the judgments they render. In some domains we can speak in terms of what is mandatory. In other domains, perhaps those that encompass butterflies and "lower" life, our judgments are limited to what is morally permissive, or, more loosely, what is simply "more welcome." Under the view proposed here, there is some shift in the aims and ambitions of moral philosophy; a shift, too, in how practical dilemmas are defined, attacked, carried to solution, and justified. Most important, it holds, I believe, implications as to the sorts of persons we aim to become, the relations we build, and the world we will leave as legacy.

Morals Matter

My CONCERN IS not with moral and legal philosophy for their own sake. Rather, the animating concern is worldly: What sort of planet will this be? The various possibilities, the conceivable futures, can be thought of as so many filmstrips laid out in front of us, side by side. The first frame of each strip is the same: a "picture" of the entire earth at this moment. But as we move beyond the "near" frames (those depicting our own life-times), the films begin to display variances from strip to strip, as the potential futures that they depict diverge. They diverge in the number and variety of human, animal, and plant populations that will inhabit the earth. They diverge in the rate at which natural resources are depleted. In some there is more consumption in the near term, and more famine in the far. In some versions the oceans are dead; in others, the atmosphere is gone. There are differences in the world's wealth, both in the aggregate and in its distribution among peoples. There are differences, too, in the sorts of social institutions with which populations are governed: various shades of totalitarianism and democracy.

What futures we can realistically aim for—the range of potential hereafters—can be considered a question of *technology*, within the constraints, principally, of resources.

Which of these accessible futures we ought to select, why one filmstrip might be considered morally preferable to any other: that is a question of *ethics*.

How we arrange our affairs so that the future we choose is the future that becomes the reality: that is the question of social institutions, of *law*.

This book is about these questions, and how we construe, and deal with, the relations between them. They are large questions, but they are real, and really upon us. Consider a basic: water. This nation's agriculture (and, indirectly, a portion of the world's food supply) depends upon vast underground water aquifers, such as the Ogallala, which few of us ever give thought to, much less can name. Yet, we are drawing them down, and poisoning them, at such a rate that by one estimate only 5 percent of the water that was available in 1800 will be available to the much larger population in 2100. This presents an inescapable moral dilemma. Ought we to restrict our own water usage, conserving it for the unborn? Ought we to invest capital into some mammoth public works project to desalinate sea water, even if the undertaking would infringe our own comforts, and would not begin to pay dividends until future lifetimes?

Or consider the problem of storing nuclear fuel waste. For us, the living, the cheapest method of disposal might be to seal the wastes in canisters and simply dump them onto the ocean floors. Although this could be done in such a way as to present little immediate hazard, the canisters would, in time, erode, jeopardizing life in the ocean, and with it dependent generations of people. On the other hand, the alternatives that would better protect the future are each billions of dollars more expensive. It has been suggested, for example, that the safest storage would be to put the waste into rockets and fire it into solar orbit—but the expense would be simply fabulous.[1] Money would have to be withdrawn from contemporary projects, including those aimed at alleviating the despair of present persons, whose plight is presented to us in vivid immediacy. Ought we to make such a financial sacrifice for the benefit of future generations of human and nonhuman life? What form would the arguments for such a sacrifice take? What appeal can one make to the skeptic who demands why *we* ought to subordinate our welfare to *theirs*, to beings whom we shall never meet eye to eye, who are (in this respect like mountains and forests) in no position to reciprocate? And even if someone can develop a persuasive argument that we ought, in moral theory, to take present steps to modify distant futures, what would be a just intergenerational distribution of goods? How much do they deserve? And how can the living be motivated to make the sacrifices required? How can the legal and political institutions be animated to respond?

It is because of problems like these that there is today a widespread feeling that our technology, our capacity to alter the earth and the relations thereon, is outstripping our ethics, our ability to provide satisfactory answers to how that power ought to be exercised. And there is the further feeling that even when we know, or believe we know, what would be the right thing to do, our social institutions, the bureaucratic machinery of courts and agencies, are incapable of bringing it about.

None of these feelings is new, of course. The gap between technology and morals is a theme that runs from Prometheus through Faustus, Frankenstein, and the low-budget sci-fi films in which our meddlings with nature inevitably linger to harass or destroy us. (After Hiroshima, it was everyone's first second thought). The gap between morality and law has been playing since Antigone.

But it would be ironic to dismiss these laments because they sound familiar (almost every epoch in human history has voiced them). Rather, the laments sound familiar because they are among the central, continuing problems of civilization. And however unoriginal, it may be no idle conceit to suppose that today things *have* gotten worse.

It is not just that ours is the first civilization that has the weaponry and the toxins to end it all. Humbler problems penetrate every corner of our lives. Every day the news media give us a glimpse of some new ethical or legal conundrum. A doctor stands trial for letting a brain-damaged newborn die. A hospitalized paraplegic asserts the freedom to expire as her right. In Canada, there is a protest over a "harvest" of seal pups. In Los Angeles, anti-pornographers and "sex industry spokespersons" confront each other over women's rights. We have, as a sort of mirror image of the present's obligations to the future, questions of the present's responsibilities for the past: Are we legally or morally obligated to make reparations for the damages of slavery? For the internment of Japanese-Americans in "relocation" camps during World War II? There is abortion, the death penalty, gay rights, and animal liberation.

Yesterday, the law was trying to establish rules for wrongful death actions. Today, we are seeing "wrongful life" suits in which health-impaired children, who would rather they had not been born, sue their parents and their parents' doctors for misdiagnosis and failure to abort. On the ballot, moral issues are confronting us not merely as traditional appendages to the candidates, in the form of campaign promises, but in their own skin, in the form of direct popular referenda: ERA, nuclear disarmament, the death penalty, gun control. Corporations are hiring resident ethicists. Books on ethics, of a traditionally "academic" depth, are popularly read, and centers have been founded for its study. Morals has even acquired, in the institutional personhood of the Moral Majority, its own lobby of sorts.

The irony is that now, at a time when the interest in moral dilemmas is so high, ethics—the body of literature one might turn to for guidance —seems so often at a loss for anything to say. In its oldest, most tenacious form, this disregard of ethics takes the shape of moral skepticism, the position that there are no right or wrong nor perhaps even meaningful answers to moral questions. On this view, "right," "wrong," "good," "evil" come down to matters of personal or class preferences paraded out in philosophic garb. The whole enterprise is fruitless and deceptive. This is a view I will have something to say about later, for no one who is under skepticism's sway (avowedly or unawares) can be expected to participate in moral discussion either earnestly or well.

But suppose we put aside the skeptic for a moment and look at the situation from the perspective of those who do value moral discourse. These people—most of us, I like to think—believe that there are some answers that are better than others. For this group, therefore, the fault with contemporary ethics is not that the enterprise is vacuous; they believe good answers are possible in principle. But there is a distance opening up between contemporary moral theory and the dilemmas we actually face, a distance that prompts a mild sense of irrelevance, if not disregard. Indeed, surveying today the academic literature in philosophy, one experiences the same sense of unreality one gets reading the economics journals. As the work gets increasingly sophisticated and abstract, many writers find themselves responding more and more to one another, and less and less to the problems. The result is that our moral and legal view of the world has in some ways lost contact with the predicaments we are interested in resolving. What is that "moral and legal view of the world"? In what ways has it become unsuited? And what is to be done to secure a conception that is more in line with the problems we want to understand and deal with?

The Historical Legacy

WHAT *IS* OUR "moral and legal view of the world"? How did we come by it? In what ways may we wish to revise it? The questions are large and abstract enough that we should expect in response many different accounts, each told in its own distinct language. The sociobiologist has one version of events, the anthropologist something else to contribute, the economists and theologians their versions. None of these versions, certainly not the abbreviated one I am about to tell, can convey more than one slant on a complex story.

At the core of my own story—my central theme—is this. Our received ways of defining and handling legal and moral problems grew out of relationships among ordinary normal persons living in a collective society. I will refer to these persons as Persons—with a capital *P*. My term *Persons* is less extensive that the biologist's *homo sapiens*. *Persons* is limited to normal adult human beings who, possessing full human faculties and living as neighbors in time and space, are capable of knitting the bonds of a common community. My definition of *Person* excludes, for example, humans who have not yet been born, those who live on the other side of the world, and those afflicted with such a serious defect that their capacity to form social bonds is impaired. All these are persons, of course, and worthy of our concern. But they are not the Persons who have been the focal concern of ordinary law and morals.[1]

The use of a single term, *Persons,* does not mean that there has been a single, stable conception of "personhood" through history. In every era there have been contesting notions of what a person is, or could become, and the prevailing view has left its stamp on our thought. From the Renaissance through Freud, there has been a gradual recognition of an interior emotional life. In both law and morals this has fostered allowance for "emotional pain and suffering," and for such mental elements as excuses, motives, and intentions. Our conception of other significant human properties has persisted through time relatively unchanged. Persons experience pleasures and pains (rather similar to each other's, we imagine) and are capable of practical reasoning. They can speak for themselves, exercise moral choice, and—living in a common moral community—assert and waive the sorts of claims needed to govern their reciprocal relationships. All in all, the legal and moral codes and, more basically, legal and moral ways of thinking, responded with a weave of rules, principles, and policies deemed suitable to the image of Persons in my restricted sense—to ordinary humans in ordinary communal relationships. Indeed, the whole texture of conventional law and morals is dominated by the fact that many potential conflicts can be forestalled by assigning Persons claims and rights which they can then assert, waive, or trade to mutual benefit.

Now, of course, like any other broad generalization, this one could stand enough qualifying to fill a separate book. Much of morality's history, and not a little of the law's, has concerned man in his relations, not with other men, but with (and through) God. And even when the emphasis has been secular, some accounting has had to be made for creatures who did not fit the Persons mold—who were not normal persons in a common community, but were too conspicuous to be ignored entirely. These unconventional entities, or "Nonpersons" as I shall call them, ranged from natural persons of "special" sorts (including infants, lunatics, and the unborn) to such nonhumans as animals, the dead, and various sorts of aggregate or corporate bodies: nations, tribes, municipalities, business organizations, and universities.

There is no fair way to summarize how each of these Nonpersons was treated in various contexts across the sweep of history. If one traces culture back far enough, there must certainly have been times when things (for example, totems) were regarded as having an independent moral and legal existence. Even in twentieth-century India we have a case in which an interfamily dispute regarding custody of the family idol was reversed with orders that on retrial, counsel be appointed for the idol.[2] Plutarch thought it quite right and natural that the gods should inflict punishments on cities for their inhabitants' misdeeds on the ground that a city is "one continuous entity, a sort of creature that never changes from age, or becomes different by time."[3] In English law after the Norman Conquest there were situations in which the brunt of responsibility fell on the community rather than on individuals. If one of the Norman conquerors was killed and the murderer not apprehended, the fine, called the "murdrum," was borne by the local civic group, known as the "hundred."

Oftentimes, Nonpersons were fitted into the Persons framework by overlooking distinctions that might have been drawn between them and Persons. Simply by the legal fiction of denominating the Nonperson a "person," it was thereby brought under the same principles as were applied to any "other" person. Some of these efforts were abandoned and now appear anachronistic, such as the occasional trial of an animal for crime that occurred in the Middle Ages (see Chapter 7). But other disregard of apparent differences persist. Most significantly, we still live by the practice that evolved, in the law at least, generally treat corporations *as if* they were natural persons, and thus to accord them much the same bodies of rights and duties as those to which Persons are subject—for example, the right to equal protection under the Fourteenth Amendment.

In other instances, the assimilation of Nonpersons involved formulating special limited exceptions to the general rules of what was expected of, and toward, Persons. Witness the prevailing treatment of infants and the insane. They are, as a starting point, *persons*—but persons under disability and therefore, while subject to the Persons framework as a start, subject also to certain specially tailored pleas and protections deemed suitable to their particular disabilities. While we owe them most of the duties owed to Persons, perhaps even some additional ones, they are not bound by their acts and promises in the same way, and are not drawn into the same body of rights.

While there were thus several "solutions" to the tensions Nonpersons introduced, the general point is this. Wherever it was felt necessary to provide (or begrudge) a Nonperson some accounting, the aim has been to do so with such minor tamperings as would preserve the Persons framework as intact as possible.

A recent California case illustrates this attitude as it operates in law. A lady had provided in her will that if she should die before her dog, the dog should be put to death. She died first, but before the dog could be destroyed, such a public outcry was raised that the San Francisco SPCA brought suit to enjoin the destruction. The California legislature was even drawn into the controversy, derailing the lawsuit by enacting a special private bill on the dog's behalf.[4] The case received wide media attention as a portent that animal rights were on the verge of judicial recognition. But in fact the bill, closely read, evidences little heresy to the Persons orthodoxy I am describing. The lady, it was reasoned, had not *really wanted* her dog to be destroyed. She just did not want it uncared for. Had she known the circumstances (that one of the attorneys would be prepared to offer it a good home), she would not have provided for its destruction. Thus, it appears that the law spared the dog's life not from consideration of the dog itself, but from consideration of the lady's wishes. By a "true construction" of the will, we were able to preserve the notion that what really counts are Persons. Of course, the dog, we can imagine, could care less about the hairsplittings of jurisprudence that rescued it. But from our perspective, the way we describe and justify what we are doing makes a considerable difference: in how we view ourselves, how we define and identify our guiding values —hence, in how our future unfolds.

To see this same phenomenon at play on the morals side, we have to go no further than orthodox philosophy's treatment of cruelty to animals. For some philosophers, animal cruelty presented no problem because it raised no conceivable objection. Descartes was persuaded that animals lacked even conscious awareness; they were, in his image, "like the clock."[5] Thus, although because of some undiscovered mechanical principle a dog howled when we cut it open alive, *as though it were in pain*, it could no more experience feelings and was no more an object of moral concern than a machine. For other philosophers, who felt cruelty to animals should be censured, the problem was to find a basis on which to condemn the practice, yet stop short of recognizing that the animals *themselves* had interests and claims, a recognition whose implications would have been subversive to the Persons framework. The favored "solution" was that uncensured cruelty toward animals could rub off, making *us* less trustworthy and nice in our dealings with one another. As far as mainstream moral philosophy was concerned (we can suppose that any sensitive eight year old knew better), concern for ourselves, and not concern for the animals, formed the basis for our duty not to bait bears and mutilate cats and poke out the eyes of pigeons.

This is a strategy sometimes called *redescriptivism*. The situation giving rise to moral unease—that some animal is being pained—is redescribed in such a way as to identify and attach ultimate significance to the indirect effects of the action on human beings. What might have been phrased and examined as a practice objectionable to the creature is recast in more familiar terms of human feelings and human virtues. The thing whose fate gave rise to the original intuition of wrongness or cruelty drops out. It is not just with animals that this practice occurs. Comparable redescriptions are ubiquitous. Feelings of obligations to wildernesses are translated into obligations (it is hard to put it unpompously) "toward one another in respect to enjoying wilderness areas"! Posthumous obligations—honoring gravesites, wills, and death wishes—are justified on the basis that acting "as though" we respected the dead provides mutually beneficial assurances for each of us while living, nothing more. In this circumlocutory manner, the originally animating perceptions and sentiments that might, if attended to, have matured into principles capable of challenging our fundamental assumptions are stunted and deflected into talk about indirect duties to other persons. No critical attention lingers either on the thing *or* on conventional modes of thinking.

In summary of this sketchy survey, it would be wrong to conclude that neither law nor morals has had anything to say about, or even lacked sympathy for, what I call Nonpersons. But in general, it is fair to say that the predominant attitude, the framework of rules, and even the preeminent rationale for the exceptions, have reflected an assumption that Persons are alone, or in some privileged way, considerate. The considerateness of other "things" has been deemed either unintelligible or purely derivative of the welfare of Persons.

4

Pressures on the Persons Framework

FOR CENTURIES, society has been able to accommodate the occasional Nonperson that seemed to require some legal or moral attention without any challenge to the prevailing Persons framework deep enough to force an articulation and defense of its philosophical presumptions. Recently, however, several developments have collaborated to make the interest in Nonpersons, and the pressure on conventional thinking, more acute and widespread. Together, they raise questions whether there might not be "other ways"—other than the received, intuitive ways—to think about our relations with Nonpersons. And these questions raise, in turn, larger questions about what we should expect from ethics as an enterprise.

SCARCITY

First, there has been an apprehension of impending worldwide scarcity. A sense of *limits* has always provided the drive for law and ethics. As Hume observed, if goods were in unlimited supply, questions of distributional justice, of allocating goods rightly, would not arise. The customs, etiquette, and property laws that grow up around a water hole in the desert reflect more elaborate consideration than those that develop in regions where water is plentiful. Today, however, it is not just a water hole, but the whole earth, that one fears is running dry of basic resources. We can understand "running dry" quite literally in the case of our vast and vital underground water aquifers. Overdrawn and poisoned, they, and that means we, are running out. The ozone shield and the oceans are in jeopardy. And the forests. In the advanced countries, and perhaps more so in the less developed world, per capita wealth may have "topped out" in real terms.

These threats have intensified and extended the interest in distributional justice: what are the ethics of dividing a stable or even shrinking pie with others whose lives are spatially and temporally remote? One reaction to scarcity, the national debt (borrowing against the future), has reached such a level that we can no longer disregard the moral dimensions of the financial burdens we are passing along to the unborn. And there are the problems of endangered species. It has been estimated that 10 to 20 percent of the earth's species living in 1975 will have disappeared by the close of this century. This is a specter that, now entered into public consciousness, puts pressure on the existing moral and legal framework to come up with new principles for the conservation and stewardship of what we are coming increasingly to think of as (in Kenneth Boulding's insightful term) "spaceship earth."

TECHNOLOGY

Accelerating advances in technology provide the second source of pressures on the conventional framework. It would probably be trite, and certainly wrong, to claim that every new scientific development is destined to multiply our moral perplexities. New advances in birth-control techniques—a "late pill," for example—may defuse the abortion debate with its slightly unpregnant question, "Is the fetus a 'person'?" A dramatic breakthrough in resource technology—fusion energy, or the capacity to extract hydrogen from seawater on a commercial scale—could soften the sense of impending scarcity and thereby ameliorate some of the distributional dilemmas.

Nonetheless, even if each and every technological advance does not promise to make our legal and moral lives more complex, the net impact seems destined to have dramatic implications, particularly on the consideration that needs be given to Nonpersons. First and foremost is the power, and the threat, of new forms of weaponry. The laws of warfare, once concentrated on the protection of soldiers and noncombatants, have since been amended to prohibit means of warfare that are intended, or may be expected, to cause "widespread, long-term and severe damage to the natural environment."[1] Thus far, over thirty nations, but neither the United States nor the Soviet Union, have consented to such a treaty. Should we? Another international pact, the Environmental Modification Convention of 1977, now with over forty signatories, invites nations to desist from "environmental modification techniques," defined as any techniques for changing, "through the deliberate manipulation of natural processes, the dynamics, composition or structure of the earth, including its biota, lithosphere, hydrosphere and atmosphere, or of outer space."

The issues technology unleashes at home are, if humbler, no fewer. In medicine, with increased power to preserve life, we have to face the question, when are we permitted to let it pass away? What is the right, morally and legally, of a human vegetable to die with dignity? With the growing power to create life (even, with genetic engineering, to create new forms of life) there comes in tow the question: What lives and life forms ought we choose to create? Scientists are prepared to give us forms that serve us better: "supertrees" and animals that grow faster and fatter. Are there any moral limits, other than risk to humans, as to what forms of life we can alter, put at risk, or destroy? Are there any obligations to genetic material per se?

We are, moreover, acquiring the power to build complex robots and to create artificial intelligence. We can connect mechanical devices with human tissue and organs to come up with biological-technological hybrids. We can repair a baby girl with a baboon's heart, clone cells, deliberately "farm" embryos and organs of the dead to service the living. What moral and legal constraints do these abilities put us under? Does an embryo have rights, and if so, who is to assert them?

And the other side of the coin: what place need we make in law and morals for robots, artificial intelligence (A.I.), and clones? Is the day so far off that we will be wondering what obligations we ought to hold toward, even expect of, *them?* In April 1985 the U.S. Centers for Disease Control reported its first documented case of a robot-caused fatality. A Michigan worker was found pinned between an industrial robot and a safety pole. The robot's pressure on the human's chest brought about cardiopulmonary arrest.

Perhaps at this stage of robot technology there is not any morally or legally significant difference between a person crushed by a robot and a person crushed by a tractor. But it is easy to imagine that as we advance our capacities to create new forms of intelligent machines, the law will have to make allowances. First, there are questions regarding the liability of the manufacturer. The manufacturer of the ordinary machine, the tractor, is liable for damages that result from certain defects of construction and design. The parents of a child, by contrast, are not liable, absent special statute, for the damages wrought by their "product," the child. The child is an autonomous actor, possessed of free will that has in general been deemed to cut off the responsibility of the parents. An advanced artificial intelligence, capable of reprogramming itself and reacting to its environment (to heat, light, voices, etc.) in ways practically unforeseeable by the manufacturer, would fall between the tractor and the child. No one doubts that the manufacturer would remain liable for such tangible defects as defective wiring. But in the event the A.I. goes awry in some unforeseeable way, would the law of design defect be expansive enough to deal with the situation, or would new doctrine be called for? It is possible that instead of assimilating the A.I. to the tractor, we would assimilate it to the child, thereby restricting the exposure of its maker.[2]

The more interesting, although more fanciful, questions involve the liability of the A.I. itself. Is there no justificatory theory of criminal procedure and no conceivable machine that would support a proceeding against the machine? On the contrary, one can imagine two developments converging. On the one hand, robots are destined to become more "mysterious." That is to say, as programs grow more complex, the outputs will become less foreseeably a product of any programmer's original intentions. Humans, on the other hand, are likely to become less of a mystery: as behavioral science advances, the range of unpredictability, of "free will" in personal conduct, is destined to narrow. As a result, even if we never come to treat artificial intelligence and robots as we treat humans under today's criminal law, it is conceivable that under a future "criminal code" the two might be treated more and more alike, with both errant humans and errant machines "reprogrammed," each in the appropriate way by comparable procedures of testing, examination, character witnesses, and so on.[3]

Moreover, advances in technology have extended the reach, intended and unintended, of our actions. The injury Cain did his brother was done on the spot, at arm's length. But with present power, the harm we do (one has only to think of toxic effluents) can stretch across the earth and linger well into the future, slaying unseen brothers, strangers to us both in space and time. These distances dilute the forces that animate and direct moral thought in kinship groups and small communities—shame, guilt, empathy, anxiety, and the prospects of retaliation and reciprocity. And at the same time, the potential universe of our obligees—the very number of persons whom we know our actions do or could affect—seems simply to overwhelm us with the impracticality of extending throughout the world the familiar moral demands that evolved to adjust relations among contiguous Persons. Can we really subscribe to a morality that impels our being responsible to *everyone* in the same way?

Moreover, it is not just technology in the narrow sense, with mass-produced goods and "better" ways of warfare, that puts us into contact with persons toward whom it is difficult to feel anything, at least as we feel for neighbors. It is a common observation, but one well worth remembering, that mass media, and television in particular, are making of us all one global community. Pains thousands of miles distant are brought vividly into our living rooms. How ought we respond to these troubling images we once could blissfully ignore?

In this globalizing tendency, television is the successor to transportation, communications, and even money (including its modern variants —stock certificates, commercial paper, and so on), which have all long operated to the same effect. Earliest commercial relationships were conducted on a face-to-face basis, goods and services being exchanged in barter. In such a society, and even in the more advanced small town, people dealt with and depended upon a relatively narrow circle of, if not friends and neighbors, at least regular trading partners and merchants whom they saw personally. But modern currencies, in combination with mass markets and extensive transportation networks, have "liberated" commercial dealings from such a personal basis. The net effect is that increasingly, people are exercising influence over others whom they never face and might not even understand if they did. Their actions radiate beyond their moral community.

THE BUREAUCRATIZATION OF LIFE

Third, the conventional framework needs to confront the growth and proliferation of bureaucracies. Traditional law and morals have centered attention upon direct, two-person situations, in which the inequities are typically *intimate*. Adultery, robbery, and deception all occur face-to-face. The classic obligations have been peculiarly personal as well: of the Good Samaritan to the destitute, of the parent to the child. Contemporary predicaments, however (one thinks of Chernobyl' and *Challenger*), do not generate from such straightforwardly one-on-one relationships. More and more, the world, particularly in developed societies such as ours, is being shaped not by individuals apart, but by workers in groups, linked together in business organizations, pension funds, labor unions, governmental agencies, associations, and all the various other formal and informal bureaucratic structures whose population explosions comprise one of the most striking demographic phenomena in this century. It is not merely human virtue these new creatures implicate, but the rectitude of organizational design: of the information pathways, command and control systems, and bureaucratic hierarchies that forge cadres of administrators, workers, and machines into uncertain, impersonal, and potentially mighty connections.

This ascent of bureaucracies gives rise to new sets of questions. First, pressure is placed on conventional notions of individual responsibility. The classic image of the culprit is an individual, the night stalker or cut–purse. The harm organizations do—I daresay the most serious and widespread harms—are ordinarily unplanned and unanticipated, not under anyone's knowing control. No one wanted or devised the debacle at Three Mile Island. Typically, the plant manager whose authority is x knows one bit of information, a; the vice-president for operations, whose authority is y, knows b; the night watchman knows there have been some peculiar hissing sounds; the control-room operator knows the pipes are hotter than usual; the vice-president for safety has received a warning communication from some regulatory agency that, buried in two hundred pages, cloaks a somber portent. We might suppose that if there were within the organization a single individual who knew a and b and this and that, and who had real power over the whole operation, that person would be morally blameworthy and perhaps legally liable to boot. But what if there is no such person, as there often will not be? Did any one person in NASA appreciate all the risks to *Challenger?*

The questions are not utterly new, but conditions of modern life make them freshly pressing. How do we judge and deal with individuals in an organization when the harms they do are blameless by traditional standards, or the product of joint effort, or the result of misplaced but well-intentioned zeal, or the outcome of insidious peer-group pressure or superior command? How do we judge and deal with persons when their actions as much reflect the office they step into as their "own" character and undertakings? What, for example, are the limits of the vicarious responsibility of a superior for the misconduct of his or her subordinates? When should those at "the top" be able to plead ignorance, and those at the bottom raise, as a defense, that they were subject to "superior orders"? These are the unanswered questions that ran through Nuremberg and Watergate, and echo through the modern corporate and governmental scandals one reads about every day.

The second set of bureaucratic problems concerns the moral and legal status of the corporate entity *itself.* When there has been, say, a toxic chemical spill, it may be possible to locate some identifiable human culprit crouched low in the bureaucratic thicket, someone who knowingly, perhaps even intentionally, caused the contamination. No one doubts such a person, in such a case, deserves punishment. But as I have indicated, bureaucratic misdeeds can occur without the wrongful, knowing conduct of any individual in the organization. When, in response to such situations, is it appropriate to (in morals) blame and/or (in law) prosecute the manufacturing corporation or municipality, entities that are, in our terms, Nonpersons? Or are blame and punishment appropriate for Persons only?

Note, too, how many of the "new" societal problems—from toxic wastes to euthanasia—are so entangled with corporations that they require us to understand and confront *corporate*, and not just human, character. To cope with massive toxic torts such as asbestos-related diseases and toxic pollution, we may be well-advised not just to fine the individuals responsible, but directly to alter the bureaucratic structure —for example, to require a delinquent chemical company to place a toxic engineer in a position of high authority and to reform its internal information pathways.[4] To deal with euthanasia, hospitals have been encouraged to take the question out of the individual doctor's hands and place the dilemma before an organizational ethics committee, composed and governed according to special rules. In many modern situations, conventional efforts to understand ordinary human properties and incentives have to be augmented by a sophisticated understanding of corporate/bureaucratic properties and incentives.

MORAL MATURATION

And finally, side by side with scarcity, advances in technology, and the burgeoning of bureaucracies, the moral and legal order is being impinged by what we might call the moral maturation of mankind. This is not to make the claim that the history of civilization has been a march toward moral progress, toward people getting better and better every day in every way (which would be a harder thesis to maintain). But it is probably true, as Darwin maintained, that history displays a continual extension in the range of objects receiving man's "social instincts and sympathies." Primitive man's concern was predominantly for a narrow circle of family and tribe. Later, "his sympathies became more tender and widely diffused, extending to men of all races, to the imbecile, maimed and other useless members of society, and finally to the lower animals."*

There are several explanations for this development. Certainly it is reinforced by intellectual sophistication generally. We have acquired a farsightedness in predicting and appreciating consequences of our actions that our forebears, frequently to their convenience, were free from. But it little matters whether we regard the moral maturation as a symptom of other developments—in technology, urbanization, commerce, leisure, media—or consider it of independent interest for the sociobiologists or someone else to explain. Whatever the cause, the consequence is to place additional pressure on the Persons framework. Throughout civilization, the more "we" have recognized that another person, family, or tribe is like us, both in the properties "it" possesses and the common fate we share, the readier we have been to connect our common relations with moral filament.

By extension of the same process, the more we are learning about animals, plants, and, in its way, all of existence, from subatomic motion to cosmic phenomena, the more we have been struck with the sorts of similarities that stir empathy (several recent studies have suggested evidence that trees communicate)[5] and the often unanticipated interdependencies that cause concern. Even appreciated differences are

*Charles Darwin, *The Descent of Man: and Selection in Relation to Sex*, 2d ed. (London: John Murray, 1874), pp. 119, 120–21. Compare Jeremy Bentham, *Introduction to the Principles of Morals and Legislation*, 2 vols. (1789; rpt. London: E. Wilson, 1823), chap. 17, pp. 235—36:

"The date *may* come when the rest of the animal creation may acquire those rights which never could have been withholden from them but by the hand of tyranny. The French have already discovered that the blackness of the skin is no reason why a human being should be abandoned without redress to the caprice of a tormentor [see Louis XIV's Code Noir]. It may come one day to be recognized, that the number of the legs, the villosity of the skin, or the termination of the *os sacrum*, are reasons equally insufficient for abandoning a sensitive being to the same fate." (Italics in original.)

significant. As Paul Taylor points out, as we pay increasingly close attention to other organisms, we achieve a richer understanding of the other's situation. This learning to look at the world from the other thing's distinctive standpoint is a major step toward respecting its moral worth.[6] From all causes, the growing recognition that we are all, even amidst so much conflict and competition, part of one fragile global community encourages rearranging the legal-moral framework so as to make more room not only for the infirm, insane, and infants, but for animals, plants—indeed, for the entire planet as an organic whole.*

---

*The evolution of morals has been expressed not only in terms of a widening of the classes of entities deemed morally considerate. There has been a parallel extension in the range of interests deemed protectable, of "harms" that are morally wrong to inflict. Witness the increased accounting, both in law and moral thought, for pain and suffering, emotional distress, and harms to "personality."

5

The Crisis in Frameworks

W HAT PRESSURES have these developments placed upon the conceptual legacy? To illustrate the growing tensions, consider a typical knot of the conventional ethics textbooks. "You see a stranger lying unconscious in the roadbed: Do you have a moral or a legal duty to drag him to safety?" (How straightforward and undivided the responsibility. You pull him to safety, he lives; you don't, he dies.) Or, "A has made a promise to B; under what circumstances is A relieved of her (alternatively) legal and moral obligations to keep it?"

Surely not every moral and legal dilemma associated with the developments I have traced above—the advances in technology, the bureaucratization, the scarcity of resources, the moral maturation of mankind —forces our thought to run along radically different channels. But there are coming to the fore today moral and legal conflicts of a more complex and, in ways I shall illustrate, multilayered kind than the traditional dilemmas; they are less satisfactorily modeled by the conventional Persons-oriented frameworks.

As a paradigm of the "new" sort of dilemma, let me use the so-called bowhead whale controversy, which can be condensed, for illustrative purposes, to the following.

The lands over which the U.S. government has dominion include the submerged bed of the Alaskan Beaufort Sea. The Department of Interior has proposed to lease the acreage to oil corporations for purposes of exploiting oil and gas that may underlie the region. To carry out exploratory drilling (and, certainly, in order to support development if commercial reserves should be discovered) drilling platforms will have to be constructed in the path that the bowhead whale, an endangered species, uses to reach its sole known spawning ground. Oil spills could have disastrous effects on their survival. Also, early-stage oil exploration often involves dynamiting (the explosions' echoes are used to map geophysical structures), and there is evidence that the procedures could destroy the whales' hearing, and thus their ability to navigate and survive. To make the matter more complex, if the whales successfully avoid these hazards by adjusting to a course that takes them somewhat to the north of their present route, they will be out of the range of a native tribe, the Inupiat Indians, who have long hunted the bowhead, a custom they claim to be integral to the maintenance of their culture.

Let me survey for a moment the various *sorts of conflicts* that appear to arise from this situation. (Later, I shall examine whether we can substantiate the intuition that these are real, and really different, conflicts calling for some revisions in the way we think about law and morals).

First, there are conflicts of *Natural Persons versus Natural Persons.* The interests of the contemporary Indians, who want the bowhead to be undisturbed (except by themselves) are at odds with domestic consumers of petroleum products who have an interest in a secure source of petroleum products, and even stand to gain some relief, as taxpayers, from the government's oil-lease revenues. Observe that while this conflict has some elements that suit it to an ordinary Persons model of analysis, it lacks others. Unlike the hypothetical bystander who practically stumbles upon the drowning person, the petroleum consumers are widely separated both culturally and geographically from the Indians. It is not evident to what extent we all share a single "moral community."

There are also conflicts of *Natural Persons versus Corporations.* The native Americans are at odds both with the U.S. Department of Interior (a public agency) and with the oil companies (private corporate bodies) that wish to participate in the lease sale. There are *Corporations versus*

Corporations. The village of Kaktovik, a municipal corporation, aligned in court against ARCO, an oil company, with the National Wildlife Federation, a nonprofit corporation, appearing as intervenor.

There is, in addition, a highly charged set-off of *Nation-States versus Nation-States*. The United States, as a nation member of the world body, is signatory to an International Whaling Convention (IWC). Other signatories include Russia and Japan, who have long been under U.S. pressure to reduce their whaling. Now, in the bowhead controversy, Russia and Japan have rejoined that if the United States is to honor *its* treaty obligations under the IWC, it must crack down on the Inupiat's "harvest" of bowheads or be subject to charges of hypocrisy on whale conservation and see its world leadership on the issue erode. Hence, on the plane of world bodies, the United States is in conflict with Japan and Russia.

There are, as well, conflicts of *Natural Persons versus Animals,* the whales being in jeopardy both from the Indians, who would kill them deliberately, and the consumers of oil products, who would jeopardize them indirectly to satisfy what economists call their "higher preferences."

We might consider, too, *Animals versus Animals,* since the decline of the bowhead would confer a benefit on the krill that the bowhead consumes (although I think most ecologists would contend that such a short-term reprieve for the prey would be likely, in the longer term, to have adverse effects on their own fate due to alterations in the ecological balance).

Even beyond these conflicts among contemporaries, there are other colorable interests to examine, which might also be said to provide the basis for other conflicts over time. First, there is the Indian tribe or even culture to account for, by which I mean to indicate not merely the interests of this Indian or that, but the value of a community freighted with ways of life that transcend and survive particular lives. Second, there are analogous problems of species to consider. The survival of a species of *whale,* presents separate questions from the survival of any individual whale. In fact, foresters and zoo keepers face such conflicts regularly. To preserve an endangered species, there may be no viable alternative but to cull out or pen in individual members. The individual (in this illustration, the whale) has intelligence and can experience pleasure and pain—has, in short, several of the properties of a natural person, at least in degree. But a species—in this regard, like a corporation—*itself* lacks these properties, has neither sentience nor even substance, and thus to talk of the interests or claims of a species raises some of the same conundrums as when we speak of the interests or claims of a corporation, tribe, or culture per se.

There are, as well, future interests to consider. Our present actions —draining domestic oil reserves, eliminating or altering the Indian culture, infringing the population of bowhead whales—are going to influence the resources that the future generations have available to them, their recreational opportunities, even their tastes.

These future generations' problems are, as we shall see, incredibly complex. We do not know (1) who—what sorts of or how many people —will be living in the distant future; (2) what consequences our present actions, such as the depletion of oil, will have on them in view of their alternatives; or even (3) what their preferences will be, assuming that we are committed to respect their preferences in some degree. For all we know, our descendants will be content to while away their time playing the progeny of Pac Man, and will consider us, their ancestors, at best quaint for having derived pleasure from the idea of there *being* whales and wild lions that almost none of us ever actually went off to see.

And, finally, there is some constituency for the affected habitat, or something even more encompassing, such as the whole ecological balance or the whole earth.

Now, as I readily grant, because some persons *feel* that there are unconventional values at play that are not adequately accounted for by prevailing frameworks, this does not mean that a coherent accounting for such values can be provided, much less that such an accounting would be right. The alternative is to maintain that there are no queer, nonhuman values or interests running around; many will claim that the apparent "conflicts" can be redescribed, without loss of morally or legally significant insight, in terms of our interests as we have conventionally conceived them. That is the issue to which we must now advance.

II

THE NONPERSON
IN LAW

Implicit in all I have written thus far there runs a major question of *care* and *respect*. What are the things we ought to care about and respect, and in what ways should that attitude be manifested? Our two principal institutions for sorting out and implementing these concerns—morals and law—have been dominated, conventionally, by a Persons orientation. Therefore, increasing regard for Nonpersons requires us to consider how suited our received ways of normative analysis are to resolve or even guide us through the evolving problems of contemporary concern. In what ways, and with what justification, might Nonpersons be accounted for in moral thought and legal rules?

At this point, we have to disengage more carefully the legal aspects of our inquiry from the moral. While law and morals share common roots, functions, and often subject matter, their emphases are different. In morals, the emphasis is on generating and justifying general standards of conduct. In law, the emphasis is on authoritatively implementing some of the standards for which morality has spoken: killing is wrong, therefore murder should be punished.

Assuming a need to divide our inquiry, there are two paths we can pursue. We could start by articulating and defending some general theory of morals, and then try to derive from that theory what sorts of moral claims, including claims to legal treatment, could be raised on behalf of various Nonpersons. Under this approach we would begin by asking on what bases *ought* we to be concerned about the preservation of rivers. We would then ask how any defensible concern could be translated into legal reform. The other approach, that which I adopt, is the reverse. It begins by asking whether giving a river various "legal rights" is intelligible and examining what doing so would entail. Once the implications are identified, we can then proceed to the moral inquiry: *ought* we to commit ourselves to *that?*

By adopting the second approach, we save ourselves the trouble of evaluating a number of arrangements that are legally unintelligible anyway. For example, we eliminate from further worry whether trees ought to have the vote, because giving trees the vote simply is not a coherent option. But other options, which are not so incoherent, can be identified and the implications assessed. The normative inquiry, thus deferred, acquires a more definite focus. The emphasis is not "Does a river have moral rights, and if so, what legal status can be derived from them?" We ask, "In what legal status might a river intelligibly be placed? And for each such arrangement of the legal system (treating a river *this way*) is it morally defensible?"

In pursuit of this plan, I intend three distinct inquiries. The first emphasizes law; the second, morals; the third, (meta-)ethics.

The first inquiry, which turns on the intelligibility of legal options, we might put this way: Considering the general character of Nonpersons, how, if at all, *could* we account for Nonpersons in law and at what "costs"? (I will discuss this in Part II.)

The second question, which emphasizes competing moral theories, is this: Having considered how we could adjust the legal system to provide various Nonpersons with various sorts of recognition in the law —that is, fit them into the legal framework coherently—why *ought* we to do so? What sort of a moral position would be required as a justification? (This is discussed in Part III.)

I will then proceed to consider whether the moral theory that is required to give Nonpersons an independent moral niche can meet the requirements of an acceptable moral viewpoint.

6

Legal Considerateness

THE NATURE of a thing's *legal status,* and, in particular, the relationship between its legal status and its moral status, can be clarified if we confront at the start two popular misconceptions. The first mistake is to suppose that all questions of *legal status* can be conflated into questions of *legal rights.* That is, people tend to identify the question "Can some entity be accorded legal recognition?" with "Can (or does) the entity have a legal right?" In fact, the motive for recognizing something as a legal person may have nothing to do with *its* legal rights. For example, the courts may give a stillborn fetus the status of "person" in order to fulfill a technical prerequisite for the parents to file a malpractice case against the doctors.[1] Giving the fetus its independent legal status is designed to secure the legal rights of the parents, not those of the fetus.

This first misconception is commonly compounded by a second error. This is the view that the only basis on which we can support according a thing a legal right (or other legal recognition) is if we can show it has something like its own moral right, underneath. That, too, is a misconception, which I shall take up in Chapter 8.

Let me begin here by placing *legal rights-holding* in perspective. The short of it is that having a legal right is one way to provide something a concern-manifesting legal recognition. But it is not the only way. When the law criminalizes dog beating it institutionalizes concern for dogs. It does so, however, by creating a prospective liability for the dog beater, who is made answerable to public prosecutors at their discretion. In no accepted sense does such a statute create a "right" in the dog. The same principle is at work in legislation establishing animal sanctuaries, and laws that compel cattle transporters to provide minimally "humane" standards at the risk of losing their certificate. The law is enlisted in an effort to protect Nonpersons, but legal rights are not required. The federal government recently issued regulations requiring fishermen who accidentally land sea turtles on their decks to give them artificial respiration. The technique is set out in detail. But the term *turtle's rights* is never mentioned. Nor need it be. The turtles are provided a measure of legal protection by creating enforceable legal duties *in regard to* them, duties enforceable by others, presumably the Commerce Department and Coast Guard. In like vein, no one is doubting that we could create comparable duties in regard to things indisputably devoid of interests; for example, we can imagine a law making it a misdemeanor to deface some special rock, such as Mount Rushmore.* Nor are relations built on duties the only alternative to those built on rights. We could give an algae colony an immunity from governmental action, say, from the draining of a stream for a federal works project.

This should remind us that while allocating rights is a fundamental way of operationalizing legal concern, and I myself emphasized it in *Trees*, such concern can be implemented through a broad range of arrangements, not all of which can be forced into the classic "rights-holding," or even "duties-bearing," mold. Therefore, let me introduce as the more comprehensive notion *legal considerateness*. A terse operational definition would look like this. Consider a lake. The lake is considerate within a legal system if the system's rules have as their immediate object to affect (as to preserve) some condition of the lake. The law's operation would turn on proof that the lake is not in the condition that the law requires, without any further need to demonstrate anyone else's interests in or claims touching the lake.

We can illustrate by reference to a lake which is being polluted by

*The point that the only intelligible *motive* for protecting Mt. Rushmore would appear to be the benefit of humans, and not the benefit of Mt. Rushmore, is a distinct contention dealt with in Part III.

a factory. Under conventional law, the pollution of the lake can be restrained at some human's behest (call him Jones) if Jones can show that he has a legally protectable interest in the lake. Jones might prove that the lake is on his land, or that, as owner of lakeside property, he has a right to the water in a condition suited for his domestic or agricultural use. Changes in the state of the lake—for example, its degradation—are relevant to Jones's proof, but his case cannot stop with the proof of such changes. As plaintiff, he has to prove that he has some right in respect of the lake's condition, which right the factory is infringing. Damages, if any, go to Jones. If the court awards him an injunction, it is *his* injunction; Jones has the liberty to sit down with the factory owners and negotiate an agreement not to enforce it, to let the pollution restart—if the factory owners make an offer that is *to Jones's advantage.*

Contrast that system to one in which the rules empower a suit to be brought against the factory in the name not of Jones, but of the lake, through a guardian or trustee.* The factory's liability is established on the showing that without justification, it degraded the lake from one condition, which is lawful, to another, which is not.

In the first system described, the lake is not legally considerate. It has no protection that is not wholly parasitic upon the rights of some person ready and willing to assert them. In the latter system, it is the lake that is considerate, not the person empowered to assert claims on its behalf.

Now, if this were intended as a jurisprudence text, we might pro-

---

*Provision for guardians can be made either by the legislature, by special enactment, or by the courts on an *ad hoc* basis after a hearing, as is commonly done for the senile or for unborn children in will contests. For examples of legislative intervention, California law gives public-interest organizations standing to commence an action for injunctive relief to preserve or restore the integrity of a work of fine art from defacement, mutilation, and so on. California Civil Code §989(a)(3)(c). In authorizing the formation of societies for prevention of cruelty to children and animals, the law empowers any such society, or any officer or member thereof, to prefer a complaint against anyone who violates a law affecting children or animals, and even to assist in the prosecution of an offender. California Corporations Code §10404. Note that such provisions, by implicitly limiting those with standing, reduce the prospect that any member of the public will bring actions, which consequently reduces the risk that the courts will be flooded. See, generally, *Trees,* pp. 17–20.

ceed to unpack legal considerateness into the whole array of terms with which legal philosophers deal: rights, duties, privileges, immunities, no-rights, and all the rest. For our purposes, however, we can simply conceptualize considerateness into two broad categories: *legal advantage* (typified by holding a legal right) and *legal disadvantage* (typified by bearing a legal duty). The question I will pursue, therefore, is to what extent and in what senses we can coherently situate Nonpersons in positions of legal advantage and legal disadvantage (hereinafter Advantage and Disadvantage), respectively.

ARE INTERESTS A REQUIREMENT OF LEGAL CONSIDERATENESS?

At this point, someone is bound to object that all this talk about "positioning" a Nonperson in a position of Advantage or of Disadvantage simply slides over the most serious problem. In regard to legislation touching some Nonpersons—as when we criminalize dog beating, for example—few would deny we are acting for the dog's benefit, *really* advantaging it. But one cannot so plausibly characterize an arrangement that nestles the lake in the protective custody of a guardian as being "for the lake's 'benefit' " in any familiar sense of "benefit." We have simply plugged the lake into the legal system roughly in the place that a person might occupy, to a person's advantage; but it is a place that can be of no advantage to the lake, only to people. The same may be said of whatever we might do concerning many Nonpersons, from ants and aquifers to zoophytes and zygotes. Because they have no self-conscious interests in their own fates (as distinct from our interests in them), it is unclear how notions of Advantage and Disadvantage apply.

How do we respond to this challenge? Inasmuch as we cannot examine all Nonpersons at the same time and with equal emphasis, I will set aside for the moment the most sympathetic cases for the Nonperson advocate to represent—those, for example, of distant persons and higher animals. To examine the general problem, we best concentrate on the most implausible of my Nonperson clients, thereby confronting the most fundamental objections. What space is there in law and morals, what toehold even, for the subset of Nonpersons I will call "Things"—utterly disinterested entities devoid of feelings or interests except in the most impoverished or even metaphorical sense?

There are various classes of these disinterested Things. There are man-made inanimates exemplified by artworks and artificial intelligence. There are Things that were not always so disinterested—corpses—and Things with the potential to be otherwise—embryos and fetuses. There are trees and algae which, while without self-consciousness and preferences, are nonetheless living organisms with biological requirements. There are what we discern as functional systems, but not systems that conform to the boundaries of any organism; for example, the hydrologic cycle. Habitats are of this sort. That is, while the habitat may include higher animals, we may find ourselves wishing to speak for some value not reducible to the sum of the values of the habitat's parts, the various things that the habitat sustains in relation. There are several sorts of natural and conventional membership sets already mentioned: species, tribes, nations, corporations. We might for completeness' sake keep in mind such "things" as in the happenstance of our language are rendered as qualities, for example, the quality of the light in the Arizona desert at sunset. Finally, there are events that might be of legal and moral concern, such as the flooding of the Nile.

Whatever might motivate and justify the lawmakers to try to make some such Thing legally considerate, how can we coherently account for an entity that has no welfare? We can imagine our interlocutor putting it this way. "All right," he says, "let us suppose that somewhere in the text that follows, you will be able to demonstrate at least some rational basis that could motivate us to devise legal rules in which a Thing—a lake, say—is made legally considerate, as you use the term. We will even agree to provide it a court-appointed guardian empowered to get up in court and 'take on' polluters in the lake's name. But now comes the tough part. The lake itself being utterly indifferent to whether it is clear and full of fish or muddy and lifeless, when the guardian for the river gets up to speak, *what is he or she supposed to say?"*

My answer will sound, I am afraid, a bit anticlimactic. As in any situation in which a legal guardian is empowered to speak for a ward, what the guardian says will depend upon what the legal rules touching on the ward provide. By definition a Thing can neither be benefited nor detrimented in the ordinary sense, so that the rules cannot orient to its best interests in the way some rules of child custody enlist "the best interests of the child." But what is implied? Not that no legal rule is imaginable. It only means that the state of the Thing for the preservation or attainment of which the guardian speaks will have to be some state the law decrees without reference to what the choiceless Thing would choose. What we should be asking, then, is this: What states of a disinterested entity (a Thing), of necessity unrooted in its own interests or welfare or preferences, are available for the law to embody in legal rules, and what would be the implications of so embodying them?

INTACTNESS AS A LEGAL ADVANTAGE

To examine what sort of legally defined Advantages might be conferred on a Thing, and with what implications, let us begin by considering a system that took as its target preserving the lake's intactness. The lawmakers could provide stiff criminal penalties for anyone who polluted the lake in the least degree. They could fortify this "advantaging" by assimilating the lake into the civil-liability rules in a way that approximated constituting the lake a rights holder with guardian. Specifically, the law could provide that in case someone violated established effluent standards, altering the state of the lake, a complaint could be instituted in the name of the lake, as party plaintiff, against the polluter. As I spelled out in *Trees,* this suit could be initiated and maintained—as suits are maintained as a matter of course for infants, the senile, and corporations—by a lawyer authorized to represent it, by *ad hoc* court appointment, or otherwise.[2] Assuming that the guardian had to show damages, the law could simply provide that the lake's legal damages were to be measured by the costs of making the lake "whole" in the sense of restoring the lake to the condition it would have been in had its "legal right" to intactness not been violated. That is, if the defendant's liability were established (if the upstream plant were found to have violated the applicable standards), it would have to pay into a trust fund, for the repair of the river, funds adequate to cover such items as aeration, restocking with fish and aquatic plants, filtering, and dredging.

If anyone considers this farfetched, note that the federal courts have allowed such a suit to be brought in the name of the Byram River (the river that forms part of the interstate boundary between southern Connecticut and New York) against the village of Port Chester, which had been polluting it.* And it is certainly plausible that some recent and important federal legislation, including the Federal Water Pollution Control Act (FWPCA) and the Comprehensive Environmental Response, Compensation, and Liability Act of 1980 (CERCLA), will be construed as authorizing comparable results. Units of the federal or state governments are empowered to sue polluters as trustees for the environment and to recover and apply the costs of restorations, even if those costs exceed the actual economic consumption value.

Commonwealth of Puerto Rico v. *SS Zue Colocotroni*[3] is a striking illustration. In *Zue Colocotroni,* an oil tanker by that name was allowed by its owners to deteriorate into an unseaworthy condition, to be launched without proper charts, and to be manned, as the courts put it, by a "hopelessly lost" and "incompetent crew." The ship ran aground off Puerto Rico, spilling thousands of tons of crude oil. Puerto Rico, as trustee for its resources, submitted an estimate of damage to an area around a twenty-acre mangrove swamp. The major item was for a decline of 4,605,486 organisms per acre. "This means," the district

*Byram River v. Village of Port Chester, 4 Environmental Law Reporter 20,816 (D. Conn., Aug. 21, 1974). (Suit in name of river and other plaintiffs to enjoin pollution by municipal sewage-treatment plant dismissed for lack of *in personam* jurisdiction and transferred to the federal court in the Southern District of New York for that reason, no reservations being expressed, however, regarding the river's designation as party plaintiff.) Ultimately, a stipulation of settlement was approved, 6 Environmental Law Reporter 20,467 (S.D. N.Y. Jan. 8, 1976) (defendant undertaking to conduct and monitor the project in environmentally protective manner).

court said, "92,109,720 marine animals were killed," largely sand crabs, segmented worms, and the like. Trying to get a handle on damages (the court's own can of segmented worms), the judge wrote:

> The uncontradicted evidence establishes that there is a ready market with reference to biological supply laboratories, thus allowing a reliable calculation of the cost of replacing these organisms. The lowest possible replacement cost figure is $.06 per animal, with may species selling from $1.00 to $4.50 per individual. Accepting the lowest replacement cost, and attaching damages only to the lost marine animals in the West Mangrove area, we find the damages caused by Defendants to amount to $5,526,584.20.

There was not a lot of precedent, as the reader can imagine. But the court of appeals affirmed the award, filing an opinion clearly sympathetic to deterring damage to nature—keeping it intact—without too finicky a regard either for human economic value or for the lower court's sympathetic but wondrously coarse technique for approximating the "replacement costs."

> No market exists in which Puerto Rico can readily replace what it has lost. The loss is not only to certain plant and animal life but, perhaps more importantly, to the capacity of the now polluted segments of the environment to regenerate and sustain such life for some time into the future. That the Commonwealth did not intend, and perhaps was unable, to exploit these life forms, and the coastal areas which supported them, for commercial purposes should not prevent a damages remedy in the face of the clearly stated legislative intent to compensate for "the total value of the damages caused to the environment and/or natural resources. . . ." In recent times, mankind has become increasingly aware that the planet's resources are finite and that portions of the land and sea which at first glance seem useless, like salt marshes, barrier reefs, and other coastal areas, often contribute in subtle but critical ways to an environment capable of supporting both human life and the other forms of life on which we all depend. The Puerto Rico statute is obviously aimed at providing a damages remedy with sufficient scope to compensate for, and deter, the destruction of such resources; and while we can see many problems in fashioning such a remedy, we see no reason to try to frustrate that endeavor.[4]

What the *Zue Colocotroni* litigation suggests is that an intactness standard may "make sense," in the sense that it can be operationalized coherently. But it may not always "make sense" when evaluated as policy. Certainly the policy of making the environment whole will be resisted when the costs of restoration or preservation are vastly out of line with the resource's consumption and use value, and the injury arises from a conscientious miscalculation rather than, as in *Zue Colocotroni*, from gross, almost willful, negligence. That is, even if one recognizes a moral claim to expend for the resource *some* sum in excess of its beneficial social value (as we do in undertaking the rescue of a trapped miner), one is rightly queasy about committing society to a higher price-tag than any moral theory we can devise will warrant. The issue of overprotection is not peculiar to entities that lack, or take no interest in their well-being. The problem arises from our uncertainty about *preferences*. It is thus one of the common "general theory" problems that has to be faced in connection not only with lakes and forests, but also with some "higher" Nonpersons such as whales, primates, and mental defectives, entities that, while possessing interests and even preferences, are at best restricted in their capacities to express them.*

To understand the difficulty introduced by the want of preferences, we must consider for a moment the significance of preferences in the legal system in its ordinary operations, that is, as it affects dealings among Persons. As the law develops, a body of rules establishes or confirms certain entitlements, such as the right of a homeowner to his home, or of a car owner to her car. In the familiar interpersonal situations, the existence of legally enforceable claims does not freeze the social ordering. They only establish ground rules for the operation of a primarily consensual, mutually beneficial system.

To illustrate, suppose that I own a house, A, in the downtown area of a city. I value it because it is near my place of work, old friends,

---

*See, however, David Lamb, "Animal Rights and Liberation Movements," *Environmental Ethics* 4 (1982): 215, 231 (remarking on potential of nonhumans to communicate preferences to us, particularly as we increase our efforts to "listen." See also "Koko's Kitten," *National Geographic*, January 1985, 110 (narrating success in communicating with gorilla via sign language).

favored theaters, and reliable restaurants. Suppose now that Developer comes along with plans to turn my present block into apartment buildings. She is prepared to offer me an amount adequate to purchase another house in the suburbs, B, plus an additional lump sum of $100,000. Although I prefer A to B, I do not prefer the present situation to her package offer; that is, to owning B and pocketing the $100,000. By selling to Developer my rights to the favored house, my interests are advanced (I am better off), her interests are advanced (she is better off), and—presuming that the beneficence of her offer reflected the higher economic use society had for the apartment house over the one-family residences—the whole society emerges better off. The point is, because human preferences are rich, revealable, and negotiable, the initial assignment of a property right to my home (my ownership) does not hinder, and in fact may significantly contribute to, an exchange and redistribution of goods that is advantageous to all.

When we move from voluntary to involuntary exchanges, the mechanisms for adjustment shift, but it remains preferences that shape the system. The person who accidentally or deliberately drives a truck into my car is not, like Developer, coming to me with an offer to negotiate. The truck driver is engaged in what we might consider his own private condemnation of my property, "taking it" from me through the sort of negligence or malice that no right to the quiet enjoyment of my car can prevent. But while the legal system cannot prevent such an occurrence, it can provide that the wrongdoer compensate me. And note how the compensation is arrived at. The ideal is to make the wrongdoer pay whatever it takes to bring me to a position of indifference. That position is the point where I have no valid reason to prefer my pre-accident situation to the situation I find myself in after the accident plus the compensation award. In the case of the damaged car, that would ordinarily mean ordering the defendant to pay me whatever it took (in body-shop costs and other expenses) to return the car to the state it was in before the accident. But this is not always the solution. If the cost of returning the car to its original shape is greater than its replacement cost—the cost of substituting another car—the wrongdoer is obliged to make the substitution payment only.

None of these approaches is guaranteed to leave everyone or even anyone perfectly satisfied. But there is much to be said for them as ways of making the best of the many conflicts inherent in community living. Some corrective justice is achieved; that is, we at least approximate compensation for the victims. At the same time, social efficiency is served. By confronting one another with the prospect of having to make amends for the harms we cause, the rules induce us all to take such care as is warranted in the circumstances (to drive more slowly, to have our brakes checked, etc.)—in essence, to accommodate to one another as sensibly and fairly as possible.

If we return now to the question of distributing legally enforceable claims to Nonpersons, we can see more clearly what the problem is. The problem is not the intelligibility of assimilating Nonpersons, even preference-lacking Things, into the system. We can give them claims, and lawyers to speak for them. The real problem is this. Suppose that the only kind of "advantage" we can dole out to Nonpersons is to preserve them from physical change, to substitute pure physical *intactness* for other measures of value. Once assigned, such an entitlement will not be reallocable to the highest use by ordinary law and market mechanisms. The implication is not just to give some special status to the entity over and above what market evaluations would suggest; it is to withdraw the entity from market accountability entirely. The implication is to impose a sort of freeze on selected aspects of the status quo. That would be ironic, since nothing seems quite as "unnatural" as enduring unchange.*

Comparable postures—rules which remove all costs and benefits from consideration at the judicial and administrative levels—are not

*Moreover, wherever we were to adopt such a "freeze" position, we would be faced with the further question whether to express it in what we might call the imperative form or a weak form. In the imperative form, the Advantage would be construed as carrying an obligation that we intercede to prevent change from whatever cause, however indirectly *we* may be responsible. For example, if the forests surrounding the Sahara were a full Advantage-holder in this imperative sense, we would have an obligation, on the forests' behalf, to set the Sahara back, even if drought, rather than human intervention, were considered the proximate cause. (What if the Sahara had an Advantage?) I presume that, in regard to most things, the assignment of a status-freezing Advantage in this imperative sense would require some more powerful arguments than I can presently imagine.

unknown in the law. We do not do a cost-benefit analysis every time someone claims a right to free speech; that is what is meant by saying that free speech is (more or less) "absolute." The Fourteenth Amendment's prohibition on racial discrimination cannot be evaded by a showing that enforcing the Constitution imposes an *unreasonable* burden. Several years ago the so-called Delaney Amendment prohibited the inclusion in any foodstuff of any substance that might, in any amount, elevate cancer risks in any degree. Indeed, this is precisely the approach the Endangered Species Act of 1966 sought to implement in its original form. Interpreting that Act in *TVA* v. *Hill*[5] the Supreme Court held that notwithstanding that $100 million which had been spent on a huge dam project, the whole project had to halt if one endangered species —a snail darter—would be placed at risk of elimination.

Now, we can arrange the system this way, that is, devise rules so that the intactness of certain things is insulated from all influence of market prices. But note that in the most celebrated instances where we have approximated such a posture, as with constitutional rights to speech, press, and jury trial, there is a strong and broadly shared political consensus for what we do. In the absence of a comparably widespread concord, rules that originate as flat-out prohibitions tend to erode the more their conflict with prevailing desires becomes apparent. For example, the result of the flap over saccharin was to amend the Food and Drug Acts in such a way as to weaken the Delaney Amendment. After the U.S. Supreme Court reprieved the snail darters, Congress amended the law to provide a "review" process designed to relax the protection accorded endangered species in some circumstances. The point is this. I have not yet demonstrated that there is *any* argument for preserving a Thing intact, a chore to which I will turn in part III. Much less have I shown that any such argument could meet the demands of a valid moral theory. But we can anticipate that if the costs to us of intactness are high, the legal arrangement, if it is not to be diluted and evaded, will require not only a moral argument to back it up, but a fairly sturdy moral argument, at that.

Just as a preliminary intuition, is it possible there are Things on whose behalf a plea of such strength could be made? In *Trees*, I suggested as a possibility the Grand Canyon, which owing to its uniqueness, grandness, and association with national heritage might find support on mixed moral bases for so privileged a position—to be treated like an environmental First Amendment, as it were. But regarding most other Things, even if people are persuaded to sacrifice something for their conservation, the costs of intactness will in many circumstances appear unacceptable—even morally unacceptable. Consider, for example, a proposal to gird a river with a series of small hydroelectric dams that will relieve the need to import $1 million of oil annually. Of course, after damming, the river cannot be exactly the same as it was before. Even if we discern a moral reason to sacrifice *something* to preserve the river intact, we may not feel obligated—it may not be *right*—to forego competing benefits, such as heating the houses of the poor. What, then? Recall that in comparable situations when the "rights" of Persons are conflicted, the law's response is to award the "victim," such as the private owner of land condemned for a public purpose, a lump sum calculated to make him indifferent. But we have no way to judge whether some compromise solution we might offer the river is *fair enough*, is *compensating*. Are we on the horns of a dilemma so fatal— all or nothing—that the assignment of Advantage to Things has to be regarded as unsupportable in all but the most extraordinary circumstances?

This, I take it, is the central challenge of the legal segment of our inquiry. The implementation of Advantages to Nonpersons threatens to back us into a corner. We would not only be handing them Advantages, but Advantages beyond the reach of compromises merited by our own legitimate claims and needs. What is required are more flexible alternatives.

IMPUTING PREFERENCES

First, while Things have (or "take") no interests by definition, the same concession is not required of all Nonpersons, for example, future and spatially remote humans. We cannot know their preferences with certainty, but we can make some good guesses within reason. Even regarding "higher" animals, we cannot dismiss the feasibility of correctly identifying and imputing at least some preferences. Note that the issue being raised here is not the conventional query of the animal rights literature—whether higher animals have properties essential for possessing moral rights. All we are asking here is whether we can project a Nonperson's preferences confidently enough to allocate it some Advantage, without locking ourselves into a position of utter inflexibility.

To illustrate how a Nonperson's preferences, where available, may be enlisted to support the entity's legal position, let me return to the case of the bowhead whales. I am not certain how clear a picture we have of what whales like, of what welfare economists might call their "preference profile." Presumably a whale's preferences are less richly detailed than a Person's, if only because the richness of many alternatives available to humans—to go bowling or sit in a movie—do not present themselves to animals for reasons both physical and intellectual.* On the other hand, we could say much the same for infants and the mentally disabled, on whose behalf the law constructs rough preferences fairly routinely. Surely, unless one is prepared to deny that whales have intelligence and are capable of exercising choice, it is fair to infer that they prefer their present route through the Beaufort Sea to any other. (If the path is not exhaustively prescribed by instinct, why do they select the variations they do?) True, we cannot be certain *why* and *how much* they would find an alternate route less preferable. Perhaps a more northerly path would take them into less comfortable waters in terms of temperature. Another route would involve a less familiar, more bewildering (anxiety-ridden), path; the food at the greater distances from shoreline, even if comparable nutritionally, might be less palatable.

We are unclear on all the details. But we do know some things about their preferences—and we could learn more. For example, I presume that marine biologists know the whales' favorite foods, and it does not seem beyond our capabilities to determine experimentally what meals

---

*On the other fin, a whale swimming in the ocean may routinely mull alternatives that would not occur to a person swimming alongside.

they would prefer to whatever they can locate on the northernmost edge of their current journey-route. And let us simplify matters by supposing that none of their favorite fare (krill, plankton, or—God forbid!—snail darters) are recognized as legal persons in their own right. The point is, the more we are able to approximate such interests, the more freely we can allocate Advantages to Nonpersons with the assurance that if we need to modify them, we can "compensate" the way we do with Persons. This considerably mitigates the inflexibility problem referred to earlier.

To illustrate how such compensation would work, let us suppose that we do regard the whales as having established an Advantage to their traditional migratory route—something like what the law would call an easement by prior occupancy or prescription. Even if we elevated such an Advantage to equivalent rank of a human's property right, it would still be subject to condemnation, just as the ordinary person's easements (such as a long-established access path across a neighbor's property) can be condemned. To carry out this line of thought, suppose that the government had a higher public use for the whale's easement. The Treasury might realize, say, $10 billion in selling the oil rights. If so, mankind could well stand to proceed with the oil sale and still "pay off" the whales with a trust fund of $1 million for making their new course more comfortable. This could be accomplished by, say, "chumming" the alternate, northerly route with whatever foodstuff whale research indicated was high on the whales' preferences. As an ideal, some such solution would be better for everyone (would constitute, in the academic lingo, an interspecies-pareto improvement). The U.S. citizens would be better off through a reduced tax burden. The oil companies and their customers would be better off through the prospect of new domestic oil reserves. And the whales would be no worse off, tided over by a trust fund expended in a way as to compensate them —and help steer them clear of dangers at the drilling site.

Let me hasten to confirm that I do not know enough of the facts about the whales to know whether such a solution would make sense as a response to the bowhead dilemma, and I offer it as an imaginative illustration. But controversies of this sort are not sheerly fanciful,* and the principle illustrated is significant. The more *interested* we have become in other living things, the more we have been able to discover about their preferences. (Experiments with pigeons have revealed something of their discount rates; that is, their willingness to defer modest present gratifications in exchange for more substantial future rewards.) And the more confidently we can construct Nonperson preferences— that is, adopt their standpoint—the more feasibly we can fit them into rules which, while putting them into positions of Advantage, do not do so inflexibly.

BOUNDARIES AND IDEALS

Unfortunately, the feasibility of such a preference-enlisting solution exists only in regard to Nonpersons at the higher end of the intelligence scale. In the case of many Nonpersons, and of all Things, that tactic has no place. They have no preferences. What, then, could comprise a workable solution?

One way to avoid inflexibility is to build some threshold conditions into the rules.† Such boundary-sensitive Advantages would not be out of character with ordinary human "rights." To take an obvious example, people have a right to a trial in certain federal civil cases if, but only if, the amount in controversy exceeds (depending on the controversy)

*An interesting episode of such a character occurred in Wyoming in 1983–84. A rancher installed a twenty-eight-mile-long fence that cut off the migration route of sixteen hundred pronghorn antelopes to their winter grazing site at Red Rim. All risked death. After a storm of publicity, some talk of legal action, and pleas from the governor, the rancher relented and cut passageways in the fence for the antelope to get through. Query: should a rancher in such a situation bear the costs personally, or should he be compensated from the public till?

†Even without express threshold conditions, judicial institutions are prone to dismiss complaints on traditionally available grounds when any harm the plaintiff suffered can be regarded as de minimis—beneath the threshold of what the law is prepared to recognize. See United States v. Chevron, 583 F.2d 1357 (5th Cir. 1978). The company was found to have discharged oil into a navigable waterway, which caused a presumption of violation of law; but the only consequence was a "sheen" on the water. The company was allowed to rebut the presumption of illegality by demonstrating that the sheen-causing discharge was "less than harmful."

twenty dollars or ten thousand dollars. By analogy, we could assign some monetary value to a Thing we chose to protect, say, $25 million for snail darters. This would mean that we were committed to forgo up to that amount to preserve the species. But if the tangible social benefits of some proposed snail-darter-jeopardizing action exceeded $25 million, then the action could proceed under the condition that that sum would be applied either to mitigate the risk, or else be allocated to some other part of the environment, perhaps to preserve some endangered, closely related species in a nearby biotic community.

Indeed, it remains to be seen whether the current administration will not propose some such construction of the toxic spill legislation discussed in chapter 1.[6] A polluter might be required to return the lake to its pre-pollution condition unless the amount required to restore it exceeded a fixed figure. There is no other response when we are dealing with mishaps that are technologically impossible to repair at any price. Instead of demanding an infinite sum in damages, we have to develop feasible alternative remedies. Something like this occurred in the wake of the notorious discharges of the pesticide Kepone into the James River in 1975. A full dredging of the river bottom would not only have been extravagant in relation to the dangers; many believe that stirring up toxins from the bottom was riskier than just leaving them lie. As a consequence, Allied Chemical agreed to fund an $8 million trust fund with the mandate to mitigate the damage to the river and to foster general environmental-health research in the area.[7]

Moreover, we do not have to express boundary parameters in monetary terms. We can employ physical definitions. If, say, a lake's level of dissolved oxygen should fall below so many parts per million (a common measure of biological degradation), or if the aggregate biomass it supports should decline below so many specified tons, then the guardian would be empowered to invoke some legal remedy, in whatever way specified. A comparable approach is written into the Marine Mammal Protection Act. Individual endangered sea mammals, such as porpoises, are not protected as such. But if a human activity, such as seining for tuna, threatens the "optimum sustainable population" of their habitat, then the courts are authorized to intervene. Indeed, at that point, as the courts have interpreted the law, "balancing of interests between the commercial fishing fleet and the porpoise is irrelevant; the porpoise must prevail."[8]

From boundaries expressed in numerical terms of dollars, parts per million, optimum sustainable population, and so on, it is but a short step to enlist some looser notion of ideals as an alternate device for preserving flexibility. That is, while we cannot orient the law to a Thing's welfare, we can orient it to some ideal state of the Thing, without (as with boundaries) undertaking to express that ideal in a specific set of numbers. An enlisting of ideals is not unfamiliar to law. Certainly there are many circumstances in which the law glosses over what an individual actually desires with normative notions of what he or she most valuably *is* and *can become*. On a parity of reasoning, we can transport into the legal rules that govern our relations with Nonpersons norms that try to capture essences. In regard to a river, rather than using a standard expressed in parts per million, or some opacity index, we would examine the issue in terms of whether the river's "riverhood" was being endangered, just as one may have standing to challenge whether an artwork's "integrity"[9] is in peril.

Within such a loose, ideal-oriented construct there is room for compromise. Suppose that in regard to a habitat, the law adopted something like ecosystem stability as a rough measure of its essential, protectable nature. In that case, the guardian would be warranted to settle a suit against the jeopardizer of one of the habitat's populations if the defendant agreed to stock an alternate species, less endangered by the particular project, but equally well linked into the ecological balance.

There are obvious questions about both the boundaries and the ideals-based alternatives. One is certain to wonder how, in selecting the critical boundary variables or supplying content to the key "ideal" (riverhood, habitathood), we can avoid being, on the one hand, totally arbitrary or, on the other, guilty of smuggling in whatever standard advances our own most "raw" homocentric interests. This is part of a larger issue that I return to in part III. Here, let me say only that we should not underestimate the capacity of commonsensical intuition, reinforced by ordinary language and an understanding of physical processes, to provide us with coherent notions about the essence of things quite independent of what we *want* those things to be. We are able to speak of the "death of a star," quite aside from what state we want the star to be in, or anything we might do about it. It is true that the classificatory categories selected in biology—whether something has vertebrae, nurses its young, climbs trees—undeniably reflect human "interests" in the broadest sense of what we are curious about. But surely we have a notion of what a genus or species is, independent of our own welfares. Hence, we can talk coherently about the design of arrangements that would preserve mosquitos and tarantulas, quite aside from whether doing so would be a good idea in terms of human welfare.

There is a second objection: at least where ideals are concerned, the concepts are likely to be too vague for courts to work with. How would a judge decide the point at which a river's "riverhood" was being infringed? I doubt that it would be any harder than judging "due process" or "negligence" or many other judgments that lawyers and courts are routinely called upon to make. Closer analogies exist in situations where a ruling will affect humans (albeit, in our terminology, Nonpersons) who are yet-unborn beneficiaries of trusts. The court hears out a guardian ad litem to decide what they, as Persons, probably will —or should—like. In other cases courts deal with those unable to reveal their preferences, such as the comatose accident victim and the severely retarded: Shall we turn off the life support systems, or order painful but life-prolonging therapy? We tend to work our way through these cases by invoking a concept of "personhood" that does not seem to me any less problematical than "riverhood."*

*A poignant illustration is Superintendent of Belchertown State School v. Saikewicz, 370 N.E.2nd 417 (1977). There, a profoundly retarded, institutionalized 67-year-old man with an I.Q. of 10 contracted leukemia. Chemotherapy could prolong his life, but the treatment would subject him to pain the reasons for which he would not be able to comprehend. Nor had Saikewicz any long-term projection of a *life*, which might have made short-term suffering bearable. The court settled upon a test based on what Saikewicz would have chosen, *were he*

Or compare an inquiry into "riverhood" with what is involved in a prisoner's rights case. Some restrictions imposed on an inmate are simply part of what is entailed and intended by the imprisonment. But at some point, the imposition goes too far. Judicial analysis ordinarily pays tribute to "cruel and unusual punishment" because that is the language of the Constitution. But the real issue is whether the prison conditions can be reconciled with the essential respect owed the prisoner as a Person: is some protectable sense of his *personhood* being violated? How does the judge judge when this point is reached? We simply trust her to come to a right result (perhaps informed by the precedents that develop over the years), even if we know that at bottom she is being guided by a somewhat intuitive metaphysics and morals. In like vein, in regard to the river, there is simply a difference we might trust judges to recognize between ribbing a river with dams but leaving the river's total flow and course intact and, on the other hand, so depleting its waters that it simply peters out and never reaches the sea.

---

able to understand the choice. How can such a hypothetical reasoning process carry forward without introducing some ideal of personhood into the analysis?

We may also invoke something like a personhood standard in instances involving compensation for a loss, where the losers are suspected of exaggerating their true preferences in order to extract a higher payment than is just, and we wish to establish what they probably *really* want.

The Nonperson in a Position
of Legal Disadvantage

T HUS FAR I have been examining situations in which the law might situate a Nonperson in a position of Advantage, epitomized by cases in which we would put it in the position of a party plaintiff. I want to turn now, if only briefly, to the other side of the coin. Can we conceive of situations in which we might intelligibly place a Nonperson, or even less plausibly a mere Thing, in a position of Disadvantage?

I will take as the paradigmatic Disadvantage being positioned as a defendant in a civil or criminal matter. But there are two prior observations. First, being placed in the position of a defendant is not the only way in which the law may place something at Disadvantage. For example, the law disadvantages deer through the establishment of a legal hunting season, although it does so by what classic jurisprudence would have called "no-rights," that is, leaving the deer powerless to make legal complaint. Conversely, being placed in the position of defendant is not necessarily disadvantaging; it depends upon the alternatives. In the light of otherwise prevailing practices, making a Nonperson stand trial may actually constitute something of a relative Advantage. There is some suggestion of this in a recent case arising in a Detroit suburb. Authorities impounded a prize sheep dog with plans to destroy it for having killed an eighty-seven-year-old woman. The dog's owners rejoined that the lady had died of a massive heart attack. The dog was tried, even allowed "character witnesses" to testify about its "gentle disposition." After a hearing that, according to press reports, took on "all the trappings of a murder trial," the dog was ordered defanged, neutered, and confined to home.[1] In Virginia, a dog sentenced to death for barking was reportedly given a reprieve by an appeals court, the death penalty being considered too harsh a punishment.[2] It is hard to judge from the newspaper accounts with what technical accuracy the hearings were characterized as making the dogs defendants in a real criminal trial. But the stories at least remind us that being made a criminal defendant is accompanied by certain procedural protections and a public visibility that an animal, such as the zoo tiger that mauls a child, rarely receives. Better to be brought to the trial than to be unceremoniously disposed of as chattel, like an old lamp.

Of course, from our point of view, putting a Nonperson on criminal trial seems, if not incoherent, at least odd or pointless.* We associate crimes with notions of blameworthiness, free will, and criminal intent, none of which applies to a tiger, much less to a tree. But these elements are not indispensable to criminal prosecution. In fact, the distinction between intentional and sheerly accidental misconduct is one that the law disregarded for centuries. In this light, it is not surprising that there were times when animals, even lower animals and inanimates such as trees, were subjected to criminal penalties, sometimes after elaborate trial. In Exod. 21:28 it was provided that an ox who gored "a man or woman, that they die," should be put to death. Plato, apparently carrying forward notions of Attic law, provided similarly in his *Laws*. Referring to a goring, he wrote, "The kinsmen of the deceased shall prosecute the slayer for murder."[3] In 1120, a bishop of Leon was said to have excommunicated the caterpillars that were ravaging his diocese, and in 1565 the Arlesians asked for the expulsion of the grasshoppers.

The case came before the Tribunal de l'Officialité, and Maître Marin was assigned to the insects as counsel. He defended his clients with much zeal.

*Although I focus on criminal cases in the text, one can conceive a civil suit against a Nonperson. Suppose that under a will, the deceased owner of a dog has established a generous trust fund to keep the dog well fed and groomed for life. The dog bites the postman. Assume that the dog's caretaker is blameless, or at any rate not so well compensated by the trust as to be able to pay the postman's medical bills. Is it so unreasonable that the postman should be able to reach the dog's estate to cover his damages? To suppose otherwise is to force the costs of the accident on the postman—why should he bear them?—in favor of the dog.

Since the accused had been created, he argued that they were justified in eating what was necessary to them. The opposite counsel cited the serpent in the Garden of Eden, and sundry other animals mentioned in Scripture, as having incurred severe penalties. The grasshoppers got the worst of it, and were ordered to quit the territory, with a threat of anathematization from the altar, to be repeated till the last of them had obeyed the sentence of the honourable court.[4]

Today, we look back on tales of that sort as evidence of a primitive legal system that no one now could possibly defend. But recall that to our recent ancestors, it seemed just as mindless to prosecute corporations (in our terms, Nonpersons) as it seems to us to prosecute oxen. Indeed, the requirement that a defendant need have criminal intent, which was gradually tacked onto the law in the twelfth to fourteenth centuries, has more modernly receded for many classes of strict and vicarious liability offenses. As a consequence, there is no doubt we *could* prosecute Nonpersons—put, say, an artificial intelligence on trial— without rendering the legal system incoherent. Historically ships were not only made parties to litigation, they were quite literally defendants. If "she" engaged in piracy, she could be made the subject of an action, quite aside from the fate of those who steered her in sin and who might have escaped capture. See, for example, *U.S.* v. *Cargo of the Brig Malek Adhel.* [5] The brig had been seized by pirates. After capture, the United States condemned and sold the offending vessel. In refusing to release the ship to the original lawful owners, Justice Story (quoting Chief Justice Marshall from an earlier case) observed: "This is not a proceeding against the owner; it is a proceeding against the vessel for an offense committed by the vessel; which is not the less an offense . . . because it was committed without the authority and against the will of the owner."

Such trials are thus coherent. But are they *wise?* That is a separate and harder question. A full answer would require us, in each case, to examine the practice in the light of traditional justifications for the criminal law.

Take first *general deterrence.* One reason we criminalize conduct is to make an example of the wrongdoer in order to affect and restrain the behavior of others. Of course no ox will be deterred by another ox's gloomy fate. (Would an artificial intelligence be so influenced?) Nor, for that matter, does anyone think it possible to deter a corporation as such. But in both cases, subjecting *the Thing* to criminal process may be viewed as an effective although indirect way of modifying the behavior of the people best positioned to exercise control over the instruments of harm. In the one situation we are sending a message to those who can tether or fence the oxen; in the other, to those who can steer the corporate bureaucracy. And by proceeding against the Thing (leaving in the background the managers, whose personal guilt may be obscure), we realize our aims without directly colliding with traditional values such as no liability without fault, the presumption of innocence, and so on.*

Another recognized function of the criminal law is *general education.* We use the trial not just to detain or rehabilitate wrongdoers, or even to deter others, but to dramatize what the society considers egregiously wrongful conduct. I suspect this is part of the explanation for having put pirate ships on trial. And one reason why we prosecute an auto company (as distinct from its executives) for the manufacture of an exceedingly shoddy car is that we want to underscore a social value: that casual disregard for life is not to be tolerated. Prosecuting the corporation, whose name has more public recognition than that of an executive, sends out a message that is destined to travel to the general public.†

There is an illustration in the Nuremberg trials of the Nazi war criminals of how these considerations may combine to operate. Several persons, including Franz von Papen, who was made defendant principally because he had preceded Hitler as chancellor and not done enough

---

*Note that the law can choose to prosecute the corporate manager and ox owner as well as the things they control. Exodus goes on to provide, "But if the ox were wont to push with his horn in time past, and it hath been testified to his owner, and he hath not kept him in, but that he hath killed a man or a woman; the ox shall be stoned, and his owner also shall be put to death" (Exod. 21:29). Corporate stockholders and officers take note.

†On the other hand, the prosecution of the errant company's officers presumably sends a "message" that more effectively travels to their corporate executive peers.

to resist his rise, wanted Hitler indicted and tried, notwithstanding the fact that Hitler was presumed by all to be dead.[6] Although under these proposals Hitler would have been tried for acts he committed while he was a moral agent, he was at the time of trial, in our terms, a Thing, a mass of burned, decaying matter. Now, surely, if punishing the guilty is conceived as the only function of the criminal law, the suggestion has to be regarded as incoherent; Hitler was beyond punishment. But the proposal need not be so viewed, precisely because there are competing and supplementing rationales for the criminal process. In all criminal trials, and quite dramatically at Nuremberg, we are deterring others from like offenses, staging ceremonies of denunciation, and engaging in moral education and development. Moreover, trying Hitler would have placed his role, and therefore that of the other defendants, in a more balanced and fair perspective. (This is what I presume to have motivated Papen.) Trying Hitler, albeit now a Thing, would have produced a proceeding that was more *just.* *

Most people probably feel that *vengeance* and *retribution*, often invoked as a warrant for criminalizing certain conduct, are out of place as applied to entities that lack free will, or, at least, a will capable of malice. But the meaning of a concept like free will is too indeterminate, the dynamics that underlie vengeance too complex, that one should reject the possibilities out of hand. Certainly some serious thinkers have thought otherwise. Consider Adam Smith:

> The dog that bites, the ox that gores, are both of them punished. . . . [N]or is this merely for the security of the living, but, in some measure, to revenge the injury of the dead.[7]

For such reasons, I do not think we can categorically aver that there is no plausible prima facie case to be made for putting at least some Nonpersons, even Things, on trial in any circumstances. The analysis

---

*One may point out that had we "tried" Hitler, one traditional element of a criminal trial—that the defendant be allowed to respond to his accusers—would have been unfulfilled. But I am not sure that the proceedings would therefore have been something other than "a criminal prosecution" (a problem now of nomenclature). Presumably, Hitler would have had a lawyer to speak for him, as had Martin Bormann, who, although presumed dead, was tried anyway and sentenced *in absentia* to death by hanging.

mirrors the analysis we performed on the Advantages side. That is, whether we might *want* or *ought* to so situate a Nonperson depends upon a fuller description and evaluation of the consequent system that would result. The considerations are complex and subtle. For example, the criminal trial of the dogs could be supported by someone who thought punishing dogs was incoherent, but who wanted to protect both humans and dogs from the consequences of a hasty, and later to be regretted, striking out in rage. In each situation, one is forced to weigh against the gains in deterrence, rehabilitation, character building, and justice the added costs of dragging a new class of defendants into an already burdened court system. There are, too, the subtle social costs of overcriminalizing conduct that is not "really criminal." And there are always alternatives to consider. For example, I can well imagine at some not-too-future date a court considering it appropriate to appoint a technically trained "Master" to investigate and make a judicial report on an artificial intelligence system that has "gone haywire," with disastrous results. But such an arrangement would not require a lawsuit against the A.I.—certainly not a criminal prosecution.

SUMMARY

In summary of this brief review of the legal recognition of Nonpersons, let me make clear that I am not claiming that each and every Nonperson could (much less should) be put in each and every position the law has carved out for Persons. There is, at the least, a threshold question of intelligibility, policy aside. For each arrangement, we have to ask, could *that* entity be fitted coherently into *that* legal provision? It would make no sense to accord a tree the right to sit on a jury, for example, or to make a will. But surely a tree could be the beneficiary of a will. And decisions to cut one down, even by its private owner, could be made subject to administrative review (some cities now do this). And while the argument for making trees defendants is one that will not root easily, it is at least *conceivable,* and therefore worth evaluation—as evidenced by the fact that it once was so. Holmes reminds us that under the laws of Alfred, if a tree fell on a person, killing him, it was to be executed, its corpse delivered to the deceased's kinsmen to chop up and put to revengeful and beneficial use at the hearth.*

The basic point I want to carry forward is this. As concerns the positioning of Things in law, the range of options we can coherently implement is much wider than is commonly recognized. However, to say that any particular arrangement is coherent is not to say that it is *wise*, much less morally right or morally welcome. We could prosecute and execute the insane, but it would strain the moral fabric of the law. Indeed, each of the many options has costs that are easy to identify: the inflexibility that comes of assigning entitlements that will be practically inalienable, the added court burden, and perhaps even the erosion of judicial credibility should judges be regarded as subordinating identifiable human interests on behalf of a constituency that could not care one way or the other. But whether these costs are "too great" in any situation turns on another inquiry—the moral dimensions of our subject, to which I shall now proceed. Which if any such arrangements are defensible, and on what grounds?

---

*Holmes, *The Common Law* (Boston: Little, Brown & Co., 1946), p. 11. At a later period, under Edward I, a tree from which someone fell to his death was deodand, that is, forfeit to the Crown, even if its owner (if it had one) was blameless. *Ibid.* p. 24, citing authorities.

III

THE NONPERSON
IN MORAL THOUGHT

With these observations on how Nonpersons could be fitted into law, let me pass on to the more fundamental questions of morals. Supposing that we *could* intelligibly adjust the legal system to provide various Nonpersons recognition in the law—that is, fit them into the legal framework through an assignment of Advantage and Disadvantage —why *ought* we to do so? What would an argument in favor of such laws look like? And, more broadly, on what basis might Nonpersons be accounted for, not merely in law, but in moral thought generally?

These, the moral questions, are, as I have already intimated, harder than the legal ones. And of these none seems more intractable than the ontological conundrum. By reference to what principles are we to carve up the world into those things that count, and those that don't? It is well known that in some conditions the survival of a herd may require the "thinning out" of individual members. If we take herds rather than individual animals as our moral unit, then presumably the "thinning" is all right. On the other hand, if the individual counts, but not the herds, then thinning is harder to defend. Hence, are *individuals* morally favored, or *herds?*

Let me emphasize that viewed from within the law, that is, from the perspective of a judge disposing of a case, such dilemmas can be contained manageably. The *Palilla* decision illustrates this.* The palilla is a rare, small bird whose sole known habitat, in Hawaii, was being

*Palilla v. Hawaii Dept. of Land & Natural Resources, 471 F.Supp. 985 (D. Hawaii 1979).

threatened. A suit was brought in the name of the palillas as plaintiffs to force the Hawaiian Department of Land and Natural Resources to take affirmative action to arrest the threat. The judicial predicament was that the apparent villains, the enemy of the palilla that the suit pressed the government to restrain, were the Islands' feral goats who were nibbling away the palilla's only foodstuff, the mamane tree. Now, a judge who had to consider this controversy from scratch would have a host of moral problems to untangle. If there is any warrant to intervene in the first place, why ought the birds be preferred over nature's apparent favorite, the goats? Why, if one is to care about Nonpersons at all, ought one care about either birds or goats rather than something else—for example, the mamane tree?

Probably to his relief, the federal judge never had to confront head-on these underlying moral problems—what *ought* the law to be? His task was simplified because there was a prior rule provided by Congress, the Endangered Species Act. Under that act's authority the palilla had been listed as an endangered species; jeopardizing its habitat was to be avoided at all costs (essentially, a habitat *intactness* standard of the sort discussed in Chapter 6). No one had thought to do the same for the feral goats, which have been fending fairly well for themselves just about anywhere from time immemorial. Hence, viewed from the perspective of the bench as a question of implementing the laws of the land, the decision was not so knotty: the law said the goats had to give.

But for the question we are now facing there is no such simple solution available. That is, imagine we are not judges applying the law that exists, but representatives sitting in Congress deciding what the *law ought to be*. How does one construct a rational argument that one rule is better than any other?

Moral Considerateness

ARGUMENTS BASED ON HUMAN UTILITY AND HUMAN RIGHTS

As WE SAW in Chapter 6, it is an all too common mistake to suppose that all questions of legal considerateness boil down to questions of legal rights. In this chapter there is an analogous error to confront: to suppose that the only basis for maintaining that X (someone or something) has a legal right is to demonstrate that X has a moral right, as it were, underneath. Here, too, there is a fragment of truth on which the mistaken generalization rests. Some legal rights associated with ordinary humans—including some of the most fundamental, such as freedom of speech and of worship—relate to strong claims of moral right that were championed long before the constitutional provisions were enacted to secure them. With such an image in mind there is a temptation, when considering whether an animal or tree or future human should have a legal right (or other Advantage), to suppose that it requires proof of some independent and prior moral right.

But this is simply not so. One perfectly plausible moral basis for making Nonpersons legally considerate, even to the point of according them something approximating "legal rights," is where doing so is calculated to advance the welfare of humans. Such an argument can be carried through quite apart from any independent moral right that the Nonperson can be shown to have, and, indeed, quite apart from whether it is even of any independent moral interest.

73

Corporations, for example, are not Persons. Yet, they are fitted into law by assigning them legal, even constitutional, rights. General Motors can sue, be sued, and raise "its" rights to be free from unreasonable searches and seizures. This is a practice that has the support of persons who would not argue that corporations are themselves moral agents to which moral rights and duties can be ascribed. To *justify* positioning corporations as holders of legal rights (and bearers of legal liabilities), one need go no further than show that a regime in which corporations are so positioned is preferable in terms of the beneficial consequences of the resulting system for contemporary humans.

On a like basis, we can support the legal personification of many Nonpersons (e.g., granting them standing in court) because it is the most sensible way of promoting our normally recognized ends, without ever deciding whether the Nonperson deserves any independent moral rights. If the preservation of a species is of commercial benefit to us, one way to fortify that benefit is to appoint for the species a guardian. A legislature, averse to the risk of toxic wastes on humans, might be well disposed to create a guardian-enforced right in bodies of water to enjoin toxic-induced changes in their status quo, at a threshold before an irreversible hazard to humans has become provable. This would be a system in which some Things were made *legally* considerate. But it does not presuppose their being *morally* considerate. To supply moral warrant for the arrangement, one need not look beyond a sheerly conventional utilitarian calculus.

Similarly, someone who was persuaded that among basic human moral rights was the right to a clean environment could well support the assignment of environmental legal rights for the environment as means of securing the moral rights of Persons. In fact, in much of Anglo-American legal history a stream's "natural flow" was as protected from interference as any environmentalist might have wished; the protection stemmed, however, not from any moral claim on behalf of the stream but from what were conceived to be the "natural rights" of the riparian (streamside) landowner.

The reader may be tempted to respond, "Then we are talking about the legal rights of humans, not those of rivers." Not necessarily. Remember that even if the judge or legislature is animated solely by a concern for human welfare, the elements which the guardian is required to prove in court in a particular case need not include actual or potential damage *to humans.* On the contrary, we are assuming that the legal rule will authorize claims on behalf of the river when changes *in the river* exceed a certain standard. Under such a system, the direct interest—what would govern the lawyers' and judges' attention—would be evidence bearing on the river: whether it was being "damaged" in the legally defined sense under that standard. There would be no call to prove any hazard to humans, or any infringement of a human's rights, if the rule did not so provide.

OTHER BASES FOR THE LEGAL CONSIDERATENESS OF NONPERSONS

There are many illustrations of this sort where the legal recognition of a Nonperson can be rested on grounds of ordinary Persons' rights and interests conceived and calculated in the most straightforward and familiar anthropocentric ways. Most people, I expect, are prepared to deal in those terms, and to reform legal and social arrangements to the extent they demonstrably inure to the benefit of contemporary (or, slightly more problematically, future) humans.

The falling out occurs when someone proposes going one step further. What happens when we are being asked to spare wilderness areas, rivers, species, and whatnot and thus to forego timber, living space, and chemicals, not from consideration of our interests as we ordinarily understand them, but from consideration of *something else?* The objection is not just that such sacrifices are unwarrantable. More severely, it is common to feel that a moral argument aimed at justifying sacrifices from consideration (somehow) of nonhumans, in particular of things devoid of interests, is not even intelligible. There is no "something else." (One Canadian writer, criticizing my views in *Trees,* paraphrases

Gertrude Stein against me: "When you get there, there's no *their* there." "The only stone which could be of moral concern and hence deserving of legal rights," the critic gibes, "is one like Christopher."[1]

The objection might be put this way. A moral dilemma grows out of, and operates to resolve, conflicts. All conflicts are conflicts of interest. We might have conflicts of interest among ourselves *in regard to* a particular river. This means that we would conserve a certain state of the river to the point, but not beyond the point, warranted by our collective interests *in it.* But the river itself has no independent interests. In our discussion of law, recall, it was possible to sidestep the river's lack of real independent interest by presuming that the lawmaking body would merely mandate whatever was to be the river's legally protected state. Legal interests and legal harms are what the law provides them to be. But when we step back to put ourselves in the position of lawmakers and ask what considerations we might mull to arrive at any environment-conserving standards, there is a corresponding question that definitions cannot stifle: How, not in legal fiction but in credible fact, can any legal position we put the river in make *it* better or worse off? The implication, it will be said, is that any apparent conflict between us and rivers is illusory.

Whatever truth there be to the claim that Things lack interests, it is also misleading. Of course, to speak of a moral dilemma presupposes interests, even some conflict: one interest that tugs one way and one interest that tugs another. That much is inherent in "dilemma." But there is no reason why the conflict cannot be a conflict within a single person, the moral agent faced with a decision. The "conflicting interests"—so far as that is required—may be one's own. Indeed, if morals are to be intelligible, it is imperative that our talk about interests (and "preferences" and "utility") allows for a conception of conflict between what we take our interests to be *before* carrying through a moral analysis, and what we take our interests to be *after.*

To illustrate, imagine Jones, who in the course of driving on his way to a business meeting sees along the roadside the baby that—as in its typical command appearances in the ethics readers—is about to drown in six inches of water. Jones's initial inclination is to hurry past, for if he stops he will forgo a favorable deal. But then Jones considers certain other things, including the value of the human life expiring in the water, the prospective parental grief, and the community's legitimate expectations. He saves the child.

How shall we analyze Jones's decision in terms of his interests? In some perfectly defensible sense of the term, we would be warranted to say that his "interest" was to save the baby, or that to do so was what he preferred or was of more utility to him. But if we elect those manners of speaking, we obscure the very process we are trying to illuminate: how moral reasoning contributes to amend our initial preferences into (and this is what finally matters) our morally reflective, more enlightened ones. To preserve the distinction, we do better to say that Jones recognized as his *initial* or *utility preference* signing the contract (sacrificing the child). But on reflection from a moral viewpoint about what he ought to do, Jones reached a *morally corrected preference* to save the child (forgoing the contract).

That distinction is vital if we are to make any sense of a nonhomocentric morality. Specifically, several writers espouse a "deep ecology" viewpoint that somehow values the environment beyond its value to us.[2] But if such an ethic is to get off the ground, how does one even state its ambition coherently?

Return to the question of damming a wild river. Ultimately, the preferences the decision reflects will be our own, not the river's. That much is true, trivially. Only persons—certainly not rivers or fish—prefer. But the real issue is how our preferences will be arrived at. Surely anyone who considers the damming of a river will want to calculate the river's utility to us. Presumably that would involve, first, an estimate of the consumption and use values of the river in each alternative state. How do the revenues that damming would garner through electricity and irrigation compare to the loss of revenues from impeding barge traffic? Next, we would uncontroversially add a "shadow price" to account for the fact that the river has values to us that do not show up in actual market-price transactions, in lost traffic tolls, and so on.

The concept of shadow price is worth a moment's reflection. The general idea is this. In comparing the social value of two ordinary commodities, such as a loaf of bread and a can of paint, the relative price people will pay gives us a fair expression of the products' relative worth. If the bread commands a dollar and the paint sells for eight, then presumptively one more gallon of paint is worth more to society than one more loaf of bread. But we can make that judgment because the benefit from the bread and paint is limited to consumers to whom the products can be packaged and, as it were, auctioned off. But when it comes to valuing the social benefits of the river, the technique of "packaging and pricing" just will not work. I cannot enjoy the bread unless I pay for it. Many of the benefits of a river, however, are so far-reaching and diffuse that not all those who benefit can be excluded from, and therefore forced to pay for, the benefits each derives. I cannot feasibly be charged for the pleasure I get from the river just through driving by and looking at it. Hence, the concept of shadow price may be enlisted to give us a closer approximation to the river's real utility. It aggregates what people *would* pay in dollar terms to preserve such benefits if they were honestly to reveal their preferences and *could* be made to pay for them.* No one evaluating the damming of a wild river would dispute the relevance of taking such an allowance for shadow cost into account.

To clarify what *is* in dispute, let us call the conventional shadow

*The shadow price would include, for example, the beauty of the river, to the extent that people would pay to view it if they could otherwise be excluded. Larry Tribe, in "Ways Not to Think About Plastic Trees: New Foundations for Environmental Law," *Yale Law Journal* 83 (1974): 1315, 1319, introduces shadow pricing in a similar context, but it is not clear that he draws a sharp line between (1) the conventional welfare-economist's usage, what those who determine market prices fully informed of their tangible benefits "would pay" if they could be forced, and (2) what morally *ought to be paid* whatever the collective preferences. The distinction may collapse if one is a conventionalist in morals, but is critical if one rejects conventionalism, as I do. Tribe does suggest cultivating "experts" to help identify "fragile values" that might be overlooked in cost-benefit analysis. Such experts may or may not be moral correctors as I use the term. That depends on whether they operate from a critical moral perspective in telling us how we *ought to* value the object in question, or simply aim to improve our estimate of how present and future persons, fully informed of the facts, would collectively value the object in fact. The former effort, but not the latter, accords with seeking the "morally corrected shadow price" described in the text immediately following.

price of the economist the "base shadow price" to distinguish it from what I will call the "morally corrected shadow price." The market value plus the base shadow price measure what I referred to as utility preferences, for example, all value that would be ascribed to the river other than through conscious moral reflection.* The "morally corrected shadow price" refers to the utility preferences adjusted as a consequence of moral reflection.[3] It expresses the value which on some moral view we *ought to* be entering into our analyses, whether that value is conventionally recognized by most people or not.

Granted, by recasting the issue in these terms we do not provide an answer. But at least it gives a handle on what an easily clouded discussion is, or ought to be, about. Let us continue with the hardest case, that of a mere Thing. Is there any moral argument touching upon a Thing that can support modifying our utility preferences, specifically, so that a social arrangement not warranted by utility (because we would be sacrificing "too much") might yet be warranted by some morally corrected evaluation? To hold that there is such a revalued "price" for an object is what I mean by calling the object *morally considerate.* To illustrate the dilemma of "deep ecology" in these terms, imagine a state governor whose staff has done a cost-benefit analysis of the damming project. His staff has accounted for all of the beneficial interests we have *in* the river. They have calculated that we stand to benefit so much from the electricity. They have offset those gains with what is lost in boating and fishing. A dollar value is even allowed for lost scenic value. "On that basis," the governor says, "damming the river pencils out to be in our interests. Still, I want to do what's right. So I am prepared to think through my preferences further, to 'morally correct them,' as you say. But on what basis ought we to give up our benefits to preserve the river?

*The phrase is not without its problems. It turns on conscious valuation. What of the person who so "instinctively" values the continuance of the river that it is a settled part of his intuitive utility function? The answer (as best as I can give) is that I am supposing an ability to distinguish through introspection what we desire from considerations of our utility in some sense, from what we desire (as Kant would put it) "from duty." See Immanuel Kant, *Groundwork of the Metaphysics of Morals*, 3d ed., trans. and ed. H. J. Paton (New York: Harper Torchbooks, 1964), p.68.

Once we have summed up our interests *in it,* there is nothing else to add to the ledger."

The governor may concede that where we are considering relations with ordinary Persons, we may find ourselves amending our original dispositions by adopting a corrective moral viewpoint. But, the governor will maintain, that is possible because Persons, we all agree, are morally considerate. Persons have interests and preferences. We can adopt their standpoint and judge what is for their "good." He may even concede that some such a corrective analysis would warrant modifying our treatment of higher animals such as nonhuman primates and whales. They, too, may be morally considerate. But no such modification of thought processes touching the river is appropriate or even conceivable. "It may be possible to make a Thing *legally* considerate through legal fiction," he will say. "But there is no moral legerdemain through which you can make them really considerate."

WHAT DOES IT TAKE TO BE
MORALLY CONSIDERATE?

How do we respond? We can grant, at the start, that Things, and indeed most Nonpersons, lack any number of properties deemed morally significant in the literature. They have not the capacity to understand what is happening to them, the power to frame a plan of life, to exercise moral choice, and so on. A person whose initial inclination is to steal can be persuaded not to steal because stealing is the wrong thing to do. Such a dialogue is out of the question with Nonpersons, which is why rampaging rivers and lions may do harm, but they cannot do wrong. All this can be expressed by conceding that, unlike Persons, Nonpersons are not *moral agents* holding preferences that are correctable by ethical reasoning. But it is a long leap from the fact that Persons are the only audience of moral discourse, and therefore the only prospective obligors, to the inference that only Persons can be obligees or have other moral significance. It is not, let me grant, an utterly irrational leap. But to make it, one must lay as a ramp some additional premise, such as that we have no obligation to behave morally except toward those things capable of responding toward us in kind. Some philosophers, who trace all obligation to self-interest, tend to give reciprocity such a foundational role. In evaluating their position, however, we have to draw a clear line between explaining moral principles and justifying them.

Viewing the development of morals descriptively, as do sociobiologists, one can see why ethical attitudes would be likely to evolve with some bias toward those who can favor us, or our progeny, in return. But there remains both in fact and in moral favor a considerable amount of altruistic behavior, even to the point of outright self-abnegation, that is hard to explain, much less to justify, solely in terms of its individual or genetic "survival value." We commonly not only regard it as commendable, but speak of obligations to make sacrifices in favor of those who are in no position to reciprocate, such as the comatose, the dead (is there nothing to be said for Antigone?),* and anonymous victims of wars we conduct in distant lands.† In sum, there is no reason to accept the premise that being a moral agent, or obligor, is a prerequisite of being a moral patient or obligee.[4]

The skeptic who concedes the obligor-obligee distinction, and who recognizes that being a moral agent is not a prerequisite for being morally considerate, may put before us a second barrier: to be considerate, a thing must be, at the least, a holder of moral rights. This is a requirement presupposed by much of the animals and abnormal humans literature. The proponents of their considerateness typically main-

---

*There is a long-standing tradition in Judaism that burial of the dead is the greatest *gimilut chasidim*, "deed of loving kindness," in part because, in contrast with other kindnesses, there is no prospect that the deceased will repay the favor.

†In fact, I would think that a strong argument could be made for federal aid to the decked sea turtle (see p. 44) precisely because it is so helpless and so unresponsible for its plight—not because it can do anything for us in return. I grant that this strikes no fatal blow to those who will maintain that sentiments of sympathy in general, even if in this instance they settle on a sea turtle, redound to "our" advantage. But then why, over the course of evolution, have our moral sentiments not grown more precise, more survival-efficient, so that we do not expend energies on so many "inefficient" sympathies?

tain that even if a whale or fetus does not possess all the properties requisite for full moral agency, it may nonetheless "hold rights." What that requires—what it takes to be a rights holder—remains a subject of considerable dispute. But most of the literature appears to assume that having (or "taking") interests of some sort is necessary. Things, by definition, do not take an interest in their well-being, if they have one. Therefore, it can be argued that when it comes to revising our inclinations touching Things, the route most familiar to contemporary moral philosophy, that via a discourse about rights, appears to be blocked.

The question whether we can raise on behalf of a Thing, or even Nonpersons, a moral right or something that plays an equivalent role in moral discourse is one to which I will eventually return. My own view is that to speak of the moral (as opposed to legal) rights of a tree or river is not appropriate. But however one comes out on the rights question, it is not dispositive of the issue here, which goes not to rights but to moral considerateness. Just as we saw in Chapter 6 that not all legal considerateness can be boiled down to legal rights, so, too, not all moral considerateness can be expressed in terms of moral rights. Consider the conventional good Samaritan dilemma: We need not reach the question whether the child in jeopardy has a right to the passerby's rescue, or even whether the passerby has a duty to the child, in order to say that it would be *morally commendable* for the passerby to rescue the child, or that the passerby would be *advancing some good*.

Similarly, to support the welfare system, one need not argue that the poor have some sort of moral right to welfare, although it is sometimes put that way.* The welfare laws may be defended as good, as morally welcome, on the grounds that they conduce to the betterment of the whole society, or rightly recognize the considerateness of the destitute. On a parity of reasoning, to support placing a Thing in a certain legal position one is not required to prove that it has a moral right to be so situated. There is support for the arrangement if it is morally better so

---

*The poor who had fallen beneath some level of poverty might indeed have a "right" to relief; I will not argue the point. I am only saying that the level of relief which is *good* is not bounded by the level (if any) to which the poor have a *right.*

to amend the law, that is, if we can demonstrate that the amendment would advance some good.

This places our skeptic in a third, fallback position. He must say this: Even if we substitute some broader notion of good for rights as the key to moral evaluation, we have not detached ourselves from *interests.* Any moral revision of our thinking still requires an accounting of the interests of the things on whose behalf our disposition is to be revised—else, wherein lies the "good" in sacrificing our more obvious desires? If we discern some good in improving the lot of the poor, even at some sacrifice of general welfare, it is because we can identify some human interests that have been advanced. On the other hand, if we are asked to make a collective sacrifice in consideration of a river and are told to exclude from our thoughts any consideration of the interests of Persons affected thereby, where is the "good" in it to be found? Indeed, when we move to the realm of Things what are we being asked to think *about?* As Joel Feinberg puts the challenge, "[A] being without interests has no 'belief' to act in, and no 'sake' to act for."[5] But even if one agrees,* does this mean that in evaluating actions affecting their condition, there is no "right" and "wrong," no "morally better," that is not fully explicable in terms of human utility and human rights? Are there no intermediate foundational possibilities?

---

*One need not. One can maintain that while plants and trees do not "take an interest" in themselves, each has a good of its own (an "interest" in one sense), and even derive a moral right from it. See Tom Regan, "What Sorts of Beings Can Have Rights?" in *All That Dwell Therein* (Berkeley: Univ. of California Press, 1982), pp. 165–83.

9

Unorthodox Moral Viewpoints

THE QUESTION, then, is not, "Can a mere Thing have rights?" The question is, "Can a Thing be morally considerate?" To understand what "morally considerate" means, we have means to imagine a context of moral evaluation, for example, "Ought we to dam a river?" An entity —for example, a river—is morally considerate if in deciding what we ought to do, its condition enters into our reflections, not exclusively as an instrument to the pleasures of Persons. We are assuming, as moral philosophers often do, the vantage point of a hypothetical impartial, morally enlightened observer of events and character. The hypothetical observer's verdicts of right and wrong, just and unjust, permissible and impermissible are not fully determined by what is welfare maximizing, or what the majority of persons (at their contemporary stage of enlightenment and prejudice) happen conventionally to approve of. But even then the puzzle remains: when the independent observer reflects, not about our interests and welfare, but about the river, what does she think about? The challenge is to devise a coherent moral viewpoint from whose vantage reflections that account for a Thing serve to reevaluate decisions reached on the basis of ordinary Person-dominated welfare considerations alone. Let me sketch five theoretical strategies from which I believe such a viewpoint could be developed.

1. APPEALS THROUGH FUTURE GENERATIONS

The first strategy may sound almost like a confession and avoidance—a confession that a "real" Thing-regarding argument cannot be made, and its avoidance by diverting appeal *through* the anticipated interests of future generations. Even if rivers lack interests, future humans may have an interest in at least some rivers. Pursuing such a line of thought, one might suppose it no trick to derive a present reason for modifying contemporary conduct affecting at least some Things, even if doing so does not serve our welfare. From our perspective alone, the benefits from conserving some endangered species may not be worth the sacrifices. But when we pool with our own interests the interests of the unborn, and recalculate, the new majority may favor conservation.

Unfortunately, much of the appeal is deceptive. On close inspection, the future-generations strategy is anything but straightforward; nor, in the last analysis, does it save us from having to address the considerateness not only of Nonpersons (which, in our parlance, includes future persons remote in time), but even of Things themselves.

Some of the difficulties of relying on the preferences of future generations stem from our present ignorance, particularly as we project to futures that are increasingly remote. We do not know what effect our actions will have on them, or even how they will care. *Who*—or *what*—will our remote descendants be? These uncertainties have been deemed so insurmountable that they have been urged as a basis for discounting remote futures entirely.[1]

Even if we set aside such factual ignorance, serious problems of value remain. At the threshold, *their* considerateness is hardly more "self-evident" than the considerateness of a natural object. It is true that they—some persons down the line—will have well-developed preferences. But why ought we to subordinate *our* welfare to *theirs*, for creatures we shall never meet, with whom there is not even the most fictitious "social compact," and who are in no better position to return our favors than a contemporary river? If, as in much of morals, we are to be influenced by consideration of earned obligations, where does the balance of earnings and credits lie? While future generations may be understandably ungrateful for some of their legacy—toxic wastes and such—they will have us to thank for their technology, their language and literature, their very lives. We have already done a lot for them. What have they done—what can they do—for us?

Even if we acknowledge the rightness, in principle, of doing something on their behalf, there are the further questions: Do what? And at how much sacrifice? Establishing principles for intergenerational justice is complex. Philosophers have a hard enough time coping with interpersonal comparisons of utility among contemporaries; that is, in a moral weighing-in, how is my gain from an action to be balanced against your loss? Intergenerational comparisons involve all that and additional headaches. How do we account for the hypothetical happiness of possible persons, persons whom we might bring into existence by our actions, but do not? (Are we obligated, on their prospective behalf, to procreate?) And there is the question of an intergenerational discount rate. In ordinary cost-benefit analysis, when we compare two projects with different time horizons, one having small but near-term benefits and another promising deferred but large returns, we decide which is of greater present value by invoking a rate of discount, which implicates the prevailing interest rate. Suppose that to build a super-safe toxic waste disposal site our generation—by foregoing $1 billion in present "consumption" of cars, appliances, and so on—will save the generations who live five hundred years from now $10 trillion in cleanup costs. How is the value of $10 trillion five hundred years from now to be compared with the value of $1 billion now? Can we even speak of the "net present value" of the $10 trillion when it is a value that will not accrue to persons now living, but only to remote strangers? When generations are crossed, the answer cannot be masked as a problem of mere economic calculations to be inferred somehow from the interest rate. It is a problem of justice.[2]

Another problem is that if we seriously decide to count the interests of each future person equally with each of us—that is, make of all humans through time one big moral community—we, the living, face an unappealing dilution. Because there are potentially so many billions of *them* relative to the "mere" five billion of us presently on the planet, the aggregate weight of their interests will simply swamp ours, effectively leaving our wants to count, in the final analysis, for naught. If the matter of contemporary Western resource-ravaging life-style could be put to an intergenerational referendum, one that gave all our descendants through time an equal vote, just imagine how austerely we would be forced to live.

If, even in the face of these difficulties, we conclude that it is right to account for future interests and are even able to settle on a discount rate, further complications remain. One might suppose that the only lingering problem is predicting their preferences, and that that task, although highly conjectural, is at least in principle factual. The burden is heavier, however, because their very tastes are destined to be affected by the legacy we leave them: whether, for example, they ever have the opportunity to experience clear skies and equatorial forests. Therefore, even if we are committed to account for their interests in principle, we cannot simply rely on our best possible projection of what those interests shall be. The wants of future persons is not some independent fact beyond our influence, like the distance to the moon. We cannot avoid constructing some ideal, glossed image of our progeny, of what they *ought to be*. And that, of course, is not a purely empirical matter, but a matter of normative choice. Insofar as it is within our influence, ought they to be the sort of persons who prefer real trees and real grass or the sort who thrill to ersatz plastic substitutes? Are we willing that they be indifferent to what we discern as the beauties of nature?[3] I do not mean these to be rhetorical questions. They are hard. The point is, they are not to be answered solely by predicting facts about future generations. They draw us into regarding—really thinking about and valuing—both future persons and Things as best we can.

Certainly, by underscoring these complications I am not aiming to reject the future-generations strategy, which many readers will consider my most (some will say my only) plausible tactic. But as we consider the problems, even paradoxes, that come of trying to fit future generations into a traditional welfare-oriented framework, three points emerge. First, many people who are prepared to take the future into account suppose the justification to lie in the moral considerateness of future persons. They suppose that their intuition simply rests on a judgment that each future person ought to count equally with themselves. I believe, however, that upon further reflection such people will discover their real concern is less with the treatment of future individuals than with the advancement of some good. That "good" is admittedly hard to define. But in all events it cannot be redescribed merely as an extended utilitarianism that simply aggregates our welfare with that of the unborn. Something less welfarist and more idealistic is involved.*

Second, whichever way future-regarders conceive of themselves— as advancers of some hard-to-define, idealistic good, or as welfarists of some complex, intergenerational sort—we should not expect to extract more in the way of moral guidance than general maxims. One such maxim is Brian Barry's suggestion that we might have an obligation not to narrow their "range of opportunities" to something less than ours.[4] Another is Joel Feinberg's position that we are obliged not to hand them over the moral equivalent of a used-up garbage heap.[5] I am not disparaging maxims of this sort which, though vague, form the basis of saying something about constraints on actions touching at least some Things: not to exhaust the land, not to destroy all life in the oceans, not to ruin the atmosphere. But it will not satisfy those whose intuitions about our Thing-affecting conduct requires a finer-grained moral guidance. How—by reference to what standards—do we quiet our moral unease about ruining particular rivers and forests, actions that seem

*The welfarist can see nothing wrong in our using up all the world's resources so thoroughly that no human life could follow. Who would complain? Brian Barry typifies the contrary idealistic viewpoint in responding that "[t]he continuation of human life . . . is something to be sought (or at least not sabotaged) even if it does not make for the maximum total happiness. . . . [The objection] does not lie in any sense of injury to the interests of people who will not get born, but rather in a sense of its cosmic impertinence." See "Justice Between Generations," in *Law, Morality, and Society: Essays in Honor of H. L. A. Hart* (Oxford: Clarendon Press, 1977), p. 284.

morally problematic but would not have draconian effects on remote futures?

The third point concerns the problem of exogenous tastes—the fact that future generations' tastes will be produced, in part, by the legacy we endow them. This means that even if our moral stance is shaped by the considerateness of future persons—a desire to do right by them— we have also to be, Janus-faced, Thing-regarders as well. There is no way we can carry out a commitment to care for our distant progeny and avoid the question of what things we want them to value and disvalue.

2. ANTHROPOCENTRIC IDEALISM

As I have indicated, what makes the future-generations strategy appealing is that it appears (somewhat illusorily) to retain human wants as the touchstone of moral analysis. But surely wants are not the only data on which moral reflection can be based. Historically, few moral theories have accepted what one wants as either given or good without qualification. More commonly, what we instinctively desire is regarded as a variable, subject to—indeed, the precise target of—some disciplining virtues. The self-interest in which the rational person acts, if it must be put that way, is our moral self. I will refer to such a viewpoint as Anthropocentric Idealism.

Of course, to make some place in moral philosophy for human ideals does not in itself place our conduct toward Nonpersons on a moral footing. It is one thing to enlist a character ideal to support the judgment that kicking dogs is wrong.* But it is not apparent why anyone should pass harsh judgment on the character of someone who kicked a flower or defaced a rock. In fact, one reason why character-based viewpoints have appeal is that while they temper the crudest welfare strategies, they do not break with welfare entirely. The virtues that most readily come to mind, such as benevolence, kindness, and justice, are

*George Eliot's archtype gentleman, Grandcourt, "never did choose to kick any animal, because the act of kicking is a compromising attitude, and a gentleman's dogs should be kicked for him." *Daniel Deronda* (New York: New American Library 1979), p. 114.

regardful of others' interests. In formulating good character—in a listing, if you will, of the virtues—is there some basis to allow for the agent's conduct in regard to some Nonpersons, even to Things? To give an affirmative answer is to adopt an Anthropocentric Idealist strategy.

Anthropocentric Idealism can take two distinct routes. The first is to adopt the position that to conceive of everything outside oneself as mere resource for one's own gratification, whether the "thing" be a woman, a slave, or a river, distorts and constricts what is worthy in human character. Sheer, unmoderated *use* of other things is akin to avarice, gluttony, and lust. The other route is to hold that there are specific virtues for the attainment of which some specific Nonpersons are instrumental, perhaps even necessary. We require mountains not because they give us pleasure as such, but because they instill a character-leavening sense of majesty and awe.

Either way, a moral reason for the protection of Nonpersons is provided, although we must note that the protection, while not instrumental to human pleasure, is instrumental to human virtue and in that sense very much Person-centered. Moreover, this strategy has to proceed with the frank recognition that particularly in regard to Things, many virtues—cruelty and uncivility, for example—seem hard to apply. (Could we be cruel to a river?) Thus, any moral relations we fabricate for Things from an Anthropocentric Idealist theory will of necessity be even less narrowly constricting and detailed than those we have with Persons. Nonetheless, it is not beyond the reach of an imaginable Anthropocentric Idealism to defend some moral ascriptions for conduct that touches upon lakes, species, pretty vistas, or nature in general. While I doubt that one can be *brutal, vindictive,* or *sinful* toward them,[6] one can show oneself *callous* or *unfeeling.* I agree with Joel Feinberg that we would, and probably should, consider it evil for a person to crush a beetle encountered in the wild, or to extinguish an insignificant species, even on the assumption (which any naturalist would challenge)[7] that the elimination of the species would threaten no risk to mankind.[8] But I am not satisfied simply to leave the misconduct labeled "a free-floating evil"—"free-floating" because we cannot ground it in any conventional notion of harm. If we are committed to work these intuitions into a coherent moral viewpoint, we do better to ground the effort in a notion of human virtue that accounts for, and provides some guidance in regard to, some of our Nonperson-affecting conduct. It is not farfetched to suggest there is a human ideal that the beetle crusher is falling short of. Of course, in the case of the beetle we might say some sort of *life* is involved. But the basis is a broader one identified by Kant, who condemned "a propensity to the bare destruc-tion . . . of beautiful though lifeless things in nature" as "contrary to man's duty to himself. For such a propensity weakens or destroys that feeling in man . . . which does much to promote a state of sensibility favorable to morals."9

In sum, it is not idle to suggest that a person who has been exposed to, and who has reacted to, the grandeur of great valleys and the majesty of mountains is *better* for it than had he passed the time, even more happily engaged, watching t.v. giveaway shows. The claim is akin to the claim that fine character requires fine art; so that the wanton destruc-tion of a beautiful artwork, even if the majority of the public is indiffer-ent to that fate, might nonetheless be judged by an independent moral observer to be prima facie *wrong*.

3. ENTITY IDEALISM

Both the viewpoints I have sketched thus far can be classed as funda-mentally anthropocentric. The first is anthropocentric in orienting to-ward the wants of future humans; the second, in orienting toward some ideal of worthy human character. Both invite us to revise our original judgments by training our thoughts on Nonpersons. But in the last analysis any claims they introduce respecting Nonpersons is contingent on the well-being (including spiritual well-being, i.e., good character) of *homo sapiens*. For that reason both alternatives will be regarded leerily by many people who support a more favored status for nonhuman entities. The preferred alternative is to develop a more radical, because less "deeply" anthropocentric, viewpoint. This is likely to take the form of valuing—idealizing—certain entities themselves, or certain qualities that those entities embody or symbolize. Those entities are to be valued not because they are instrumental to anything else—i.e., that because of them people will be more happy or more virtuous. They are good *intrinsically*. The contrast with the preceding approach is that Anthropocentric Idealism would condemn the destruction of an object if it could be shown to provide potential support for valued character. Under the view now being examined, Entity Idealism, the act would be condemned because the object itself was morally considerate and its destruction wrong irrespective of consequences for human virtue or welfare or anything else.

The notion of an Entity Idealism seems hard to advance without assuming a somewhat dogmatic stance of claiming that some property "X is a good because X is a good." Yet, all moral philosophies have their hardest going at the very same starting point: identifying the basic good or goods they will champion, and persuading us to apprehend their goodness. Kant grasped that something had to be recognized as an end in itself, toward whose good everything else was instrumental. His solution was to make persons the things that were ends in themselves, and things (everything else) the things that were not, that were at best valued as instruments for man. Utilitarianism adopts a particular psychological state, pleasure, as the intrinsic good. We are asked to discern that a universe with more pleasure is morally better than one with less. John Finnis, in his recent revitalization of the Aquinian tradition, champions several equally fundamental values, including knowledge: everything else being equal, it is better to be in a state of knowledge than of ignorance.[10] For Finnis, the ultimate validity of his table of values (which includes life, play, sociability, and aesthetic experience) simply has to be apprehended as self-evident. But to do so is no more occult than to accept the principles of rational inquiry in other fields; in logic, that we should adhere to the rules of self-contradiction and syllogism; or in the empirical sciences, that theoretical accounts that are simple, predictively successful, and explanatorily powerful are to be preferred over rival accounts.[11] These principles are self-evident not in the sense that we (merely) *feel* them to be right; the point is, we cannot *prove* them because they are the very principles our proofs deploy.

Other systems of morals adopt other bedrock goods, from the contemplation of beauty to the "good will." It is not my task to examine each of them critically, for as I shall maintain below, the development of an environmental (or other unconventional) ethic need not refute and displace rivals that govern interpersonal behavior. My self-imposed chore is a harder one: As the basis for an unconventional ethic, can one plausibly defend as an intrinsic good—is it moral to make sacrifices out of regard for—properties other than the familiar ones of self-understanding, pain, and so on?

As far as intuitions go (deferring whether those intuitions can be, or need be, fleshed into a body of general principles), the answer, I do not hesitate to say, is yes. The environmental movement is testimony to the widespread feelings of support for nature's inherent worth, even when those sentiments do not prevail politically. And in many instances we see enough concern being mustered for wilderness areas, for example, to pass laws protecting them from disturbance. (A bumper sticker recently appeared in Southern California proclaiming, "I save water for Mono Lake.") It is true that conservationists, if pressed to justify their sentiments, incline to adopt a welfarist language ("so others can enjoy it"), perhaps with a future-generations gloss. But that, I suggest, is not a true reflection—indeed it handicaps the development—of the genuine moral feelings that lie behind these movements. As I wrote in *Trees,*

> [w]hen conservationists argue this way to the exclusion of other arguments, or find themselves speaking of "recreational interests" so continuously as to play up to, and reinforce, homocentrist perspectives, there is something sad about the spectacle. One feels that the arguments lack even their proponents' convictions. I expect they want to say something less egotistic and more emphathic but the prevailing and sanctioned modes of explanation in our society are not quite ready for it.[12]

One way to "ready" the society for another way of reasoning about nonhuman, even inanimate, parts of the environment is to examine the view that the moral considerateness of some entities can trace to their being good intrinsically. That is, like pleasure to a utilitarian, their existence is a bedrock of further reflection.

Such an approach is forcefully and impressively illustrated in Paul W. Taylor's *Respect for Nature*. [13] Taylor maintains that respect for nature constitutes as defensible a foundation for an environmental ethic as respect for persons does for the ethics of ordinary interpersonal relations. He rests this position on the rationality, which he supports at some length, of recognizing the noninstrumental worth of all living organisms. Even if lower organisms lack interests, each has its own good: while it may not care what happens to it, we, by a close examination of the biotic community, can learn to see the world from the organism's standpoint, to see its good in that sense. By contrast, Taylor holds, an inanimate, such as a river, has no standpoint to adopt, no consequent "good," and therefore no moral considerateness.

If we accept life as the intrinsic or inherent good, then a foundation is laid for claims on behalf of animate Things, but claims on behalf of the inanimates are at best derivative. A river would not be morally considerate as such, but we would have duties to treat it in a certain way in order to fulfill our duties to the living things that depend on it. One might suppose that this distinction would be of little moment to an environmentalist. Life in one form or another is so ubiquitous that to protect life seems to be a handy and plausible way to protect the entire environment. If a lake were utterly lifeless, or unconnected to the support of any life, we would have no duty to it; but it is hard to imagine such a lake. Even the Dead Sea is not quite dead.

Nonetheless, the use of life as a foundational good has drawbacks for an environmental movement. For one thing, it may be intuitively disingenuous, like pitching the case against cruelty to animals on the basis of human betterment. Revert for a moment to the campaign to save Mono Lake from destruction as its freshwater feeder streams are increasingly diverted to meet Southern California's water demand. The lake is remote from population centers and, aside from brine shrimp and gulls, only subtly life-supporting. If there were no brine shrimp and gulls, would morality have *nothing* to say?

More important, a life-maximizing principle leads to odd choices. Suppose that two water plans were being weighed, each of which would supply the same amount of water at the same cost. In other words, imagine the present utility of the two projects to be identical. Further, imagine future generations to be indifferent as between which project we should choose. There would be this difference only: different amounts of life are to be affected, whether life be measured in terms of absolute biomass or diversity. The first project would destroy a grand, unique geologic formation that took shape over thousands of years but supports very little life (it is all the more rare for that). The competing water-delivery plan, by requiring reconstruction of some cement-encased man-made water courses, would eliminate tons of life in the form of bacteria and algae. Does the fact that the second project would eliminate more *life* mean that the destruction of the unique formation is therefore preferred, and that all further moral conversation is cut off?

If we can establish respect for nature as grounding for a life-favoring ethical position, it does not seem much odder to make some allowance for the worth of a nonlife process. Indeed, do we not make some such allowances when, in selecting wilderness areas to set aside, we sometimes select a relatively lifeless area over a teeming one? The irrigation (and hence destruction) of a desert area may be defensible on the basis that more humans will be fed thereby. But if we put human welfare to one side, is the irrigation plan clearly right because it will bring forth a more abundant, even a more varied, life? Is there nothing to be said for retaining the relatively lifeless desert, even if doing so taxes us extra biomass somewhere else?

Along these lines, consider our treatment of the Antarctic, mile for mile one of the planet's most lifeless areas. Yet, international treaty has made it the most stringently shielded massive region on earth. Although there were obviously many motivating factors, including the protection of native flora and fauna and the preservation of "clean" areas for possible scientific value, the permit system appears to go beyond what life and science require. I am rather inclined to credit the word of the principal draftsman of the United States' treaty-implementing legislation, Steve Burton, a former student of mine, then at the State Department. Professor Burton reports that the principal regard of the parties with whom he worked was not to keep the Antarctic preserved for others to enjoy or otherwise benefit from, nor even for its hardy and unusual life. The negotiants all felt, as each of us would feel, an awe for *it,* for the region, for the fact that of the entire earth, nothing on that scale had remained as little touched by human intervention.

This is not to disparage life as an important intrinsic good. But there may well be other goods, even further removed from human conscious states, that can contribute to value (although perhaps less strongly and with less certain direction). A respect for nature may engender a preference for natural processes: for example, the natural flow of a river. Untouchedness strikes me (as it did the Antarctic negotiants) as a plausible good, and so does beauty.

To say that such goods are intrinsic is not to suggest that their introduction puts an end to moral conversation. To the extent life is a good, questions follow about how to rank the states that are thereby preferred (tonnage of biomass, diversity, stability, etc.). And different dialectic strategies remain. Suppose the question is the preservation of Mono Lake. The preservationist might call attention to the creatures for whom the lake serves as a habitat, and dwell on the strangeness of their adaptation. She might focus on its natural (nonliving) features: "Just look at the lake." ("Look at it from an airplane; from the north rim; consider its age, its uniqueness.") The dialectic is not unlike that of a docent in an art museum helping a visitor to appreciate a portrait. The docent alternately directs our attention to the work's good-making properties (its originality, boldness, fineness of detail) and to the combination of those generally-to-be-valued attributes into something, in their substantiation here, uniquely to be valued. We resist saying that the goodness of the artwork can be adequately explained in terms of its antecedents (*because* Da Vinci made it) or in terms of its consequences (*because* it gives us pleasure, or informs us how ladies dressed at such and such a period). Once the work is placed in a proper focus of understanding, it is to be valued simply for what it *is.* It is good *intrinsically.*

Now, an intrinsic-goods strategy is headed for unnecessary controversy if its proponents insist that the properties to which our attention
is aimed can be intelligible without reference to humans. For example,
if one maintains that beauty, in whatever it resides, is intrinsically good,
the character and feelings of the valuer, the beauty finder, are obviously
implicated. Nonetheless, when someone describes the Grand Canyon
as awesomely beautiful, what he is describing is not his feelings (as
though he were describing his toothache). He is describing, that is,
locating the awesome beauty in, the canyon. And if he subscribes to a
moral theory that includes awesome beauty as a foundational good, he
is suggesting that in determining the rightness of our actions regarding
the canyon, that quality, that magnificence, is significant. It is every bit
as significant as whatever psychological states, such as feelings of beauty
or terror, it inspires in us.

Of course, beauty is not the only property which, established as
intrinsically good, would have implications for conduct affecting Nonpersons, and not all the conversation has to be quite docent-like. The
goodness of life invites us to make comparisons between actions on the
basis of more and less life. Such a standard would imply at least the
prima facie rightness of noninterference with the lives of trees, although
it would require no moral accounting in respect of a rock. On the other
hand, so far as we can establish the value of beauty and uniqueness, it
would seem to imply giving Oregon's Crater Lake preference to a
"competing" tree that it was undercutting. To value flow, mightiness,
and hoary age would provide some basis for preserving a river.

Granted, the development of moral concern for Nonpersons from
such an intrinsic-goods basis has special problems to confront. Which
properties are to be supported or apprehended as goods-in-themselves,
and on the basis of what dialectic strategy or presentational experience?
In cases of conflicting indication—the awesome age and unique clear
depth of a lake versus the hoary, untouched beauty of a forest—there
is an obvious quandary, if we should be put to choose between them.
Moreover, an intrinsic-goods approach is imperiled with collapse into
the rankest relativism. Someone will say, "Assuming beauty makes

something morally considerate, X may be beautiful-to-you, but it isn't beautiful-to-me"; or, "I agree that the river is majestic, but then I find more majesty in the grandeur of a great hydroelectric project, and I say the river be dammed." And there are conflicts of perspectives. It is common experience that something which seems, from a distance, unsightly (unsymmetric, insipidly colored), yet may appear, under a microscope, breathtakingly beautiful. Similarly, something ordinarily conceived as inanimate—for example, the soil—can, considered in functional context, be valued by those who identify life as a good.[14]

There are these complications, among others, that have been contended with in the literature.[15] But I shall show that none of them is unique to, or necessarily more intractable than, those that plague any moral viewpoint. Most of us, I believe, are unpersuaded that all moral judgments can be referred to a single psychological state, such as happiness, or to a thinly veiled conventionalism which reduces all questions of value to what the majority favors or fancies. If so, then some other referent, some other "goods," are called for. It is not surprising, nor indefensible, that candidates for morally significant goods should include the living, the beautiful, the majestic, the rare, the untouched, the intricately complex, and the profoundly simple.

4. ATTITUDINAL IDEALISM: THE MENTAL COMPLEX STRATEGY

Another approach has recently been proposed by Donald H. Regan,[16] elaborating upon an idea of G. E. Moore. Moore had proposed as an intrinsic good (perhaps the highest good) not beauty, per se, nor even beautiful things, but the contemplation of beauty. More specifically, Moore, at least on one interpretation, can be read to suggest that what is intrinsically valuable is a complex consisting of (1) the beautiful thing, (2) the person contemplating the beautiful thing, and (3) the contemplator taking pleasure in the thought of the beautiful thing. Regan suggests a comparable analysis applicable to what I term Nonpersons.

On his view, it is not necessary to suppose that a species or the Grand Canyon has any value *itself*. On the other hand, Jones's contemplating the Grand Canyon, taking pleasure in the existence of the canyon itself, and wanting to know more about it can be intrinsically valuable, that is, "good just for what it is." Conversely, what would be intrinsically evil would be a complex involving (1) the canyon, (2) Jones's contemplation of the destruction of the canyon, and (3) Jones's taking pleasure in contemplating the canyon's destruction.

Sketched so summarily, Regan's view may strike the reader as an unduly complicated way to achieve so uncertain a foothold. It may seem that we have done nothing but shift attention from puzzles about objects to puzzles about complexes. Which complexes, then, are intrinsically valuable? We are faced in a direction, but given little hint of the path. Nonetheless, this approach does circumvent a principal obstacle to accepting the ideal entity view, namely, that it lodges intrinsic value in a mere thing, independent of persons. Regan seats the value (more comfortably, many will feel) in some human mental furniture. Moreover, Regan demonstrates that he can make advances on a number of quandaries more satisfactorily than the competing noninstrumental viewpoints. And while the emphasis on attitudes sounds at first strange, it is far from eccentric. The idea brings to mind a commentary of E. H. Gombrich regarding the Buddhist influence on Chinese art:

> [N]othing was more important than the right kind of meditation. To meditate is to think and ponder about the same holy truth for many hours on end, to fix an idea in one's mind and to look at if from all sides without letting go of it. . . . Some monks . . . meditated on things in nature, on water, for instance, and what we can learn from it, how humble it is, how it yields and yet wears away solid rock, how it is clear and cool and soothing and gives life to the thirsting field; or on mountains, how strong and lordly they are, and yet how good, for they allow the trees to grow on them.[17]

5. THE TRANSCENDENT SELF

The final viewpoint sounds the most unfamiliar—the most mystically oriental, one might say. It goes something like this. Western moral philosophy is preoccupied with individualistic egos. Witness the fashion to employ contracting and games as models for moral behavior. The underlying assumption is that the world is broken down into separate persons, each negotiation to his or her personal advantage, or playing to win. Some writers, doubtful that all this selfishness is destined to yield the best of all possible worlds, tamper with the conditions of the contract or game. Others (in particular, contemporary game theorists) seek to accommodate our intuitions by demonstrating that cooperation with one's rival may prove for the rational egoist a successful strategy.

Another response is to retain the rational individualism, but to rinse some of the egoism by qualifying the self-interest that is deemed "rational." After all, rationality is a flexible concept. As we have seen, some hold that to be defended as "truly rational," one's conduct must account for certain human virtues; or, it must account for the intrinsic good of certain things (which therefore must not be treated as a means to your ends); or, an accounting must be made for some intrinsically good attitude or life.

This fifth viewpoint contrasts with the others by aiming not to constrain our notion of the rational moral self, but to expand it. To understand the strategy it invites, one may conceive morality as evolving through a progression of ever more inclusive advances.

The most primitive "morality" (conceptually if not historically) is pure hedonism, self-interest of the narrowest and most immediate sort. From this shallowest self-interest, a concern only for the gratification of the persons we *now* are, we advance to a sort of qualified hedonism. At this second stage, each actor continues to satisfy his own interests exclusively, but in defining those interests, present pleasures are weighed against concern for future pains. Here we incorporate into our sense of self our egos through time, to include the selves we will become. Altruism, the next stage, extends our boundaries outward to include other persons, recognizing thereby a communal self.[18] Even if we go no further, the communal self supports the instrumental considerateness of such Nonpersons as historic landmarks that integrate with and conserve the community.

But there is no need to stop there. Globalism, or some more inclusive holism, goes the next step to introject Nonpersons within our sense of self. One remains, we might say, *self-interested.* But the self in which one is interested is more encompassing than the human community. One broadening principle is *life,* favored by Paul W. Taylor and championed by Albert Schweitzer in the following terms:

> A man is ethical only when life, as such, is sacred to him, that of plants and animals as that of his fellow men, and when he devotes himself helpfully to all life that is in need of help. Only the universal ethic of the feeling of responsibility in an ever-widening sphere for all that lives—only that ethic can be founded in thought. The ethic of the relation of man to man is not something apart by itself: It is only a particular relation which results from the universal one."[19]

(This passage, incidentally, was quoted by the court in the California controversy, discussed in chapter 3, in which the law refused to carry out the testamentary instructions of a lady that her dog be destroyed.) But are we compelled to stop even there, at life? So much of life and nonlife being interdependent, there is the temptation to press further and ask, On what theory of moral philosophy is it more rational to identify one's extended self with the community of living things rather than with the biotic community or some larger planetary whole? The intrinsic good is something in addition to and other than Man and Thing; it is something that, ignoring boundaries, encompasses both. This is the view that produces as the basis for objecting to some action, such as the elimination of a species, "the cosmic impertinence" of it all. As I suggested in *Trees,*

> [t]he time may be on hand when these sentiments, and the early stirrings of the law, can be coalesced into a radical new theory or myth—felt as well as intellectualized—of man's relationships to the rest of nature. I do not

mean "myth" in a demeaning sense of the term, but in the sense in which, at different times in history, our social "facts" and relationships have always been comprehended and integrated by reference to various "myths"—that we are co-signers of a social contract, that the Pope is God's agent, that all men are created equal. Pantheism, Shinto and Tao all have myths to offer. But they are all, each in its own fashion, quaint, primitive and archaic to modern ears. What is needed is a myth that can fit our growing body of knowledge of geophysics, biology and the cosmos.

In this vein, I do not think it too remote that we may come to regard the Earth, as some have suggested, as one organism, of which Mankind is a functional part—the mind, perhaps: different from the rest of nature, but different as a man's brain is from his lungs.[20]

I suspect that Japanese Prime Minister Yasuhiro Nakasone had such a view in mind in his dramatic plea for the environment before the United Nations in late 1985. Reciting his own haiku to underscore the view that "man is born by the grace of the great universe," Nakasone went on to explain "that all living things—humans, animals, trees, grasses—are essentially brothers and sisters."[21] Many today share the sentiment, testifying that the holistic, transcendent self strategy is gaining a growing foothold in popular consciousness. Yet, in truth, if this tactic has special appeal, it brings with it also special problems.* If everything—the whole—is good, what can be bad? To put it another way, the familiar moral frameworks are all built upon the boundaries which holism deprecates, between mine and thine, and between your rights and my duties. Perhaps those boundaries have to go. But what is to take their place? That is, how would a holist *judge?* Even a holist would have to countenance some divisions, as of "brothers and sisters" and strangers, that which we prefer to preserve and that which we prefer to sacrifice, and to work out the principles on which "family" harmony is to be adjusted.

---

*See the discussion of the biotic community and the Gaian viewpoints in chap. 16.

WHERE DO THESE VIEWPOINTS BRING US?

Certainly these five strategic viewpoints do not collectively exhaust the alternatives from which a disputant, seeking to influence our Nonperson-affecting conduct, might launch his appeals. Nor are they exclusive. The entities whose contemplation is favored in the attitudinal (fourth) strategy will almost certainly be defended as intrinsically good in the third strategy. To some degree, therefore, when it comes to justifying the validity of these viewpoints, the case for several will be pitched on common grounds. Moreover, in several circumstances, whichever theoretical strategy we adopt, the indications for action—what is good and what is bad—are likely to be the same. Where, then, has the analysis brought us?

At this point, I shall not aspire to elaborate, defend, and carry through (that is, apply to each and every class of Nonperson) all or even some of the strategies the viewpoints invite. I will be satisfied if I have thus far established simply this niche for Nonpersons: One cannot dogmatically dismiss some considerateness of at least some Nonpersons, a considerateness not based sheerly on appeals to present human welfare. To put the matter in terms of our law-reform inquiry, a rational person may have several prima facie reasons to place a Nonperson in a position of Advantage (or Disadvantage), even if doing so should entail some subordination of our original, morally unreflected preferences. In parts IV and V, I will have more to say about the meta-ethical burden that a proponent of such a theory has to carry: Can any of these Nonperson-accounting viewpoints meet the requirements we can rightly demand of a moral theory? But first we should recognize that establishing the prima facie considerateness of Nonpersons is not the only chore that a moral theory has to contend with if it is going to make much difference in how we think and act.

First, what is being sought is not merely a moral viewpoint that accounts for Nonpersons in principle. We need a moral viewpoint rich enough to advance us through the ontological conundrums. By reference to what principles is the moral and legal world to be carved up into those "things" that will count? Is the unit of our concern the ant, the anthill, the family, the phylum, the genus? Why a river, rather than a watershed, or the whole hydrologic cycle? A holistic, global perspective has its own burdens. The whole is continuously in flux. On what basis can we distinguish changes that are good from those that are bad?

Second, suppose we can dispose satisfactorily with the ontological conundrums, the carving up and so on. Suppose that on the basis of one of the viewpoints sketched above we are able to justify how prima facie moral regard for some Nonperson might originate. There will remain the question, how can the regard (the obligation or whatever) be discharged?

The distinction may sound overly fine. But a moment's reflection will show that it is easier to say how moral regard respecting a Nonperson might originate than to say what it entails the regarder to *do*. Consider, for example, a will under which Jones establishes a trust with directions that the trustee expend the funds on behalf of Jones's favorite tree after his death. Whoever accepts the position of executor comes under an obligation to act for the tree. That is so notwithstanding the fact that the obligation would have originated in actions of Jones, rather than in anything the tree did to earn them. Nor are the trustee's obligations toward the tree diminished because they involve the discharge of continuing obligations toward Jones at the same time.*

Thus, it is not hard to illustrate how an obligation toward a Nonperson might come about. After all, not every obligation needs to be earned by the obligee's worthy conduct, as by pulling a thorn from a stranger's paw. The more thorny question is how the obligor, for example, the trustee, would do right by a Nonperson. Perhaps in the case of a living organism such as the tree, our sense of its needs provides adequate guidance. Although the trustee cannot make the tree happy, she is obliged to dispense the trust funds to assure that it be watered and fertilized, and to pay a tree surgeon's fees when it gets sick. But in the case of other Nonpersons, our ever-hounding lake for example, deter-

---

*Indeed, as the testator is dead at the time the trustee performs, talk of the testator's benefit is no less problematic than talk of the tree's benefit.

mining how to discharge our moral obligation is more complex. Of course, in the context of the will, we can imagine special instructions that would obviate the need to ponder what was in the lake's benefit. For example, the will might simply specify that the lake be stocked with a certain sort of carp. But that would be sidestepping the real issue, which can be better illustrated by asking what the testamentary trustee for a private lake would be obliged to do, assuming that the will failed to spell out in detail any specific obligations such as "stock with carp," or "keep free of algae," and simply said in general terms, "take care of my lake after I'm gone."

The problem is that we customarily discharge a general duty with an eye toward benefiting the thing: for example, advancing the child's "best interests." Once again, the fact that many Nonpersons cannot be benefited in any familiar or straightforward way rises to vex us. What do we do with regard to the many things incapable of being benefited even in the way we can "benefit" the tree?

What is needed is some notion of an action morally commendable in regard to X that is not dependent upon benefiting X, upon X's own good. Let us put it this way. In default of any welfare of the lake, is there nothing the lake trustee can further, other than the welfare of contemporary Persons? Clearly there is. Each of the five moral viewpoints sketched above could be mined for some rational guidance not reducible to the welfare either of contemporary humans or of the lake. For example, on the view that the lake is to be conceived as intrinsically valuable, the trustee might regard herself as obliged simply to preserve the lake as best she can, within constraints of the sort discussed in connection with the legal rules, namely, in accordance with some flexible notion of the lake's ideal essence.[22] Or, adopting a virtue-centered theory, there are duties discharged (or, at least, good acts performed) by acting in the right way. Consider the recent litigation seeking to forbid the mass burial of aborted fetuses without religious graveside rituals.[23] The argument that the fetuses would be made no better off by the ritual is correct, but does answer to those who favor the ceremony. Their position is grounded on an ideal way of life. Under other theories the morally commendable performance may be indicated once the ontology is established, by reference to the same principles. Under a theory that provides an accounting for riverhood on account of majesty, the prima facie wrong would be to drain the stream to an unmajestic trickle.

The hardest problems are probably those I have left for last: the distributional dilemmas. It is not enough to carve up the world, establishing what is to be deemed morally considerate. Nor is it enough to agree how that regard translates into prima facie good (or at least bad) acts. What are we to do in the case of conflicts, not always conflicts of interests (because Things lack them), but conflicts of *indication?* For example, suppose that working within one or another of the above viewpoints, a prima facie case can be made for preserving an endangered species of animal, such as the snail darter. If it is to make any difference in our conduct, the presumption in favor of preservation needs to be sturdy enough to resist rebuttal on the slightest showing of a conflicting human utility preference. In other words, even if the continued existence of a species, or the state of a river, is granted to be "a good," how do we make adjustments in the face of other competing goods?

In mediating competing claims among Persons (directly and through the powers of the state), the most common strategy is to combine welfare principles with rights principles. Some writers invoke welfare-improving principles as a basis for social action, with moral rights introduced as side constraints on how far the majority can go. To promote the greatest good of the greatest number we devise institutions designed to stamp out crime, such as police, courts, and jails. But on the view that Persons have rights, we do not go so far as to eliminate an individual's right to counsel, or to a jury trial, on the grounds that to do so would be best for (and might well be approved by) the majority of the law-abiding public. Other writers favor the converse; that is, they begin with rights, rather than welfare, as the foundation for social relations. For example, I start out with a presumptive right to control my property; the right-protected outcome can be overridden, if at all, only in the face of the strongest showing of countervailing general welfare, or of some conflicting "higher" right.

Either way, rights are given a pivotal role. Small wonder, then, that much of the contemporary Nonpersons literature, particularly in regard to animals, fetuses, and the terminally infirm, has been drawn into a discussion of whether the things with which they are respectively concerned "have rights." Having rights is ordinarily regarded as a way, perhaps the exclusive way, to secure the benefits of moral considerateness. Thus, the standard gambit of animal and fetus advocates is to survey the properties of ordinary Persons that have been proposed as the basis for human rights, and then to search for enough of the same properties in their unorthodox clients to warrant granting them rights on the same basis.

I myself am skeptical, however admiring, of these efforts to account for the considerateness of higher Nonpersons such as animals by assigning them "rights."[24] Insofar as rights are a useful foundation for moral discourse, they seem more at home relating Persons to one another. In large part, this is because only Persons, moral agents living in a common moral community, are capable of waiving and trading claims of their own volition, and thereby of creating the richly textured moral fabric in which rights belong. The implication is not to remove Nonpersons from all considerateness. In Chapter 16, I will have more to say about why the notion of assigning a whale rights might be resisted even by one who is sympathetic to whales. I will also show why this does not entail eliminating the whale from moral significance, since it leaves open our potential duties toward the whale.

This is not a matter about which I am adamant, particularly since the stakes of shifting from a semantics of rights-against to duties-toward seem so uncertain. Certainly, the emphasis on rights cannot be predicated on the idea that rights are absolute and in that sense the fundamental unit of moral analysis. To judge from the way rights are ordinarily employed, while the asserted right cannot be overridden merely by general welfare or because most people would prefer it overridden, almost everyone concedes that some showing of some countervailing interest will do. I have, perhaps, a "right" to liberty. But surely my right is not beyond being overridden if prosecutors should convince a jury that I engaged in murder. Those who maintain otherwise, "absolutists" of some sort, are generally defining the right (my liberty) in a way so abstract as to avoid recognizing the conditions under which it can be abrogated. Rights expressed on such a broad level of generality are possibly effective in contouring moral discourse, but are fated to exercise weak gravity on the final outcomes of actual conflicts. This suggests that the difference between mere moral considerateness, on the one hand, and rights holding, on the other, is more a matter of degree than is suggested by the emphasis accorded rights discourse in much of the literature.

What one seeks to accomplish by denominating a claim one of rights is to distinguish it from other claims as sturdier. It deserves special weight when squared off against competing interests and values. When we so regard rights functionally, we see that much of what is sought can be equally well secured, and, I think, in the case of Nonpersons be more plausibly secured, by speaking of our duties. We have already seen that it is quite coherent to express duties in regard to a Nonperson without becoming entangled in assertions about the Nonperson's rights. The executor of the tree-benefiting will has a duty to water the tree whether or not the tree has a right to be watered. Rights are equally dispensable when regard for the Nonperson originates not from a testamentary will, but on other bases, for example, when we consider conserving a Thing because of its intrinsic value or on account of a way of life to which it is integral. The conduct someone wants to persuade us to adopt by arguing that "a river has a right," say, that we not pollute it (without some strong showing of conflicting value) can be equivalently expressed in the form, "we have a duty not to pollute the river" (without the same showing).

Of course, even if, as concerns Nonpersons, an analysis built on duties is more congenial than one built on rights, we are still left with the task of establishing those duties. If I defer getting down to that, I have reason. Neither discourse, neither one framed on rights nor one framed on duties, can be understood independent of a larger construct of supportive and underlying principles. Any inventorying of properties (does *this* look like the sort of thing that will support a right or duty?) has to depend upon an investigation of the whole construct, the moral world view, in which the right or duty is situated. To illustrate, let us suppose that my having promised Jones to play chess gives Jones a right to expect me, and gives me a duty to be there, at the appointed time. I subsequently discover that I cannot both make the chess appointment and also plug a toxic leak that is destroying the ecological balance of a stream. In what sense does Jones's "right" that I show up for the match or my "duty" to be there answer the question of what I ought to do in the final analysis, after everything, including the emergency, is considered? If "right" and "duty" are to be understood in a conclusionary sense, as the final product of some moral equation, then one wants to know what were the premises, and how the conclusion was drawn. If "rights" and "duties" are not being used in a conclusionary sense, if there are, as one assumes, other principles lurking in the background, one wants to bring them into the light.

The point is, wherever the existence of rights and duties is entered in controversy, we are pressed to look behind and around them to whatever set of moral principles they are alleged to derive from, as well as to companion principles. Hence, neither rights nor duties can be the indivisible atoms of our attention. As tools of analysis they appear to be intermediate and perhaps eliminatable, depending on the framework. What we are after then are not just principles that embed Nonperson rights or duties, but a whole moral framework that supports Nonperson considerateness. Moreover, I am holding open the possibility that in our relations with Nonpersons both rights-talk and duties-talk are too stern. A framework that adopts some milder tone may be required. But are there other alternatives that can do the job, that are rich and fine-tuned enough in their guidance to adjudicate among at least some competing courses of action, each of which enjoys a prima facie basis for being considered morally welcome? It is to this larger question, that of frameworks, that we must now turn.

IV

WHAT CAN WE DEMAND/
EXPECT OF A MORAL
FRAMEWORK?

A BRIEF FOR PLURALISM

One popular inspiration for the environmental movement is a passage in Aldo Leopold's *Sand County Almanac:*

> When god-like Odysseus returned from the wars in Troy, he hanged all on one rope a dozen slave-girls of his household whom he suspected of misbehavior during his absence.
>
> This hanging involved no question of propriety. The girls were property. The disposal of property was then, as now, a matter of expediency, not of right and wrong.
>
> Concepts of right and wrong were not lacking from Odysseus' Greece: witness the fidelity of his wife through the long years before at last his black-prowed galleys clove the wine-dark seas for home. The ethical structure of that day covered wives, but had not yet been extended to human chattels. During the three thousand years which have since elapsed, ethical criteria have been extended to many fields of conduct, with corresponding shrinkages in those judged by expediency only.
>
> This extension of ethics, so far studied only by philosophers, is actually a process in logical evolution. . . .
>
> The first ethics dealt with the relation between individuals; the Mosaic Decalogue is an example. Later accretions dealt with the relation between the individual and society. The Golden Rule tries to integrate the individual to society; democracy to integrate social organization to the individual.
>
> There is as yet no ethic dealing with man's relation to land and to the animals and plants which grow upon it. Land, like Odysseus' slave-girls, is

still property. The land-relation is still strictly economic, entailing privileges but not obligations.

The extension of ethics to this third element in human environment is, if I read the evidence correctly, an evolutionary possibility and an ecological necessity. It is the third step in a sequence. . . .

The land ethic simply enlarges the boundaries of the community to include soils, waters, plants, and animals, or collectively, the land.*

I would be pleased to have the present enterprise associated with Leopold's entreaty that we develop a "land ethic"—or something, or some things, of that sort. For the disappointing fact is that neither Leopold nor any of his successors have been very successful explaining, much less justifying, what a land ethic would involve. Leopold's categorical imperative is generally understood to be the equivalent of, "A thing is right when it tends to preserve the integrity, stability, and beauty of the biotic community. It is wrong when it tends otherwise."† Sometimes Leopold sounds surprisingly like nothing more than an enlightened utilitarian, i.e., one arguing that the warrant for protecting the land is our ultimate dependency on it, and that therefore protecting it redounds to human benefit. This leaves open the question whether there is any cause to condemn an action that radically disturbs the environment but represents a net welfare gain for humans, even when the reduced value of the environment is accounted for. A true earth ethic would answer "yes."

I have argued that the commonest objections people raise—that things are not moral agents, have no interests, etc.—are not fatal to some endeavor along the respect-for-earth lines. I have offered five possible viewpoints from which, separately or in supportive combination, an ethic like a "land ethic" might be developed.‡ And I have

*Aldo Leopold, A Sand County Almanac, (New York: Ballantine, 1970), pp. 237–39.
†See James D. Heffernan, "The Land Ethic: A Critical Appraisal," Environmental Ethics 4 (1982): 235.
‡There is a separate question: How feasible is it to expect an earth ethic (somehow defined) to emerge? It is popular today to take a dim view of the prospects so long as and wherever capitalism and Christianity dominate. In that regard consider the following:

We must discover and conquer the country in which we live. It is a tremendous country but not yet entirely ours. Our [prairie] will truly become ours only when we come with columns of tractors and break the thousand-year-old virgin soil. On a far-flung front outlined in rough contour the chores such a framework would have to perform. It should give a justifiable account of (1) how prima facie considerateness for a thing originates, (2) how the ontological conundrums (which things are considerate?) are to be resolved, (3) the manner in which the prima facie considerateness ought to be manifested, and (4) the distributional dilemmas: how we are to resolve conflicts when more than one course of conduct appears morally welcome.

But where do we go from here? Did Leopold have in mind an ethic that would govern all moral questions, but by reference to a grander, more encompassing set of principles? Or was the land ethic to be an ethic that governed man's relations with land only, relegating interpersonal relations to independent principles? To press ahead, we have to know something more about the constraints an ethics builder is under. *What is an ethic supposed to look like? What is it supposed to do?*

Presumably, to produce an ethic is to produce a framework for testing and if need be "correcting" our initial dispositions on other than narrowly prudential grounds. To render such a project coherent, I am supposing it may invoke an independent "moral observer" for whom the community's conventional notions of welfare, interests, and the good, are, although relevant, not conclusive. (Even if the majority of the community regards genocide as in its interest, and good, the moral observer may yet deem it wrong.) But of what mental material is the platform from which that independent observation to be made—principles, maxims, paradigm examples of good and evil, or something else?

---

we must wage war. We must burrow into the earth, break rocks, dig mines, construct houses. We must take from the earth . . .

The passage happens to be lifted from a 1929 textbook designed for the education of twelve to fourteen year olds in the Soviet Union. (Only the word *prairie* has been injected to replace the original *steppe*.) Albert E. Burke, "Influence of Man Upon Nature —The Russian View: A Case Study," in *Man's Role in Changing the Face of the Earth*, ed. William J. Thomas (Chicago and London: University of Chicago Press, 1956), p. 1048. The quotation is not misleading. The Soviets have proceeded to compile quite a bad environmental record unassisted by either capitalism or Christianity. Nor, I presume, do those who potshot at the West read much about the Third World's performance. Technology, surely, East and West, is a problem, in whatever ideology it is cloaked. But the point is, the forces which bring man into conflict with the environment are complex, deep-rooted, and often as worthy and simple as a desire to feed the hungry and advance knowledge; it strikes me as a disservice to our understanding, and flimsy eschatology, to lay our entire predicament on Scripture, Adam Smith, or mindless greed.

Must we provide, for each moral dilemma it recognizes as a dilemma, one right answer? Or is it enough to identify several courses of action equally acceptable, perhaps identifying for elimination those that are wrong or unwelcome? And as among contending frameworks, are we constrained to select one and reject all the others? That is, may we proceed to put forward several sets of principles, each to govern a specific moral jurisdiction, such as our relations with Nonpersons and our relations with Things, on its own peculiar terms? Or need we provide a single coherent set of principles that will govern throughout, so that any ethic we champion has to absorb its contenders with a more abstract and ambitious creation?

At this point, the inquiry extends beyond the question of an earth ethic, or the moral considerateness of Nonpersons as such, and enters a subject of much broader interest, one that brings us to the very bedrock of moral philosophy.

Moral Monism

So MUCH IS going on in contemporary moral philosophy that one hesitates to generalize about what is and is not orthodox today. At the hazard of some caricature let me offer a few sweeping, but I trust not unsympathetic, impressions. Much of the effort appears divided, as all academic and artistic endeavors divide, into camps. The camps are typically assembled under the banner of some set of general principles the camp's adherents are committed to carry and defend. We have already referred to some of them. In one camp there are those, typified by utilitarians of various schools, who orient morality to the consequences of our actions. An act (or general rule) is good if it brings about a state of affairs better than any other state of affairs within the actor's influence. The "better" state is variously associated with that containing the most pleasure, or achieving the most welfare-satisfying compromise among competing preferences. Within such consequentialist schools, the general boundaries that fence off alien positions having been drawn, most of the internal activity is dedicated to such matters as defining what consequences are good, and assessing how we compare one person's welfare with another's.

Other camps, the deontologists, typified by the Kantians, emphasize duties and ideals. The word *deontic* comes from the Greek verb "to bind." The notion is that there are at least some things one ought to do because one is morally bound to, the consequences to be, if not wholly damned, at least deeply discounted. Kant, for example, fairly fumed at the Benthamite notion that the punishment we mete out to a criminal should be determined with forward-looking regard to the consequences on deterring others. Even if there were no prospect of deterrence (if the wrongdoer was, say, discovered alone on a desert island from which she could never escape, and thought by all to be dead), we should be bound to punish her for what she did in the past, just because she deserved it. In camps of this sort, most of the internal effort is spent in considering how our duties originate and where they lie, and in testing in the light of universalized principles particular intuitions about how we ought to act in concrete situations. Contractarians, such as John Rawls in his *Theory of Justice* mood, share much of the Kantians' viewpoint but seek to overcome some of Kant's perceived shortcomings. They identify moral constraints by reference to rules that rational persons would subscribe to if they were in a hypothetical original position—"behind a veil of ignorance," as it is put—not knowing what contingencies of ability, wealth, and so on would be their own lot in actual life.

These camps have their major and important differences which are well discussed in the literature. The point of interest here is only that underneath all the rivalry, there is a striking if ordinarily only implicit agreement on two tenets that together endow moral philosophy with what might be called its prevailing sense of mission. Each school is *monistic,* and as a sort of corollary, each is *determinate.* By monistic I mean that the enterprise is conceived as aiming to produce, and to defend against all rivals, a single coherent and complete set of principles capable of governing all moral quandaries. By determinate I mean that the ambition of that one framework is to yield for each quandary one right answer. I suspect that anyone who wavers between doctrines, or who shows second thoughts about the most ambitious powers of his selected orthodoxy to solve all problems, would arouse suspicion of "not taking morals seriously."

Sometimes these suppositions are made fairly explicit, as when we are told that the task of the ethicist is to find "a complete set of valid ethical principles from which all true ethical statements can be deduced." These principles are to "have roughly the same relation to the totality of valid ethical statements that Euclid's axioms and postulates have (or were intended to have) to his theorems."[1] More often, the Monist spirit is veiled, and has to be inferred from the form that assault takes on the rival camps. The accepted maneuver is to volley onto one's academic foes a hypothetical quandary that their principles cannot handle, or that they can solve only in a way that seems intuitively unsatisfactory. So strafed with embarrassments, the besieged contenders are expected to splinter into confused, undisciplined factions, primed for surrender. The underlying assumption is distinctly Monist: if an ethical system cannot satisfactorily dispose of every conceivable dilemma, it will not do, and must withdraw entirely across all fronts.[2]

To illustrate, the neo-Kantians typically try to confront the utilitarians with a hypothetical in which a welfare-advancing state of affairs (to which the utilitarian appears committed) is produced by an evilly motivated act that would discredit the actor. Jones, with the intention of blowing up a school bus, inadvertently saves it from an avalanche. "How," asks the Kantian, "can you say that a bad act was 'good'?" Little systematic attention is given to the alternative we will examine in chapter 14: that the morality with which we judge actions might be severable from the morality with which we judge the character of the actors.

I am not saying that everyone engaged in moral philosophy would declare themselves Monists if the question were expressly posed. Some would certainly try to disassociate from the idea.[3] Occasionally there even appears in the literature projects that can be construed as laying claim to a limited turf only. For example, John Rawls expressly recognizes that his notion of "rightness as fairness"

> fails to embrace all moral relationships, since it would seem to include only our relations with other persons and leave out of account how we are to conduct ourselves toward animals and the rest of nature. I do not contend that the contract notion offers a way to approach these questions which are certainly of the first importance; and I shall have to put them aside.[4]

Such disavowals are, however, the exception. Indeed, the prevailing assumption—that a moral system has to be uncompromisingly universalistic—appears so ingrained that even a philosophy that originates with limited territorial ambitions may find its backers championing its banner in every corner of the moral globe. Bernard Williams suggests that such has been the history of utilitarianism.[5] Bentham, the father of the movement, was animated by a desire to reform social institutions, typified by the prison system. Hence, utilitarianism's original emphasis was to provide guidance to lawmakers in devising standards for general legislative rules that would apply across broad populations. But once unloosed, the basic idea was generalized to every corner of personal conduct, including, for example, interfamily relations.[6]

Whatever may be the status of Monism in academic circles today, no one, as far as I am aware, has undertaken to examine expressly and in any detail the case for its antithesis, Moral Pluralism. As a rough start, the Moral Pluralist holds that a public representative, a senator, for example, might rightly embrace utilitarianism when it comes to legislating a general rule for social conduct (say, in deciding what sort of toxic waste program to establish). Yet, this same representative need not be principally utilitarian, nor even a consequentialist of any style, in arranging his personal affairs among kin or friends, or deciding whether it is right to poke out the eyes of pigeons. And surely, being committed to utilitarianism as a basis for choosing legislation does not entail judging a person's character solely by reference to whether, on balance, he advances the greatest good of the greatest number of Persons.

The fact that no one has come forward to champion a Pluralist analysis is odd. For one thing, the ambitions of the Monists, to oust all rivals from the entire moral terrain, seem hard to jibe with prominent features of moral life and reasoning. A grasp of these features is essential not only to understanding the moral status of Nonpersons, but to carry forward moral philosophy itself.

Monism's first flaw is a failure to account for the fact that ethics involves not one but several distinct activities. One involves making personal choices: What is the right thing for me to do in these circumstances? At other times, we are prescribing conduct for others. At still other times, the emphasis shifts away from current choices, our own or anyone else's, and involves a special moral describing or grading. We may be assessing an actor (was Napoleon, as Tolstoy argued, evil?), an action (was it wrong to drop the atomic bomb on Hiroshima?), a social rule (is the death penalty unjust?), a prevailing practice (discrimination). Sometimes we are evaluating neither actions nor character, but emotional attitudes or other mental states. Envy and vengefulness are bad; feeling guilt (in fitting circumstances) is virtuous. Sometimes moral language arises in an explanatory mode: "His goodness held him back." And moral talk comes up in other ways: in punishing and rewarding, invoking justifications and excuses, and building up moral credit.

Of course, all these activities are related. In morally evaluating a historic figure or a character in fiction, we are practicing the use of moral predicates, and in some sense committing ourselves to how we will use them in various "live" situations. Yet, it does not follow that the bases for our moral judgments remain identical throughout, as we shift from activity to activity. For example, what is right for us need not be right for others. We might be obligated to hold ourselves to a higher standard; presumably then, different rules or principles apply. Moreover, the way we decide what is right for us personally needs not track the same considerations as ought to guide us in a particular social role, as parent or friend, legislator or prosecutor. In the evaluation of actions, the consequences, while perhaps not conclusive, play a large role in most persons' thinking. In evaluating a terrorist attack, some accounting will be made for the effects, for the number of victims. But in the evaluation of an attitude—for example, the harboring of prejudice, or indifference to sufferings—there are no effects to consider.

Nor is it self-evident that the way we decide that an act is "a good act," meaning merely that it is permissible, needs follow the same line of thought we employ in deciding whether it is commendable or mandatory. Surely one can intuit the possibility of different thought procedures, an intuition whose logical structure I examine in Chapter 13. In like vein, to regard eating animals as "wrong" does not seem to me to entail not eating animals. We might consider someone a better person, morally, who is a vegetarian on principle, and credit his or her character accordingly. Or we might think the practice wrong in the sense that some justification was owing ("my doctor said beef liver would alleviate my anemia"), but not a justification that had to carry the weight demanded of a person who has killed another person ("self-defense"). Hence, the Monist project faces this burden: can all the moral activities, with all their nuances of judgment, be brought under the governance of even the most blandly general parent principle, such as Kant's Categorical Imperative* or utilitarianism's Greatest Good?

There is another way to divide morals into separable activities, which, properly considered, puts the burden Monism faces in sharp relief. There appear to be (1) activities that involve the alteration of our tastes; (2) activities that take our tastes as a given, and involve alteration of our preferences; and (3) activities that take both our tastes and preferences as a given, and involve the alteration of our conduct by appeal to how they should be combined with the tastes and preferences of others.

To illustrate, suppose a person, Jones, who likes—has quite literally "developed a taste for"—pâté de foie gras. Smith does not want Jones to continue to indulge his tastes. Smith is concerned with the way pâté de foie gras is traditionally (although, hopefully, less universally now) produced. Geese, almost from birth, are force-fed huge amounts of grain by grasping them firmly with braces, inserting a funnel down their throats, and turning on a machine pump-feeder. A band is placed around the bird's neck to keep it from regurgitating. Their livers swell to occupy most of their deformed body cavities until eventually the liver membrane may even break. The process, known as *gavage*, produces a particularly tender, and many find palatable, pâté.

Now, there are, as I have just indicated, several strategies available

---

*Kant actually states the Categorical Imperative in several forms, including, "Act only on that maxim through which you can at the same time will that it should become a universal law" (H. J. Paton translation of *Groundwork*, p. 88), and what Kant deemed to follow from that: "Act in such a way that you always treat humanity never simply as a means but always at the same time as an end" (p. 96).

to Smith, each of which can be regarded as part of a separate moral activity. The first is for Smith simply to show Jones the paragraph above, together with similar literature. Jones, having read them, may find the process for making pâté so revolting he will lose his taste for it. Note that pursuant to this strategy Jones is not brought to the point of a conscious moral decision, in that Jones never denies himself on moral grounds something he wants. That is, he never corrects his initial preferences in the sense of Chapter 8. He has not been argued out of wanting the pâté as much as jarred out of wanting it by a sensitive and selective presentation of the facts. His tastes have changed.

In the second strategy Smith goes beyond a graphic narration of how the pâté is made. He structures the presentation with some references to moral principles or examples. He might emphasize considerations for the geese, because they suffer. He might invoke concern for mankind: goose *gavage* contributes to callousness and brutality. The aim is not to change Jones's taste for the pâté (let us imagine him still salivating at the very thought of it), but to alter his preferences, to get Jones consciously to decide not to eat pâté henceforth because he has been persuaded that he ought not to do so.*

To illustrate the third approach, imagine Jones unshakable both in his taste and his preferences. Smith might yet adopt as a strategy that under some morally defensible collective-choice rule which combines different persons' preferences *justly,* Jones should consent to subordinate his own preferences to those of others. "Although you would prefer a rule that allowed the sale of pâté, most people are against it (or, the greatest weight of preference is against it) and have passed a law forbidding it, and the relevant institutions, the legislatures and agencies, being appropriately constituted, you are under some obligation to comply with their verdict."

Now, I consider each of these activities—certainly the last two—to be moral activities. But they operate in different spheres and aim at

*Note that not all principled considerations would be moral. Smith might point out that eating the pâté presents danger to Jones because toxic substances tend to concentrate in the liver. But appeal to such blatant self-interest would not constitute a "moral argument."

different things. To take them in reverse order, the third strategy would seem to provide the neo-utilitarians their most comfortable home grounds, allowing them to take preferences as given and undertake to work out rules for their combination. On the other hand, if someone is engaged in the second activity, that is, seeking to "correct" individual utility preferences, there is something out of bounds in insisting that those preferences have to be regarded as given. There is no reason to assume that preference combining must proceed according to the same rules, principles, and so on, as preference determining. Similarly, the point of the first activity is to alter the fundamental tastes on which are based the preferences given in the second activity. If taste changing is regarded as part of morals, subject to principles, the "principles" are more those in virtue of which we educate tastes in music and art. They are not the same principles that govern the other activities. Failing to hold these activities distinct adds to the plausibility of Monism, but it is deceptive, and does not do justice to the complexity of morals.

Monism's second weakness stems from the diversity of entities that have at least a colorable claim to moral recognition. Some have sentience (higher animals); some are abstract or membership class concepts (corporations, cultures, species); some have intellectual talent, at least of a sort (A.I.s and, coming soon, androids); and some are genetically human, either capable of experiencing pain (advanced fetuses) or non-sentient (early embryos). At this point, I do not want to beg the question which is my burden to carry forward: Is there some rational framework into which at least some of the Nonpersons can be fitted as morally considerate, and in what way? But as a start, both the popular media and the academic literature testify to growing sentiment that moral discourse has to provide at least some Nonpersons some sort of moral accounting that they are not now receiving. Among the conventional schools, acknowledgment that some revisions are in order takes the form of an occasional determination to show how that school can accommodate some of our sympathetic intuitions according to its own lights. A Kantian, for example, can substantiate objections to cruelty toward animals. These are laudatory and in some degree, certainly, successful efforts. Yet, when we consider the diverse and peculiar properties that the entire range of Nonpersons presents, it seems doubtful that any single framework—not one of the conventional frameworks certainly—can make many adaptions without stretching itself so unrecognizably as to jeopardize its original appeal.

For example, since utilitarianism can be extended to anything that experiences pleasure and pain, future persons and animals can be drawn into the moral community, at least as obligees if not as obligors.[7] But as we have already seen, utilitarianism's efforts to handle future generations ties it into some awkward if not paradoxical knots. Is there warrant to include those who *might* be born—obliging us to bring them into existence on the basis that the more people, the more pleasures? Is a future earth containing 50 billion humans, moderately miserable in their overcrowding, better than (represent an advance in welfare over) the same planet with 1 billion beamingly happy inhabitants?

Nor is it clear that utilitarianism can satisfy the concern that backs the animal liberation movement. A utilitarian, who has troubles enough providing an adequate account of human rights, is all the more tested to provide their equivalent for animals. Suppose that bears *count* along with the rest of us, that is, that right and wrong are determined by lumping together the pleasures and pains of bears with those of persons. Even so, if the pleasures derived from bearbaiting, or, for that matter, eating bear meat, outweigh whatever welfare losses the practices occasion the bears (and the squeamish human onlookers), then those practices, for a utilitarian, are morally right.[8] Those opposed to the bearbaiting are, for a utilitarian, morally nonsuited. Moreover, there is no way to extract from utilitarianism any direct, as opposed to instrumental, support for species as such, since species (like tribes, nations, and early embryos) experience no pleasures or pains.

It is not only the utilitarian whose capacity to account for unconventional entities appears to fall short of satisfying popular—or, at any rate, growing—intuitions. The utilitarian's principal contenders all require, in various ways and with various justifications, putting oneself in the place of another (by dint of what it is in vogue to call "thought experiments") and testing whether we could really will the conduct under evaluation if we assumed the other's position and/or natural endowment.[9] While such a hypothetical trading of places is always problematical, it seems least so when we are trading with persons who share our culture, whose interests, values, and tastes we can therefore presume with *some* confidence. But even that slender assurance is destined to erode the further we venture our imaginations beyond the familiar Persons domain. With what conviction can we trade places with members of spatially and temporally remote cultures, with aboriginal tribes, or with our own descendants in some future century? And of course, if we wish to explore our obligations in regard to the dead, trees, rocks, fetuses, artificial intelligence, or species, trading places is essentially a blind alley. It is one thing to put oneself in the shoes of a stranger, perhaps even in the hooves of a horse, but quite another to put oneself in the banks of a river. ("How would I feel if I were a river, and ribbed with dams?")

What does all this demonstrate—the multiplicity of moral activities and the variety of Nonpersons? Certainly, the fact that orthodox moral philosophies, each with its own Persons orientation, have difficulty accommodating various things, except perhaps as resources, is not in itself *proof* that these conventional moral schools are wrong or have to be amended beyond recognition. One alternative, the position of a die-hard adherent to one of the predominant schools, is that any Nonperson that the school cannot account for, except perhaps in a certain limited way, cannot (save in that limited way) have moral significance. But there is another response to the dilemma, one that is more challenging to the assumptions that animate conventional moral thought: How monistic need a moral order be? Need we accept as inevitable that there be one set of axioms or principles or paradigms for all morals, operable across all moral activities and all diverse entities? What would a Moral Pluralism look like, what would it commit us to, and how would we deal with its own dilemmas?

Calling Moral Monism to Question

Moral philosophy as it stands today might be compared with astronomy in the Middle Ages. From the ancients, medieval science had inherited the view that the earth occupies the center of the universe. The other celestial bodies were conceived to be rotating about us in a flattering obeisance of perfect spheres and circles. Over the years, increasingly careful and accurate observations of planetary and stellar motion produced observations that did not square with this simple schema. In effect, heavenly bodies were showing up at the wrong place at the wrong time.

Of course, today we explain the deviations that puzzled early astronomers by a revised conception of the whole system. We are no longer bound to the view that the earth is the immobile center of the universe, nor even do we consider it stationary. The earth is spinning about an axis (itself not stationary to a plane) and is, with the other planets, traveling about the sun in nearly elliptical orbits. A few heretics did interpret the data in some such more complex way, at least to the extent of positing heliocentric orbits. But wholesale acceptance of such a radically revolutionary model would have torn the elaborate fabric of beliefs that had been woven into the geocentric cosmology. It would, at the very least, have called to question the authority of common sense, of the ancients, and of the Church. Indeed, to some extent the whole prevailing social order was modeled on the imagined orderliness and hierarchy of the planetary system. Viewed psychologically, there was investment, too, in the conceit that God has placed the creature of His image in the center of the cosmos. Geocentrism was homocentrism was egocentrism. For centuries, therefore, astronomers selectively edited the data, as in the possibly apocryphal story about Galileo's contemporaries refusing to look at potentially unsettling evidence through his telescope. When data appeared that could not be disregarded or dismissed, the adjustments they permitted were as meager and cautious as possible. The aim was to provide an explanation that was more conservative than heliocentrism, less "costly" in terms of the associated beliefs they would otherwise have had to relinquish.

The universe, the early revisions had it, was indeed earth-centered and built upon circular motions, but in a more complex and wondrous way than had theretofore been appreciated. Retained was the fundamental tenet that the paths of celestial bodies about the earth were perfect circles, but—here, the amendment—sometimes the circles served not as the path of the body itself, but as a "deferent," the locus of the center of a lesser circular orbit ("epicycle") on which the body itself was actually traveling. In other words, rather than to suppose the planets were moving along ellipses around the sun, the preference was to conceive their paths as circles that spun upon circles around the earth. As new, additional observations turned up further inaccuracies in the contemporary model, another epicycle could always be added to keep the system's predictive capacity in line with the data that the improving observational technology and skills were able to provide. In such a manner the central tenet, geocentrism, was long preserved, although the simplicity of the allied beliefs (of theology, politics, and so on) was purchased at the cost of cluttering the sky with deferents, epicycles, and epicycles on epicycles.[1]

In suggesting a parallel with contemporary moral philosophy, I do not have in mind only the obvious substantive point, the tenacity of propositions that place humans in the center of things. There is a methodological parallel, an analogy to the way we are responding to our own explosion of hard-to-fit moral "data." By moral data, I mean the everyday phenomena we see all around us that strike us as right or wrong or morally problematical, and seem therefore to warrant some further ethical inquiry. These data include all the pressures on conventional frameworks surveyed in part I: medical advances that empower us to "farm" organs from embryos and the dead; military advances that threaten to draw the environment into warfare on a scale never before imagined; a growing sense of resource scarcity that has focused interest on future generations; increased understanding of nonhuman life, with an accompanying increase in empathy; and so on. So far as these phenomena cannot, like the moons Galileo saw circling Jupiter, be disregarded, they put pressure on our contemporary models either to provide them a clear place or to justify the exclusion.

Hence, the more such problems have surfaced, the more each school has searched about for its own ingenious conceptual devices—its own deferents and epicycles—to preserve its conception whole, whatever the clutter. Take, for example, philosophies that base all moral obligations on consent. Finding it awkward that people in many modern relations are not in any real sense *consenting,* they simply imply the consent; or, as with Rawls's veil of ignorance, they understand it to mean consent that hypothetical ideal beings *would have given* had they hypothetically known certain facts but not others. And consider the assumptions about human motivation that have to be introduced to "smooth out," simplify, and thereby preserve popular philosophical systems, such as that the whole of human conduct can be explained in terms of individualistic egoism, and that selfishness is the sole spring of human conduct. Did ever any medieval astronomer so oversimplify his data?

It is not the point of the analogy to make light of anyone. On the contrary, much of mental activity has always aimed at synthesis, at bringing wholeness out of diversity. William James supposed we found aesthetic satisfaction in it. "Our pleasure at finding that a chaos of facts is the expression of a single underlying fact is like the relief of a musician at resolving a confused mass of sound into melodic or harmonic order."[2] Given this inclination to systematize, it is not surprising that people engaged in ethics, like people who do most anything else, attempt to conserve the beliefs in which they have a psychic investment. The fortification of invested beliefs has several lines of defense. First, there is a highly selective regard and disregard of data. Many of the "facts" that we would rather not see, we don't Other subversive facts slip through, threatening to perturb the harmony of the defended system. But it is still possible for the more centrally entrenched tenets to be preserved intact from these invaders by modifying, complicating, or even trading away our more expendable, peripheral beliefs.

As a consequence, one would expect to find throughout intellectual history a tendency, as one force among many, in the direction of Monism. There was perhaps a time, not too long ago, when theology would have claimed itself qualified to provide the unifying principles for all areas of human thought, from astronomy to physics to zoology. On the other hand, I doubt that many theologians today would claim that their principles subjugate so broad and unruly a domain. Nor do contemporary geometricians still believe, as did their predecessors, that Euclid's is the only geometry. In mathematics, Gödel and others have laid to rest any hope of discovering the one grand and complete set of axioms from which all true statements of math can be derived.

A comparable partitioning has taken place in the empirical sciences. Today we conceive the body politic to be comprised of humans and human conduct; the human body, of cells; cells, of molecules; molecules, of atoms; and atoms, of subatomic particles and/or waves. What happens at one level of description is undoubtedly affected, in some complex way, by what is occurring at another. Many, perhaps most, scientists feel that "in principle" there is a single unifying body of law —the laws of all nature—that at some level of simple generality holds throughout. If so, one may harbor the hope of connecting phenomena on one plane with phenomena on another, of *someday* drawing together, say, the laws that govern the movement of subatomic particles with those that govern social conduct. But we are far from it.

In fact, "verticalism," as the ultimate unification of layers is called, may have been considered a more realistic prospect by scientists one hundred years ago. Whatever the theoretical hopes, this century has witnessed an increasing parceling of the scientific enterprise into different layers of activity: political science, anthropology, sociology, molecular biology, and quantum mechanics. No level actually annuls the laws of the other; there is ordinarily no reason even to quarrel across boundaries. By and large, Schrödinger's equations, so central to the quantum physicist, do not matter to the sociologist, nor even to the biologist. Each layer, occupied with its own depth and resolution, partially closes from the others socially and intellectually. Each goes its own way, evolving its own network of concepts, tied together by its own characteristic logic, vocabulary, and techniques. Perhaps "in principle" they can all be unified, geopolitics reduced to molecular biology. But what we actually have are separate bodies of law and knowledge.

The issue I am raising is this. If, as I maintain, ethics consists of several entity groupings as distinct, roughly, as physics from sociology —that is, if it has to deal with subject matter as diverse as persons, dolphins, cultural groups, and stars—why has ethics not pursued the same path as the sciences? That is, why has *it* not partitioned?

Part of the answer (although only part) stems from the heavier empirical burden that the sciences bear. In sciences, hypotheses are continuously confirmed by or collide with the facts with which they claim to deal. One effect of such collisions is that the hypotheses, or "the facts," or both, need to be continuously reevaluated, refined, and restated—in effect, kept in rough equilibrium with one another. Overly broad generalizations are honed down, and erroneous hypotheses— those most difficult or unrewarding to hold onto—are discarded. A view that all matter is comprised of fire, earth, air, and water, sorted about by fate, is not insightful enough to endure. As part of this process, some exceedingly general, basic truths are presumed to hold throughout, such as the conservation of energy. But as regards more detailed investigation, initial hunches break off into the separate, or at least separable, sciences, each enmeshed with its distinct technology, concepts, and principles.

In ethics, the nature and impact of the collisions between theory and reality are not of the same character. Suppose that one scientist, A, relying upon one set of principles, claims that a certain liquid will solidify at − 100 degrees Fahrenheit; B, relying on his assumptions, says it will not. In science there are well-accepted conventions regarding thermometers, pressure, and so on, with respect to which the one scientist can be proved right and the other wrong. Whoever's principles yield the wrong prediction are called into question; those on which the right conjectures are based are (thus far) confirmed. Indeed, it is ordinarily presumed that a scientific statement, to be even meaningful (let alone true), must be subject to experimental confirmation. The contrast with ethics is this. If A, invoking his moral principles, claims that a promise made in such and such circumstances should be kept, and B, invoking her principles, says that there is no such obligation, there is in a sense a contradiction. But we are dealing with contradictory claims about what ought to be, rather than contradictory descriptions of states of affairs that empirical testing can moderate. That is not to deny that there may be absolute and universal ethical positions—answers to moral quandaries as correct or false as the value of pi or the distance to the moon. But we have not produced the relatively uncontroversial techniques for determining them. I do not want to overstate the classic, easily exaggerated antithesis between science and ethics (or between fact and value). But whatever qualification the distinctions require, moral principles probably have greater resiliency, more capacity to survive with their imperialist ambitions unchecked, than their counterparts in science.

Such reasons may help explain the persistence of Monism in morals. But that hardly justifies our pursuing the same path without reflection. Even science sanctions some dual versions of the world. Quantum physics includes side-by-side wave versions and particle versions for the same phenomenon. Why, then, not ethics? In ethics, the determination to purge all but a single version appears especially quixotic because the domain of morals is so vast, variegated, and subtle. Monism's ambitions are, moreover, distorting. The commitment to make every moral judgment responsive to the dictates of one Big Comprehensive Theory forces us to disregard some of the data, to settle for an increasingly bland generality in our rules, and to estrange our moral thought from our considered moral intuitions. Hence, the more we try to force every diverse dilemma into one common mold, the less we can expect detail, insight, and direction in the real, concrete choices we face; the less will our final judgments carry, and deserve, genuine conviction.

12

Foundations for Moral Pluralism

IF THE AMBITIONS of Moral Monism are delusive, what alternative is there? In the last chapter I raised an analogy between contemporary moral philosophy and medieval astronomy. Here, let us note where the analogy ends. To replace geocentrism there was a coherent rival model, heliocentrism, waiting in the observatory wings. In the case of moral philosophy, its most embedded tenet—its geocentrism—is, rather than a particular schema, the presumption that there is any single schema to be found (whatever it may turn out to be). Rather than offer any rival all-encompassing schema, I am suggesting replacement of the notion of the single schema itself. The alternative is to develop a conception of the moral realm as consisting in several different schemata, side by side. This is the view I call *Moral Pluralism.*

Moral Pluralism ought not to be confused with *moral relativism.* The latter is the familiar position (or positions, for the doctrine emerges in several garbs and even disguises) that each moral claim must be related to a particular place, its validity turning upon whether it correctly identifies the prevailing moral sentiment of the relevant community. For example, to the moral relativist, the assertion "Clubbing baby seals to death for their pelts is 'wrong'" is fatally incomplete until one identifies some specific reference group: ". . . is wrong among the Xs." Thereupon, having fixed the reference, the inquiry resolves itself into an empirical question about communal preferences: clubbing seal pups is "right"—that is, "right" among the Ys—if the majority of the Ys approve of it morally; it is "wrong" if they disapprove. For the relativist, there is nothing more to be said. Ethical discourse is reduced to a sort of grand Gallup poll.* So understood, morality affords no independent, critical perspective for people who want to call to question society's prevailing conventions. Are we prepared to concede that some country's genocidal policies were "right" because a majority of its citizens approved? Would even the whole world's approval make it right?

Because of these implications, moral relativism is not an ethical position I would defend—if, indeed, in its hasty abdication to anthropology it is an ethical view at all. Nor is Pluralism meant to suggest merely that one finds in ordinary human affairs a plurality of values in potential conflict, such as freedom and equality—an important fact that liberal political theory must account for. I mean something that is at once more far-reaching (in that it reaches beyond traditional human interests) and more elaborate (in that it is girded on a more complex and intricate set of variables than competing values).

Pluralism conceives the realm of morals to be partitioned into several planes. The planes are intellectual frameworks that support the analysis and solution of particular moral problems, roughly in the way that algebra and geometry provide frameworks for the problems to which they are respectively suited. Each plane is composed of two fundamental elements. First, there is an ontological commitment, that is to say, a foundational judgment as to which things are to be recognized and dealt with.

To illustrate, in doing plane geometry we make an ontological commitment to a world that consists of points, lines, and angles. Solid geometry posits a less flat citizenry of spheres and cubes and their surfaces. Arithmetic posits numbers. In the same vein, each moral plane embeds its own posits as to what things are to be deemed morally considerate within that framework. In some planes it is essentially

---

*It is possible to develop a more defensible view of relativism that makes rightness turn on conformity with deeper conventions. That is, an action can be viewed as right depending not on whether the majority would in fact approve that particular action. Instead, the question is whether the action conforms with fundamental conventional principles of which the majority actually or impliedly approves, but whose implications in the specific instance the majority has failed rightly to recognize.

sentient creatures whose interests count. In others it is Persons, species, or nation-states. But (the Pluralist maintains) just as the rules of solid geometry are not the rules of arithmetic, so the rules that govern our relations with animals are not the same rules that govern the relations among corporate bodies.

Thus there is for each plane a second element, what I call its governance—essentially the rules that apply. In the various geometries, the governance is the system of postulates, axioms, theorems, and corollaries that determines the range of questions that can be asked about the points, lines, and planes, the strategy of their analysis, and the quality and substance of the solutions. In the context of our inquiry, the governance for each moral plane is the body of rules, principles, and so on, to which that version of the world is subject.

A concrete illustration of where I am coming from—and heading —may be helpful. Under recent law, all federally funded institutions using live animals for research are required to establish review procedures to assure that the animals are being treated in a "humane" fashion. As the programs have developed, there has been increased vigilance to avoid the infliction of pain on the animals; but there is not the same reluctance to impose death. For example, if an animal awakening from an invasive procedure faces any prospect of continuing pain, it is almost certain to be sacrificed: "put out of its misery." By contrast, in dealing with a convalescing human who is unable to consent, we are ordinarily prepared to impose a regimen that entails considerable suffering if we believe there to be the faintest possibility of salvaging further life (even further pain-racked life). The exceptions, if any, are almost always where the human has become a (we say "vegetable" but we mean) lower animal, a Nonperson.

I presume that these distinctions have little appeal to a Monist. The moral world comprises one group of morally relevant entities ("rights-holders") all treated the same way ("equally"). Either animals don't count, so that we can use them for our benefit without constraint; or they do count, and have the same rights as we do. The implication of the either-or choice may be to dismiss the animal entirely. As one defender of animal experimentation has recently argued.

> If all forms of animal life . . . must be treated equally, and if therefore
> . . . the pains of a rodent count equally with the pains of a human, we are
> forced to conclude (1) that neither humans nor rodents possess rights, or
> (2) that rodents possess all the rights that humans possess.*

Unsurprisingly, this chain of reasoning leads the author to conclude that animals have no rights.

Pluralism is an attempt to view the situation in a less binary, more flexible manner. The Pluralist is in no way surprised to find us being at once more considerate of animals' pain than of their lives, and of Persons' lives than of their pain. Both animals and Persons are considerate, but our relations with each are separately fabricated. With animals, it appears that those charged with making actual (nonphilosophic) decisions have adopted something close to a pure utilitarianism. That is, in selecting between courses of animal-affecting conduct, society is increasingly committed to minimize their pain. In dealings among Persons, we also seek to minimize pain; but we blend into our judgments an additional, sometimes conflicting consideration, what a Kantian would call respect-for-persons. What we have here, in the terminology presently being examined, are two separate worlds (Persons and animals) across which separate rules (moral governances) are in operation. People and rodents both experience pain, a morally salient fact that is accounted for by each of the two standard institutional review committees, those for humans and those for animal subjects. The respective committees divide—they invoke distinct governance considerations—when life is to be taken. Our duties toward rodents are shaped by doubts (which should remain open to examination) that a rodent forms self-conscious, detailed plans about the future. By contrast, normal *homo sapiens* project a life rich with goals, dreams, aims and far-reaching intentions.

*Carl Cohen, "The Case for the Use of Animals in Biomedical Research," *New England Journal of Medicine*, 315 (1986): 865, 867. Cohen's ultimate conclusion, if not his reasoning, suggests more flexibility; although he would not weigh the pains of all animate beings equally (p. 868), and thinks we ideally should be conducting more animal experimentation than at present, he appears to stop short of dismissing the pains of animals, since he considers us required to desist from experiments on them wherever we can accomplish the same result using alternative methods (p. 868).

If our conception about the "richness" of animals' lives is accurate and significant, then the prevailing tendency to divide man and animal, and to be more solicitous of the animals' pain than of their lives, is not mere speciesism but an attempt to recognize and deal with morally salient differences which warrant some systematic accounting. Of course, no one is persuaded that in our early and still unfolding attempts, we have gotten it right. Thus, in carrying out the details of a Pluralist project, there are lots of blanks to fill in. If we are to sort out entities, why according to the richness of respective lives, rather than according to life expectancy (so that Galapagos tortoises and elephants are grouped with *homo sapiens* and valued in the same way)? If richness controls, who is to say what richness is? Our perceptual world is in some respects more impoverished than that of insects. Supposing a separate framework for lab animals, are there no limits on the pain we can impose, so long as human benefit is demonstrable? One alternative Pluralism exposes is that while animals may have no "right" to be free of the minimum pain required of a valid experiment, they may have at least a right to be free from agony.*

Moreover, the lives of nonhumans, even if not as valuable as human lives, appear too readily dismissed in current thinking. As a member of an Animal Care and Use Committee, I am often frustrated to find that my fellow committee members, while alert to mitigate the pain to which laboratory mice will be subject, are less readily motivated to challenge experimental protocols which will result in the deaths of nonhuman primates, *so long as the deaths are painless.* Unfortunately, the position I want to espouse is one whose development Monism has discouraged, and for which there is consequently little support even in

*It is noteworthy that the University of Southern California's animal use guidelines (how typically, I cannot say) essentially appeal to human benefit to determine the validity of an experimental procedure ("a reasonable expectation that . . . [it] will contribute to the advancement of knowledge which may eventually . . . improve . . . health and welfare . . ."). But that decision once made, thereafter human benefit ("economic consideration or convenience") is no justification for not mitigating pain. U.S.C., *Policies Governing the Use of Live Vertebrate Animals,* rev. ed. 1986, pp. 1–2. The right to be free from agony would of course go further; agony could be defined as pain of such quality and intensity that we imagine the animal would rather be dead than continue to suffer it.

the animal rights literature: that (animal) life does count, but that not all life counts equally, or comes under the same rules and considerations.

The coherence of such an enterprise, the development of these intuitions, is what Pluralism commits to explore. To return to the general level, let me expand upon its two elements, the ontological commitment and the governance, in turn.

MORAL MAPS

To grasp the ontological element of Moral Pluralism, the notion that different moralities are based on different versions of the world's salient qualities, an analogy to mapping, albeit rough and incomplete, provides an instructive starting point.

Perhaps the most striking characteristic of mapping is that for a single terrain we can plot many maps, depending upon our interests. Consider the United States as a map subject. There are road maps, political maps, weather maps, topographical maps, soil maps, maps of populations, manufacture, and mineral deposits. Each map presents its own salient features in a coherent way, depending upon the anticipated interests of travelers, politicians, or mineral explorers. Most of them conform in some common, dominant features—the national boundaries and perhaps some major reference points, such as the seacoasts, Great Lakes, and principal rivers. But each of the maps also etches in, eliminates, or accentuates those variables that respond to *its* questions: average climatic conditions, altitude, roadside services. There is no one map that is right for all the things we want to do with maps, nor is one map, the topology map, more valid than another, the demographic. Indeed, we do not regard them, because of their variances, as inconsistent. We may in fact choose to overlay maps, that is, combine salient features. The hiker may want a map that combines the altitudinal isobars of a topographical map with the rain data of a climate map and the paths of a trail map.

In considering the analogy to morals, one principal parallel has already been intimated: the possibility that moral discourse can be

partitioned into different domains depending upon the entities subject to like consideration, or the moral activity in which we are engaged. To illustrate the latter, as we move from one moral activity to
another, there are shifts in the evidence that is deemed salient, or
perhaps even "admissible." For example, in judging a person's character, we incline to map considerable data that bears on the person's
life, his entire past, his projected future. By contrast, where the emphasis is on evaluating societal rules and institutional arrangements, it
is persuasive to argue, as Rawls does, that there are certain things
about one's own personal abilities and prospects which those doing
the evaluation *ought not to know*, that must be considered hidden
behind a "veil of ignorance."[1]

There is food for thought, too, in the multiple functions of a map.
They assist us in evaluating practical alternatives, for example, to plan
journeys. But at other times we consult an atlas just to satisfy curiosity,
to evaluate actions of others: Hitler's armies repeated some of the same
mistakes in Russia as did Napoleon's. In none of these uses are maps
decisive. Both the trip we finally plan and our ultimate evaluation of
someone's strategy will depend upon independent information and
feelings. No map, we might say, provides by itself the full basis upon
which a conclusion will be drawn.

But this incompleteness ought not to be misunderstood—in particular, it is not to say that the map has no effect at all. Consider a map
in the service of selecting the route for a trip. Typically, we start
inclined toward an initial destination. We want to get from *here* to
there, from Los Angeles to Boston. Let us assume that the inclination
to make the trip arises independently from and is not to be altered by
any information on any of the maps available. Nonetheless, we are
bound to learn from the map that there are only so many routes, or that
there is no road along *this* way that can be counted on as positively
passable in winter. Or we may see that if we go *that* way, we will
encounter disagreeable conditions—road construction, or whatever.
Thus, even under the assumption that nothing on the map will dissuade
us from traveling to Boston, the map may still modify our behavior in

important ways: as to which route is best (or which routes to eliminate), when to take the trip, what to expect, how to prepare.

The map analogy will raise objections from anyone who is committed to the view that to every moral quandary there is only one morally correct answer. Intuitively, this mold seems to fit the many dilemmas where there is a concisely defined option, and we cannot avoid choosing between a solution that is incontrovertibly right and another that is downright wrong. But it would be a mistake to generalize this model across all situations in which ethical reasoning is invoked. It may be that no choice is "right," or that several are, or that each is within what James Fishkin calls the "zone of moral indifference."[2] These alternatives tend to be obscured by the strong emphasis traditional ethics places on "the Good," as aesthetics does on "the Beautiful." But what we want of practical reasoning (as preachers and art critics are aware) is more often to identify and eliminate the bad and the ugly, an endeavor that does not require, and may not even be advanced by, a full-blown theory of the Good or the Beautiful. Indeed, I doubt that the typical knot in our moral lives comes in the form of deciding which of two alternatives is morally mandatory. Practically speaking, the issue is more likely to be, which of several alternatives is morally impermissible? Which will build up moral credit? For which will some sort of justification or explanation be owing? What we want, in order to identify the boundaries of our permissible—and praiseworthy—conduct, is something much like the map of the moral terrain. To assign numbers, even words, to the situation may abstract too many salient features that do not number or name well.

This can be seen more clearly if we consider the way in which maps support thinking and convey information. Like pictures, maps operate in a particularly vivid, readily graspable way. A road map does not make a discursive statement about the road between cities A and B. It *shows* something about the road in the context of other roads, cities, mountains, and so on. Moreover, by variations in color tones, the map's imagerial capacities can be enhanced. For example, by increasingly darker hues a map of population or of vegetation can represent increasing densities of people or plants.*

This quality, the graphic presentation of relations and degrees, is particularly useful in developing a conception of practical ethical reasoning in which morally salient qualities of the world, including rationality, sentience, and autonomy, are not qualities that humans, dolphins, or pigs either possess or do not possess. It is, I think, a truer picture of the moral world, and the source of much moral perplexity, that qualities we deem morally significant are often present in subtle and delicate distinctions that do not lend themselves to numerical orderings. Some of our most pressing moral questions arise because of such shadings and the consequent confusion in trying to bring an entity under one heading or another. (Consider the question "How human is the fetus?" in analyzing abortion, feticide, and other prenatal controversies.)

Another distinct attraction of the map analogy is that maps are provisional. One reason is that the territory being mapped may change. Over time, coasts recede, deltas form, rivers meander, lakes dry up, continents even drift. Other changes owe to a filling in of detail as our knowledge of what has always been out there advances and the focus of our interest shifts. Ancient maps recorded the most obvious geographic details, such as major continents and oceans. Today's record air quality and subsoil water tables.

In this there is a strong parallel with the development of ethics, even for those like myself who are not out-and-out relativists. Some basic duties and virtues make an early appearance in civilization, such as certain interfamilial obligations and certain virtues, such as lovingness. These, we might say, are as apparent to a primitive eye as mountains and as slow to drift as continents. Some of civilization's moral progress

---

*Traditional philosophy feels most at home with thinking that takes place in words, with, for example, the deduction of some propositions from others. One valuable if unanticipated by-product of computer science is the prospect of making systematic advances in our understanding of thinking in images as a distinct, and distinctly analyzable, process. See Emily Isberg, "Thinking in Visual Mode," *Harvard Magazine*, March–April 1986, pp. 28–32, reporting on the work of Harvard psychologist Stephen Kosslyn.

owes to the discovery of new terrain: power over the atom and the gene work real changes in the moral landscape, exposing paths that did not exist heretofore. Some of it comes about because the world has changed: populations expand, resources deplete, technology advances. But much of morality's evolution reflects not changes in the world so much as a refining outlook in the qualities of the world we are inclined and able to discern. We want to emphasize, or recognize in new perspective, the special moral relevance of things that have always been around us: the deserts and the disabled.

Finally, we would be wrong to suppose that a map has the potential to affect the details of a decision, while dismissing its role in overhauling our original objective entirely. In terms of the travel analogy, the mapped information may not only influence how we get to Boston, it may lead us to consider and select another destination that we would not otherwise have thought of.

In summary, what mapping offers ethics is a model for grasping how Pluralism might be conceived, that is, how morals might be partitioned into coherent subgroupings for definition and analysis. Unstructured, the ethical world, no less than the physical, presents itself as (in William James's phrase) "a blooming, buzzing confusion." The other extreme, a single, unified Monism, may be equally unsatisfactory for its own reasons. In between lies the alternative of groupings, systematic gatherings of diverse data, along the lines of maps. One set of mappings might accord with the type of activity in question, for example, whether our concern is prescribing action or evaluating character. Another set may divide according to type of entity. As I shall illustrate below, for some analyses, dominated by considerations of pain, one wants to map all sentient creatures affected. Another plane might map abstractions such as corporations, nations, species, tribes, cultures. These are entities to which "pain" and "harm" as it is understood in familiar Person discourse do not apply, and which can therefore receive an independent accounting only by reference to their own special principles and pleadings.

MORAL GOVERNANCE

Granted, even at its most useful, the map metaphor illuminates only a part of what is required to conceptualize Pluralism. Maps are simply familiar examples of how varying ontological interests or commitments can be presented in separate but nonconflicting ways. But a map does not tell us either what to map or what to do with a map when we have got it. Those are matters of governance, of the rules, principles, and so on, to which each domain is subject.

At this point, let me say a little more about the thesis that morals be partitioned. The idea that there may be different domains across which different rules apply is an intuition of long standing, although it has not received the elaboration which it warrants. One can find the suggestion in the remark sometimes made that between friends there is no need for justice. In a provocative essay, Stephen Toulmin writes:

> In our relations with casual acquaintances and unidentified fellow citizens, absolute impartiality may be a prime moral demand; but among intimates a certain discrete partiality is . . . only equitable, and certainly not unethical. So a system of ethics that rests its principles on "the veil of ignorance" may well be "fair," but it will also be—essentially—an ethics for relations between strangers.[3]

Some people will object that to make such distinctions is indefensible. If all morality is based upon the equal intrinsic value of each human being, then the favoritism toward kin and friends over strangers, however widespread (and sociobiologically comprehensible), must be regarded as morally suspect. Is there any defense for defining and assessing according to different rules our friend-dilemmas and our stranger-dilemmas? Our dilemmas involving Persons and those involving animals?

I believe that there are at least two general reasons to apply different governances to different domains. The first has to do with differential access to information as we cross domains, that is, what we can and cannot know about friends, strangers, or animals, respectively. The second involves the fact that we stand in different positions vis-à-vis strangers and different entities, and this leaves us no choice but to weave separate moral fabrics.

The Informational Differences

Almost all conventional human morality takes an account of the actor's knowledge of, in particular, others' preferences. That does not mean that the satisfaction of preferences is the exclusive consideration. But within some constraints, an action is better if it comports with the preferences of others; worse, if it conflicts.

The knowledge we have about the preferences of others varies systematically, however, according to different categories of "other." In regard to those close by, kin, neighbors, and friends, we have some ability to judge the relative intensity of our preferences, that is, to rank them *cardinally.* * Rummaging through a bookstore, I may come across a book that I would like to own. I have a friend who I reckon would get twice or three times as much pleasure from it as I. (Having that sort of knowledge is an element of friendship.) I can thus discern the goodness of my presenting it to him, and perhaps even see a certain iniquity if I should keep it for myself. And while I would get pleasure from planting another loquat tree in my backyard, I am quite sure that my neighbor, who objects to the consequent fruit flies, would be twice as put out as I would be pleased. I can thus grasp that putting the new tree in my yard would be wrong. It is not just a matter of what I want versus what my neighbor wants, which would be a one-to-one standoff. Because of the rough cardinal information available to me in those circumstances, I can make a more richly informed decision: the real balance of wants goes two-to-one.

As we move outward to increasingly distant and numerous popula-

*In an *ordinal ranking* of A, B, and C, such as we might make with ice-cream flavors, we are able to put them in order ("Ambrosia is my first choice of ice cream; banana, my second; coffee, my third"). By contrast, if we know that Abe is eighty years old, Barbara is forty, and Chuck is twenty, we not only can order them in terms of oldest, next older, youngest (an ordinal ranking), but can also express comparisons of degree, that Abe is twice as old as Barbara and four times as old as Chuck, and that Chuck is one half as old as Barbara. These comparisons of degree or quality involve the assignment of numbers in such a way as to yield a *cardinal ranking.*

tions, we gradually lose access to a certain amount of cardinal data. Our fellow citizens are known to us largely as statistics whose preferences we can estimate, at best, in a mere ordinal ranking, with no weighing for varying intensities. For example, we know that many Americans want agricultural price supports to continue, and that many others, including many farmers, are opposed. We may be able to establish, by poll or political process, how many stand on each side of that issue, and proceed to compare the number who would prefer agricultural supports to those who would prefer to subsidize medicine. That is to say, over a broad range of issues it is possible to conclude that a certain percentage of the population prefers X to Y, and Y to Z; and that some other percentage ranks Z first, then Y, then X. But with interpersonal distance and large numbers, any effort at cardinal rankings becomes increasingly unfeasible. Do those who prefer the farm subsidy to the medicine subsidy feel twice, or half, as deeply on average? It becomes virtually impossible to say.

As we radiate still further outward, to persons truly remote in space (and culture) and to those faraway in the future, we find ourselves increasingly blind not only to cardinal orderings—whether they will value lakes three times as much as we do or will like a pristine lake three times as much as they will a virgin forest. We lose the ability to estimate even their ordinal rankings with any confidence. With future persons in particular, the familiar mechanisms to identify strengths of feeling (polls and politics) are simply out of the question.

Comparable difficulties obtrude when it comes to defining moral relations with animals. That is to say, even considering animals that we believe in principle to have preferences, it is not easy to rank those preferences, and even harder to form judgments as to comparative intensities. (That does not mean that there are no cardinal orderings, nor that cardinal comparisons are beyond our grasp in all cases. My wife enjoins me to report that one of our cats, Stardust, favors a particular goosedown pillow at least twice as strongly as my wife does, and the two of them are prepared to adjust their sleeping habits accordingly.)

Now, these informational limitations do not, of themselves, compel us to apply different principles to different populations. Suppose that we did know for certain that a certain act that would save ten neighbors today would kill a thousand persons one hundred years from now. (Or, even more troubling, that saving ten neighbors can be accomplished only at the sacrifice of a thousand persons across the globe.) Someone will say that *if* we had that information, and *if* all morality were based on the equal intrinsic value of each human life, then, indeed, it would be wrong to trade the thousand for the ten. All ethics seeks some degree of general application, an ambition that would seem to mean, at the very least, that distinctions based upon space and time as such are what lawyers call "suspect classifications": the proponent of the distinction bears the burden of defending it. In other words, just as I cannot claim goods simply "because I'm me and you're you," so it seems inadequate to lay claim "because I'm here and you're there." In both instances, something more needs to be said if the situations are to be distinguished morally.

What more might be said? First is the fact that as we venture into the regions of Nonperson relationships, there is some information relevant to framing our ordinary obligations that is virtually inaccessible to us. Do earthworms *suffer,* and if so, what is their suffering like? There is an often cited article in the philosophy journals titled, "What Is It Like to Be a Bat?" which concludes that such knowledge is simply beyond our grasp.[4]

One might rejoin that we are called upon to make moral decisions each day in the face of a certain amount of ignorance. There are the risks the bridge engineer has to account for, such as the probability that the bridge will collapse, killing so many people. But our ignorance of the risks of human harm is not the same as our ignorance of the earthworms' suffering. We don't know the likelihood of a bridge collapse, but we do know what a bridge collapse is like. Using rules of inference and mathematics, we can compute the probability that a certain event, the nature of which we can comprehend, will occur. In the case of the worms, our ignorance of their suffering is not like our ignorance of the likelihood of an event occurring. We can improve our estimate of the bridge collapse by simply acquiring more data. But what data, what tests, will bring us closer to understanding the worm? Note: I am not pointing toward the conclusion that our treatment of worms is not subject to any moral constraints. What I am suggesting is that to guide those constraints, avoidance of suffering cannot play the same role as it does in the shaping of interhuman conduct.

In the future-generations context, also, we run into significant information barriers. There are the effects of unforeseeable shifts in taste, which could render remote future generations of humans more "distant" from us emotionally than contemporary primates and cetaceans. And there are "objective" data that are inaccessible at any price, including whether a present act that will save the lives of ten contemporaries will kill *in fact* a thousand in the remote future. Again, the ignorance involved is not just the ignorance that shields the bridge builder's conscience. Ignorance of the remote future introduces another element: between our epoch and theirs, millions of intervening human agents are destined to nullify and amplify present acts in simply unforeseeable ways.

We thus have to consider whether in dealing with different groups, differences in what we know and can know are morally significant. One might maintain that there is an objective right and wrong which invariably depends upon certain consequences, whether we are aware of them or not. An adherent to this position might say that the rightness or wrongness of our treatment of worms and remote humans depends upon whether we cause them suffering in fact, that is, quite aside from our knowledge, or even the knowability, of that suffering. But it seems to me that ignorance of this sort is so deeply irreducible that moral theory has to account for it by the introduction of special rules. Consider by way of analogy how the fundamentals of physics have had to account for the Heisenberg uncertainty principle, essentially, the restriction that in examining subatomic phenomena, we simply cannot know both the exact location and the exact velocity of a particle at any instant. Some information is so inaccessible that we are forced to abandon the pursuit of the facts that familiar principles would require, and formulate unfamiliar principles instead.

Moral Fabric

The second consideration is that there are insurmountable distinctions that alter the fabric of obligations we can weave between ourselves and different entities. By definition, I have reserved the term Persons for normal adult *homo sapiens* living in a common community. Persons therefore not only have, along with sentience and intelligence and life plans, a good grasp of one another's tastes and preferences. They have the capacity to understand what is happening to them, to consent, to raise, waive, and trade entitlements; they have some shared ideas of the Good. The fabric of inter-Person relationships is a product of these many fine threads: of expectations of reciprocity, of rights that can be waived, of claims that can be forfeited, of risks that can be accepted, of obligations that can be earned and discharged. When we move beyond the domain of Persons, some of these threads simply are not available. If there is to be some moral fabric between us and them, it has to be woven of another cloth. Any claims we give animals, future persons, and natural objects will have to be of a sort that they cannot waive or trade with us. If these are "rights," they are not identical with most human rights, which are waivable. Nor can Nonpersons earn obligations or reciprocate our good acts. They cannot consent to our risky maneuvers, as we are sometimes wont to do among ourselves, either because someone is paying us or because we can see that the activity advances the common good. Once more: the point is not that Nonpersons are morally inconsiderate. Their considerateness is in doubt only if we suppose that the moral fabric that connects us with them has to be embroidered with the same governance that embroiders our relations among ourselves, as Persons. The Pluralist is not so committed.

Even if we knew that the earthworm suffers, and could comprehend that suffering as well as we can comprehend the suffering of another human, and were persuaded that its suffering was morally significant, we could still not establish moral relations with the earthworm on the same basis that the bridge builder establishes relations with us. The builder knows that we know a bridge may collapse. If we consider the risk higher than is warranted by the benefits of crossing the bridge, we can avoid the bridge. We can honor or ostracize bridge builders. All those things permeate the expectations and obligations, the rights and duties, that obtain between us. Our relations with an earthworm cannot be twisted of the same stuff.

HOW MIGHT GOVERNANCES DIFFER?

What is implied is that different governances prevail, domain to domain. But if we are to pursue the notion that our relations with different things may be subject to different governances, then how might the governances differ? What are the variables as we move from domain to domain?

One possibility I have already touched upon is that different substantive principles may apply as we cross from one activity or domain and enter another. With those close by, some sort of Kantianism seems most fitting. Surely one does not save one's own child from drowning because it would be "best on the whole." We do it because it is our duty. At the same time, utilitarianism has appeal for legislation (an activity) affecting large numbers of moderately distant persons (a domain). But as our concern radiates outward to groups even more remote, calculations of utility become increasingly crude and even inappropriate. The implication is that in some domains the principles of governance will have to rely less upon calculation of welfare and more upon loose ideals about a "good" world or "just" conduct.[5]

An application of different substantive principles, domain to domain, would yield a sort of Pluralism. But particularly if we consider accounting for Nonpersons, which present a broad and finely shaded range of properties, we need to prepare ourselves with a richer range of governance variables than is afforded by canvassing the familiar substantive rules that have emerged in the traditional Person-oriented debates.

The issue is most sharply brought out when our interests shift to Nonpersons, but the one-sided emphasis on substantive rules seems to me to be a weakness of contemporary moral philosophy even in its ordinary application to interpersonal affairs.

What I mean is that the literature tends to concentrate on the substantive rules and some of the critical terms which those rules are believed to embed, such as *rights* and *duties*. In the process, other elements of moral discourse that ought to be emphasized are correspondingly slighted.

These "slighted elements" I will refer to as elements of logical texture. The notion derives from a proposal made by Friedrich Waismann that we conceive all language activity to be divided into different discourses that take place on different "language strata," in Waismann's terminology.[6] Ethics, to be sure, was not Waismann's principal focus. His background was scientific philosophy and logic, and in large measure he was reacting against the dogmatism of the logical positivists, who had insisted that there was only one set of correct standards—the "scientific" one—for such basic semantic and epistemic concepts as meaningfulness, verification, and truth.

Waismann responded that that positivist account was oversimplified even as regards empirical science, whose most fundamental buttresses often seem accepted because of their "elegance," that is, their aesthetic appeal. Positivism was worse when generalized, for it fell ludicrously short of accounting for most of the language that people engage in. Sense-data statements ("I see red"), material-objects statements ("There is a cat on the mat"), statements about people in novels, statements of mathematics, statements of scientific laws, statements of our feelings—these are all marked with coherent but distinct "logical styles," or "logical textures."

The logical styles or textures—the elements that distinguish one stratum from the other—Waismann supposed to include the characteristic texture of a stratum's concepts, its standards of meaningfulness, its methods of verification, and its criteria of truth. That is to say, each of these variables fluctuates in systematic ways as we move from domain to domain, from ordinary descriptive statements ("There is a fly on the wall") to statements of scientific law ("Water boils at 212 degrees Fahrenheit") to mathematical statements ("The sum of the angles of a triangle is 180 degrees") to statements of our feelings ("I have a toothache") to aesthetic verdicts ("The ballerina's performance was superb") to statements about the motives of someone in a work of fiction ("Hamlet's motives were thus and such . . .").

Consider some illustrations. In mathematics, an artificial language self-consciously created, the concepts are mutually defined (that is, point and line are defined by reference to one another) and governed by rules that impel a high degree of consistency and precision. By contrast, in natural nontechnical languages, concepts are subject to ambiguity, vagueness, and open texture that no rules of governance can fully anticipate and eliminate.

As we move across strata, moreover, these differences in the character of the concepts are associated with other differences in the logical style that imbues each stratum. Considering the precision of ideal scientific and mathematical languages, the law of excluded middle holds. That is, any number is either a prime number or it is not. Any substance is either an element or it is not. But in other languages, poetry for example, or the language of reporting dreams, we may not be able to impose the same sharp demands.

Likewise, meaningfulness and truth are not invariant notions throughout all strata. One may concede the positivists to have been correct that a statement that lies beyond any empirical confirmation whatsoever has no scientifically valid meaning. But those standards suspend when we move to statements about characters in fiction—for example, to an explanation of why Hamlet hesitated. Such a statement need not be disparaged as meaningless, as a mere broth of words, just because it cannot be confirmed in the same way that we confirm a statement about planetary position. The meaningfulness of the literary statement, and its truth, simply have less to do with "correspondence" to reality than with coherence, with how it ties in with other statements we have reason to believe "fit" the drama. (In this regard, at least, the stratum of fiction resembles that of mathematics.)

The picture that emerges is one in which, as we move from stratum to stratum, there are shifts in the prevailing styles of rationality. Geometries are axiomatic; deductive reasoning prevails. The sciences are more (although not thoroughly) inductive, and each epoch's laws have to be considered contingent, leaving larger room for conjecture and growth. In aesthetics, it is unclear whether the application of such terms as *beautiful* and *graceful* is governed by rules at all.[7]

To illustrate with a contrast, in chemistry definitions are "tight" enough so that if a substance is an element, and a metal, and liquid at room temperature, it is mercury. Those conditions are necessary and sufficient to judge the substance to be mercury and nothing else.[8] Consider, however, the judgment that a particular painting is somber. To support the judgment, the proponent may point out its dominant color (brown), certain masses, the heavy layering of the paint, the lack of contrasts, and so on. But surely no one will advance as a general rule that *that* sort of massing with *that* predominant color with such a layering guarantees that a painting will be somber rather than, say, noble or brooding or perhaps ugly.[9] What makes a statement of chemistry true is not what makes true the verdict of an art critic. Moreover, in considering stratum variables, we do well to heed the observation that even "truth is not the bottom line."[10] In sorting out which beliefs to embrace, reject, pursue, and defend we are ordinarily concerned about the criteria of rational acceptability, from which "truth gets its life."[11] That is, there is variance not only in how we judge the truth and falsity of statements, and systems of statements, but also in each stratum's demands of precision and of adequacy. There are variances, too, in the rules of evidence. What sort of test does a statement have to pass before it is rationally acceptable? Surely that which makes a statement rationally acceptable in math is not what makes it rationally acceptable in poetry.

It is interesting to conjecture in what ways the texture of the concepts, the standards of meaningfulness and rational acceptability, shift as we move from intellectual endeavor to endeavor, from geometry to hard science to aesthetics. But these far-ranging comparisons are not my principal concern at the moment. Nor even does my interest here lie in comparing ethics in general with science and aesthetics in general. We were led to this point by a question about morals. We asked, if moral governances vary as we move across domains, with respect to which properties might they vary? The comparisons among broadly diverse endeavors such as science, geometry, and aesthetics offer the prospect of examining what may be large-scale variances. But our task is to identify the variances that may occur, perhaps on a finer scale than variations between physics and literature, as we proceed from one "mapped" domain to another. What different "logical textures" or "logical styles" might be displayed within morals?

The Logics of Moral Discourse: Prescriptions

I HAVE MAINTAINED that it is a mistake to assume that all ethical activities (evaluating acts, actors, social institutions, states of affairs) in all contexts (among natural Persons living in a common community, across many generations, between species) are dominated by the same features (life, intelligence, sentience, capacity to form preferences), or even that they are subject, in each case, to the same overarching principles (utilitarianism, Kantianism). We should think of ethics as partitioned into several strata, or planes. Launching the analysis of a moral problem, we begin by selecting (or constructing, if need be) the appropriate "map." Furthermore, the analytical framework, the governance we bring to bear, varies "map" to "map." The distinctions include differences in the substantive principles that are applied. Certainly, pain-regarding principles are significant with regard to entities that experience pain. Other principles, perhaps invoking a natural unfolding, may be appropriate to things like plants, which while alive are presumably beyond pain. And so on. But there is more at variance than just the principles. In my view the contemporary literature tends to overconcentrate on the familiar substantive principles and the terms (such as "rights" and "duties") that they entrench. In the process, other elements of moral discourse are correspondingly slighted.

These "slighted elements" I have referred to as the textural variables of logic or style.* Without identifying and resolving the textural varia-

*The text presents the textural variables (such as the grain of description, below) as separable from the substantive variables ("Advance the greatest good of the greatest numbles, the solutions of moral quandaries are woefully undetermined even if there should be no dispute as to the applicable "principles". That is, even if we can agree that a certain problem is amenable to, say, utilitarian analysis, there remains considerable room for variance until these questions of texture have been resolved.

But what, more specifically, are the textural variables, how are they related to the more familiar substantive principles, and what do they contribute to moral conversation?

The project might be put this way. It has become popular to speak of developing and testing our intuitions and tentative moral conclusions by recourse to "thought experiments." By exploring texture, I am examining how far we can advance the notion of "thought experiment" into something less metaphorical and more rigorous. Can we point the way to more specific and systematic intellectual procedures that might vary from domain to domain, so that even Nonpersons might be regarded as morally considerate, subject to their appropriate rules?

This is a venture that will take us through a thicket at once more dense and more abstract than any we have faced thus far. Keeping a single illustration in mind may provide some useful continuity. The following episode (drawn verbatim from the magazine *Natural History*) goes to a specific dilemma involving "natural management philosophy." But considered from the perspective of logical character, it presents elements we can call upon to illustrate moral analysis generally.

---

ber"). But of course, here, as elsewhere, the supposed line between form and substance is hard to draw. For one thing, the textural variables are presumably subject to some principles of their own, even if those principles can be (as I maintain) detached from the substantive principles. The moral direction of the textural variables is less conspicuous than that of the substantive, but I am not maintaining that the textural variables are themselves purely formal in a sense that makes them utterly "value-neutral." On the other hand, the fact that the boundary between substance and logic ultimately blurs is of no embarrassment to my position. I am perfectly satisfied to regard the examination of "logical styles" as advancing the search for variables of moral governance in addition to, whether or not of a different type from, the more familiar variables of "substantive" principles. The aim is to enrich the selection and detail of the planes we have to work with and choose among. It is of no ultimate significance that any element be characterized as logical or substantive since in the last analysis they operate together to endow the plane with its governance character.

Last February, in the middle of a cold morning, a bison bull plunged through the ice-covered Yellowstone River near Fishing Bridge in the center of the park and was unable to extricate himself. Water vapor steaming from its nostrils in the crisp air, the 2,000 pound animal struggled in vain, succeeding only in enlarging the hole. About 10:30 a.m. park employee Barbara Seaquist, a member of the Young Adult Conservation Corps, discovered the drowning bison and contacted park headquarters. A park ranger replied that the incident was a natural occurrence, and the bison should be allowed to sink or swim on its own. Meanwhile, several persons who had heard about the struggling beast appeared on the scene to photograph it.

By about 5:00 p.m., as dusk was settling on the bison's struggle for life, a party of nine snowmobilers approached the bridge. After learning from Seaquist that assisting the buffalo was against park policy, one of the snowmobilers, Glenn Nielson, a vice president of Husky Oil Company from Cody, Wyoming, became outraged. He was struck by what appeared to be the callous attitude of the photographers, who were merely filming the incident. "If you're not going to help it," Nielson said, "then why don't you put it out of its misery?"

The snowmobilers left the scene, and after a brief caucus four of them returned, Nielson carrying a sixty-foot orange nylon rope. Seaquist was gone when they returned, so they fashioned a loop, tied it around the animal's horns, and walking gingerly out on the ice, tried to haul the animal to safety. At this point Seaquist returned and repeated her request that nature be allowed to prevail. She also warned the four men that they were endangering their own lives by walking out onto the ice. They ignored her. According to Nielson the bison had almost made it out of the water when the rope broke. "The sad thing," he said, "is that he [the bison] knew we were trying to help. He laid his head at my feet just exhausted." As it grew too dark for the rescuers to see, the attempt was abandoned. The temperature fell to −20°F that night. In the morning the bison was dead, frozen into the ice. Coyotes and ravens soon descended on the animal. When the warmth of spring melted the river and freed the remainder of the carcass, a grizzly bear was observed feeding on the bison downstream. A shred of orange nylon rope was still fastened to its horns.

Upon his return to Cody, Nielson wrote a letter to the right-wing radio commentator Paul Harvey, describing what he felt was the Park Service's cruelty. Harvey seized on the dramatic incident and, in three venom-filled broadcasts, tore into the Park Service's policy of nonintervention, calling officials "knee-jerk ecologists." "It is not a scientific question, it is a moral one," Harvey said. "The reason Jesus came to earth was to keep nature from taking its course."[1]

PRESCRIPTIONS AND MORAL GRADING

To identify the textural variables—to get at what they are and what they imply—we best proceed under two headings. The first category deals with actions. Here, our subject matter is, generally speaking, *prescribing* conduct: "You ought (or ought not) to save the bison." The focus is always dynamic: on how to act, on whether to bring about or permit changes in states of affairs. The second category deals with a particular type of *description*, the moral grading of agents (or institutions, or things): "The would-be rescuer of the bison is a good (or bad) man"; "Nature, as it unfolds, independent of human intervention, is a 'good.' " The focus is always static, on whether a particular label applies. The character of grading is distinct enough that I will defer dealing with it until the succeeding chapter.

The Grain of Description

Prescriptive discourse, our focus here, is concerned with changes in states of affairs. The first group of textural variables involves settling the appropriate vocabulary for describing those states. The world can be described from several stances, or editorial viewpoints if you will, each of which involves its own standards for sorting reality into classes of relevant categories, and for systematically weighting and accenting some features and deleting and supplementing others.[2]

One stance, favored by the would-be rescuer, is relatively fine-grained in its selection of categories, focusing on the individual animal. The Park Service, in contrast, consigns the individual animal to the background and emphasizes the larger unit, the park ecosystem. An intermediate view might emphasize species. Each focus brings along an allied stock of concepts. Focusing upon the individual animal, one scans for such properties as its capacity to feel pain, its intelligence, its understanding of the situation, and its suffering. None of these terms apply to the park. Instead, the ecosystem version brings out stability, resilience, uniqueness, and energy flow. An analysis that emphasizes species favors concepts such as endangered and adaptive fitness (relative to a habitat), and requires portrayal of uniqueness, breeding boundaries, population size, and genetic variability.

By alluding so uncritically to these different levels of description, I am not suggesting that each of them is equally valid. At this point I am only saying that each "editorial viewpoint" has some prima facie validity. Any further evaluation and comparison is attendant upon a filling out of detail—a detail of descriptive categories, as well as of other textural variables to which I will turn.

To emphasize these variables of texture is not to derogate from the significance of principles. Indeed, subscription to a particular substantive principle has obvious implications for texture, for favoring some descriptions over others. If we declare ourselves utilitarian so far as a governing principle goes, we eliminate concern for any species, per se, inasmuch as the species cannot experience pleasures or pains. A description in terms of habitats and reserves would be most congenial with a holistic viewpoint. But I am skeptical that the description and other textural variables can be derived from the substantive principles in any straightforward way. The questions of whether to count the pleasures and pains of all sentient creatures, or of some only, is a threshold decision for the utilitarian. But its derivability from an acceptable statement of the utilitarian principle is in doubt, as witnessed by the debate among utilitarians whether to count all sentient creatures equally.

The notion of equality, moreover, which makes an appearance in just about every philosophical system, brings along its own problem of grain, of the appropriate level of generality. To say that two things (persons or creatures) have to be treated "equally" must be understood as "to be treated alike in relevant ways." But what are the relevant ways? By what actions do we treat a struggling bison and a ravenous raven "alike"? The point is, we cannot derive from the categorical imperative the texture of such critical terms as "equal," "similarly situated," and "alike" without which the imperative to treat all alike is only loosely directive, at best. To put it another way, lacking consensus on texture, two people can agree that the principle "Equals must be treated equally" holds, and yet remain in wide disagreement as to the application. Hence, to subscribe to one of the dominant substantive principles does not determine how one will resolve the underlying textural variables. There are, I shall show, several sets of options left open, each of which will produce considerable differences in the moral plane that is deemed to govern analysis of any particular problem.

Mood

The significance of mood as an element of texture can best be appreciated by contrasting morals with law. In both activities we often use negative injunctions of the form "Thou shalt not . . ." But the law never stops there, with "Thou shalt not kill . . ." or "Thou shalt not park in the red zone . . ." In law, one always proceeds to specify a sanction which expresses the relative severity of the offense, namely, " . . . or face the death penalty," ". . . or face a twelve-dollar fine."* By contrast, much of moral philosophy is conducted at a level of abstraction which assumes every act to be either good or bad. There is either a duty to rescue the bison or no duty to do so; a right to rescue or no right to rescue. Most moral discourse lacks a counterpart to the law's gradations of sanction.

*While I emphasize negative injunctions in the text, the law sometimes speaks in terms of "thou shalts"—of affirmative duties enjoined upon governors and executors; but the same process described in the text in connection with sanctions can be found working in connection with the affirmative duties: the law is often pressed to evolve nuances far finer than have been recognized in academic ethics. It is true, however, that in many contexts the law is as bivalent as morals. Consider its stress on valid/invalid, guilt/innocence, and so on.

There is a consequent tendency for people engaged in moral philosophy to disregard distinctions that would be considered important not only to the lawyer, but to the ordinary person in the street—distinctions marked by considered nuances of feeling and belief. Compare, for example, the relative treatment of abortion in law and in morals. At the time of the Supreme Court's decision in *Roe* v. *Wade* (restricting the power of the states to criminalize abortion), abortion was generally illegal. But the highest penalty was ten years, rather than, as in the case of taking a postnatal life, life imprisonment or death. This did not mean that the law did not consider the fetus a person, or that it condoned abortion. It was just that the taking of a fetal life via abortion was not considered as bad as taking the life of an ordinary full-term person. There is a degree difference that the law expresses in gradations of punishment and reward. Should the abortionist be subjected to the penalties of murder or of misdemeanor, or be let off? Should federal funds be provided so that abortions will be cost-free to all? Should a person who desires an abortion be compelled, as a condition of the procedure, to read certain moral and medical literature?

In approaching these questions, moral considerations enter. But legal debates are far less likely than moral debates to fixate upon questions like "Is abortion good/bad?" or "Is a fetus living/nonliving?" The law's agenda, after centuries of honing on practical applications, is at once too concrete and too subtle to have remained so flat and abstract.

This relative poverty of moral discourse is another face of Monism. Monism not only presumes there to be one framework with its one right answer. It forces that one right answer to be expressed in binary terms of good/bad, right/no right, duty/no duty, stripped of all nuance of force and mood. In effect, Monism sends us clambering out over the most complex surfaces without providing us the fine variety of footholds that have evolved in law. A failure to license degrees of rightness and wrongness has been taken to imply that there are no questions of degree in moral matters—or, at least, to distract attention from them. If one is restricted to speak of rights and duties, and to assign those terms a homogeneous meaning that holds throughout, then there is no allowance for distinguishing between the duty not to kill a person and the duty not to kill an animal; between the rights of a fetus and the rights of a neighbor. We are led to suppose not only that the same principles apply from one case to the next, but since no distinctions in "sanction" are allowed, that arguments of equivalent strength are required in each case. If morality is all this rigid, then an argument on behalf of a lake has to meet the same standards as an argument on behalf of a person, or else it fails.

To inject some systematic richness into moral discourse, the least we can do is to endorse the efforts of deontic logic to inject (at a minimum) three distinct modal auxiliaries to separate out three distinct moods.*

To build upon the thoughts expressed in ordinary discourse by "ought," let us employ the operator symbol O, so that "O(Rescue)" will be read, "The bison ought to be rescued."[3]

For morally "permitted", P is employed, so that "P(Rescue)" will be read, "It is permissible that the bison be rescued."

To express the idea of an action being "morally mandatory," ! is employed, so that "!(Rescue)" will be read, "The bison must be removed from the river."

What this does is fix attention on the mood variables. The task of morals is usually conceived as determining the rightness of actions. However, these expressions are all consistent with the rightness of removing the bison—each, however, in a different sense or mood. It is one thing to conclude that it is permissible to remove the bison; another to say that one ought to do so; another, to say one must. "Permissible" presupposes an actor whose taste inclines him in the direction of rescue, and conveys the sense that it is all right to follow his inclination. "Mandatory" presumes to address everyone, those who are not, as well as those who are, so inclined. Rescue is morally better than nonrescue.

*Whether three operators are required, or whether less will do, is problematical. Certainly, given the right logical connectives, it seems possible to make at least some translations from expressions employing one operator to expressions employing another, without apparent loss of nuance. I choose to employ all three operators as sufficient to insure a range of nuances warranted by distinctions I believe are rightly made in conventional moral discourse. See "Symposium on Deontic Logic," *Theory and Decision* 2 (1971): 1–77.

Further, to say one ought to rescue, O(Rescue), does not carry the same sense of dogmatic urgency as !(Rescue), that one morally must rescue. These distinctions would seem to accord with the conventions of ordinary conversation, in which we often make a distinction between that which it is morally better to do and that which one is absolutely obligated to do, what is perhaps "one's duty." In terms of our illustration, is the would-be rescuer morally justified if he can establish P(Rescue), or is it his burden to establish O(Rescue)?*

I recognize that this proposal, that we accentuate, even formally entrench, these nuances through independent operators, is not uncontroversial. Some will support the Monist position that all judgments should be collapsed into one single mood operator: morality speaks with an imperative voice, or not at all. In favor of formal recognition of these distinctions there is, however, not only the fact that mood variations resonate through ordinary moral talk; there is also the fact that the richer the fund of variables, the broader the range of moral framework options we shall have to build with. Hence, the greater the likelihood of plausibly carrying out one of the Nonperson-regarding viewpoints. A morality that says one is strongly obligated (!) to rescue a bison or a butterfly may be absurd or unlivable. If all morality is impelled to come down to must or must not (! or ! —), finer shadings of feeling, less absurd and unlivable, are never expressed. By contrast, a morality that draws out our relations with Nonpersons in O or P terms may have enough plausibility to gain some foothold in thought. I shall proceed to demonstrate that once established, it may enable us to develop measures of insight and direction that would otherwise be suppressed.

Contradiction

When we try to transport into the area of prescriptions correspondents to the key axioms of familiar logic, another complication becomes apparent. Suppose that somehow (fortified by some substantive moral

---

*We will see in our analysis of character in chap. 14 that special appeals to an agent's predefined character might warrant P(Rescue) in circumstances where O(Rescue), regarded as a more universally applicable prescription, might not be valid.

basis) we can advance our analysis far enough to invalidate the prescription O(Rescue). But from that, what follows? That is, what conduct have we ruled out? In ordinary logic, the key axioms of excluded middle and noncontradiction* make comparable questions unproblematical. If there is a bison, which we conclude not to be in-the-river, then we know where the bison is: It is not-in-the-river. But when we try to transfer the laws of noncontradiction and excluded middle to prescriptions, we run into a systematic ambiguity. One way to contradict O(Rescue) is to place the negation outside the operator, thus: −O(Rescue). This construes the contradiction of O(Rescue) as, "It is not the case that you are obligated to remove the bison from the river." (But what does this leave open? Might you yet be required [!] to do so? Might it be permissible [P]?)

There is, moreover, another alternative, an "internal" negation generated by placing the negation sign between (hence, internal to) the operator and the state description: O−(Rescue). This construes the contradiction of O(Rescue) to be the assertion, not that there is an absence of obligation to rescue the bison, but that there is an obligation not-to-rescue. One is obligated to forbear rescue, to let nature take its course—the view, apparently, of the Park Service. And there is also the alternative O(−Rescue), read to mean that there is an affirmative obligation to do whatever is within one's power to prevent the state of affairs, the bison being in the river, from transforming into the state of affairs, the bison being out of the river. If you see the bison making it out on his own, you are to drive him back with a good *thwack*.

The same sort of ambiguity occurs when we shift to the permission, P, or mandatory, !, operator. For each there is both an external and two internal negations possible, not just a single, unambiguous opposite. These ambiguities we would expect the "axioms" of a finely textured system to dispel.

*The law of excluded middle holds p or $−p$, that is, a proposition, p ("The bison is in the river") is true or it is not true; there is no middle ground. The law of noncontradiction holds $−(p$ and $−p)$, that is, that p and its negation cannot both be true. The bison cannot both be in, and not be in, the river.

Most people who have considered deontic logic regard these wobbles as discouraging. But, once more, for the Pluralist the ambiguities that turn up can be turned to advantage, made less a problem than a promise. The more variables to choose from, the more governance options from which to fabricate a fitting moral version—or versions—of the world.

For example, in regard to wild animals and species it seems to me morally quite intelligible to maintain the position that one is obligated not to place them in jeopardy (without reason), yet also that one must forbear rescue, should they be in jeopardy. Such a position would not imply that animals and species are of no moral considerateness. But we would have fabricated from logical texture a relationship that few would suppose to hold among Persons—that, though we ought not to harm a person, we ought also to forbear rescuing them. Interestingly, some commentators, including Garrett Hardin, have argued something of that sort in connection with the spatially remote: that we are morally obligated to withhold famine relief in some circumstances, that "triage" may be an imperative.[4] Whether or not there is a sound basis to this intuition is not merely another question of Person relations, to be analyzed the way we analyze our relations with neighbors. It is a question that may implicate a separate plane, shaped by its own principles and logical style.

Thus far I have concentrated on the properties of prescriptions that are most nearly expressible in a form of language that mimics, even if it does not reproduce, the artificial language in which conventional logic is expressed. But as I have suggested, there is much more to the logical texture of moral reasoning than this skeleton of operators, connectives, and so on. We could multiply variables by focusing, for example, on ethics' equivalent to verification. Classical utilitarianism is mathematical: the moral truth is sought by summing units of happiness. Other moral viewpoints aspire to imitate geometry, to verify by deduction from unchallengeable "axioms." Yet other approaches might orient to paradigm cases, accepted examples of good and bad conduct. An action is good if it fits the paradigm of "good." A loose concept of "fit" plays the role that counting and deduction play in the other systems.

Another type of "style" distinction, favored in much of the contemporary literature, is that between moralities that are consequential or teleological ("goal" oriented) and those that are nonconsequential or deontological ("duty" oriented). It is generally supposed that in consequentialism the person faced with a choice refers the rightness and wrongness of the decision to the state of affairs it brings about. Utilitarianism is ordinarily offered as the paradigm example: "Save the bison if the consequences are best on the whole." Nonconsequentialism, by contrast, is taken to suggest that there are certain duties one is bound to perform ("Save the bison") irrespective of consequences. Kantianism is ordinarily offered as the paradigm example, although, of course, the Golden Rule, or the Silver Rule ("You ought not to do to others what you would not have them do to you"), serve to illustrate as well.

Unfortunately, these supposed dichotomies, which have been well criticized in the literature,[5] turn out to be easier to "feel" than to state intelligibly. Without getting mired in the issue we can say that for whatever merit the distinction may possess in some contexts, it is at any rate not useful here, where we seek to divide moral systems into groups by reference to the logical styles they display. The division I will advance is between those systems which refer all moral (prescriptive) questions to a single maximand,* and all other systems. In this division, too, classic utilitarianism serves as a paradigm of the first group; classic Kantianism can serve as a paradigm of the second. But the properties that lead to their separation, and the systems with which they are associated, are different from those associated with the purported consequential-nonconsequential dichotomy. Moreover, the division I employ groups alternatives in a way that generates further insights.

SINGLE-VALUE TRANSITIVE SYSTEMS

The first group of moral systems regards as the sole standard for evaluation the maximization of some single value capable of fully ranking all

*A maximand is that which is being maximized. For a corporation the maximand might be net profits, or it might be sales dollars; for a nation, gross national product.

alternative states of distinct moral interests.* Perhaps the key element to which such a system aspires is transitivity.

To understand the nature of transitivity, and its implications for moral systems, consider three lumps of coal, A, B, and C. The lumps exhibit several common properties with respect to which we might wish to compare them, including their relative weight. What is interesting about the weight relationship is that if A is heavier than B, and B is heavier than C, then A is heavier than C. This is expressed by saying that the relationship "heavier than" is asymmetric and transitive. Where A stands for lump A, and $>$ for "greater weight than," we can represent the transitive relationship as follows:

$$A \; > \; B \; > \; C$$

Because of this relationship, a weight measurement system can be established in which the heavier object is assigned the larger numeral (in pounds, kilos, or whatever), providing the advantages of indirect comparisons. What "indirect" implies is that to compare them we need not directly "play off" every object against every other in the weight scales. We can compare them indirectly through a system of common measurement.

Utilitarianism and the various other systems I group with it represent efforts to achieve for morals what the weight system achieves for objects. With utilitarianism, the "objects"—its lumps of coal—are states of affairs. The property of the objects, the states, is happiness (or, in a variant, units of utility called "utils"). This property is presumed to be measurable, like weight, and the sole "good" with respect to which all states of affairs, S1, S2, S3, and so on, can be compared. Specifically, S1 is morally superior to S2 if it displays more happiness; worse, if it displays less. Moreover, because the property that defines the good is transitive, we can produce a rank ordering across all states that a moral agent can bring about.

$$S1 \; > \; S2 \; > \; S3$$

*One can imagine a system that enlisted a single maximand with the ambition only of identifying the best alternative across a choice set, that is, without any ambition to rank the remainder. I know of no proponent of that variation.

Ambitions to yield such an ordering are not unique to utilitarianism. The same may be said of any moral system that purports to employ a single maximand in such a way that (1) all morally relevant differences among states can be referred to the same measurable property, and (2) in all cases, the morally better state is identified with the higher number.* Environmental ethicists whose ultimate value is life might maximize the tonnage of the planet's biomass on the view that more life (in whatever form) is better than less. One can conceive of a moral system that regarded the amount of Christian love, Agape, as overriding any other possible considerations. A world with more Agape, somehow measured, would be necessarily better than a world with less, notwithstanding that the world with more love happens to exhibit more pain as well.

Putting aside how defensible such alternatives would be as compared with utilitarianism, in at least one important element of logical style the two would be the same. In each system, the rightness of rescuing the bison depends upon comparing the state of the world in which the bison is left in the river to that in which it is rescued. In each system, the dominant technique is simply mathematical: the relevant property in the alternative states is summed and compared. In the case of utilitarianism, the calculations would take into account, among other things (depending upon how "extended" the scope of those creatures whose feelings are counted), the pleasures and pains (1) of the bison's would-be rescuer, (2) of the onlookers, (3) of the bison, and (4) of those creatures, including the bear and the ravens, who might dine on the cadaver.

But once such calculations are performed, what is a single-maximand advocate claiming? Even for a system as apparently straightfor-

---

*Strictly speaking, a moral system could aspire to transitivity by assigning numbers to something other than states of the world. Surely actions have properties, such as meanness of intention and goodness of motive, and there are moral views that would rate act A "better than" act B in virtue of A having a better motive. However, no moral viewpoint I know of aspires to measure degrees of meanness or beneficence and to arrange actions in a rank order accordingly. In fact, most action-evaluating systems incline to rely on multiple criteria, for which reason I treat them in the succeeding section.

ward as utilitarianism, there remains the ambiguity in selection of operators, referred to earlier. Certainly there is one conceivable version of utilitarianism which integrates with the ! operator only. On this view it is not merely P, "permissible," or O, in the sense of morally better to bring about the happiest state of affairs; in all cases, one must (!) do so—no ifs, buts, or ands.

Perhaps this is the logical texture of utilitarianism that most of the literature assumes. But is there not some appeal to adopt, across some domains, a system expressed in O-based commands? Under such a governance, to identify rescue as the best (welfare-maximizing) state would entail that the onlooker ought to rescue the bison. So far as morals has a say, it is recognized as the best choice of a morally permissible set. But that need not carry the sense that the rescue is morally mandatory.

In a system that gave such an independent status to O, as distinct from !, we could say that it was morally better if the bison were rescued than if it were not. But the passerby would not rightly be subject to the ostracism or whatever informal sanctions the society attaches to failure to make the *required* choice. Much less would it be right for criminal codes to penalize a person for failure to rescue.* Such a toning down from the imperative mood might be the sort of adjustment required if we are to extend the realm of moral considerateness from Persons to some classes of Nonpersons. One might maintain that "*this* extension of considerateness to certain Nonpersons is rational; but only in the context of a moral governance that speaks in *that* (diluted) mood."

More generally, the point is this. To support Moral Pluralism is not merely to suggest that we consider the applicability to different maps of different moral systems distinguished by their substantive rules. Potential systems are distinguishable by fine details of logical variable, as well. To identify oneself as a utilitarian, or to subscribe to utilitarianism across some maps, leaves the commitment considerably underdeter-

---

*Or, as I suggest in the chapter following, we may wish to develop an O-based discourse in connection with character: there are acts neither mandatory nor impermissible which, however, as part of a pattern, an agent has to answer for in evaluations of *him*.

mined. This underdetermination goes beyond such well-recognized problems as how to measure and compare the relevant states. (What *is* pleasure? Is it measurable on a single, continuous scale along with pain? How are different persons' preferences to be combined?) There are open variables of logical character to be resolved as well, namely, is one committed to draw judgments of a must-based, permissions-based, or ought-based character?

How one responds—for which domains—contributes to the logical character of various moral planes with which a rational moral agent constructs his/her moral world view. The potential significance of these toned-down operators ought not to be disparaged. Legitimating even the slenderest moral considerateness can "tip" outcomes that are otherwise closely balanced. Consider the question of warning remote future generations where we have stored high-level toxic wastes. Because the hazardous "life" of some of the material extends so long, the warning message—to the effect, "Danger, toxic hazard"—must be presented in a way that will be comprehendible by persons whose language will presumably bear little relation to any contemporary language. In fact, a Human Interference Task Force has been designated to, among other things, convene etymologists and linguists to try to design the optimal message.[6] In terms of national budget, it is a modest undertaking. Yet, to warrant the expenditures, some considerateness has to be attributed to future generations, so as to make the deviation of funds from current consumption, if not mandatory, at least morally permissive.

MULTIPLE VALUE SYSTEMS

It is thus clear that anyone who wants to impose a utilitarian governance (or that of any other single-maximand system) over any particular domain has several ambiguities, or open variables, to resolve. Nonetheless, the attractiveness of such systems is that they hold the promise, or illusion, of simplicity: all actions can be sorted and ranked by reference to a single measurable "good." On the other hand, even if the ambiguities could be resolved satisfactorily, the utilitarian has to convince us that all moral conduct, with all its complexities and irregularities, answers to a single index of measurement. And that is not easy to do.

The literature fairly bulges with illustrations in which we would stand to advance utility by conduct that appears, to almost any sensitive conscience, immoral. Amitarya Sen asks us to imagine a London mob whose utility gain from the pleasure of "bashing" Pakistani students outweighs the utility loss to their victims.[7] Is the action therefore "right"? One conventional response is to abandon utility in favor of some other standard.[8] Another is to retain utilitarianism as one element of moral analysis, but to employ it in association with some other standard, the one to operate, somehow, as a "side constraint" on the other. We are enjoined to maximize utility up to the point that someone's rights are trampled.

Unfortunately, whether our response to the limitations of a single maximand is to replace or to constrain it, the alternatives leave us with most of the same uncertainties to resolve—plus some new ones.

The Orestes Quandary

First, there is the obvious problem that once we abandon a single maximand, there may be no rule to give guidance in a situation in which we can feel the moral perplexity. The idea of there being "no rule" is itself worth unpacking. There might be no rule in the sense that while there is a moral system, it is simply silent as to the problem at hand. For example, the system might govern man's relations to man in exquisite detail, but have nothing to say on the rightness or wrongness of actions toward animals—on the moral difference, say, between a world in which bison are suffering and one in which they are not. But I am more interested here in the prospect of there being no rule for reasons of formal ("logical") defect. This can occur not because the system is silent on the issue, but because we find ourselves with prescriptions that conflict.

The classic illustration is the quandary of Orestes in Greek tragedy. We may regard Orestes as being subject to one rule obliging him to avenge his murdered father; another rule obliges him to honor and protect his mother. What, then, is Orestes to do, considering that his mother was his father's murderer, and that therefore the avenging would amount to matricide?* Note that in a completely determined, single-maximand system, one outcome or the other—state 1 (mother alive, father unavenged) or state 2 (mother dead, father avenged)— would, one presumes, be indicated. But when, as here, no single overriding principle is available, the two rules taken together (protect thy mother; avenge thy father) amount in their own way to no rule at all. To pose the same quandary in terms of our bison illustration, suppose rule 1 obligates us always to come to the aid of a living creature in jeopardy, and rule 2 obligates us never to interfere with nature's course.

The issue that the Orestes Quandary raises, one which reverberates throughout this subsection, is whether a system of moral governance that lacks the capacity to eliminate such quandaries should be regarded as fatally defective, so that the entire system has to be amended or withdrawn, as we might a system of geometry whose postulates allowed us to conclude of two triangles both that they are and are not congruent. Is it a requirement of every valid moral viewpoint that it yield one and only one right prescription for every dilemma it recognizes?

One contemporary moral philosopher, Richard Brandt, labels inconsistency in a group of moral principles "a fatal defect, a mortal thrust."[9] But he proceeds to acknowledge that the codes people live by are latent with conflicting directions, with no overriding principle that tells what to do in cases of collision. His own example is drawn from the Ten Commandments, which enjoin us both to honor our fathers and not to work on the Sabbath. What if one's parent demands Sabbath labors? Brandt responds, "A difficulty like this is inherent in *any* set of

---

*Orestes' choice, to slay his mother, raised so knotty a question of liability that Athena, although having proclaimed it "too grave . . . for mortal minds," nonetheless impaneled a jury of citizens who heard the arguments on the Areopagus. When they divided evenly, Athena cast the tie-breaking vote for Orestes on the curious grounds that she considered herself "verily of the father," and thus that avenging the father was the right choice. However uncompelling her reasoning, the event gave mankind, it is said, the jury trial. See Dudley Fitts's commentary to *The Eumenides* in *Greek Plays in Modern Translation,* trans. and ed. Fitts (New York: Dial Press, 1947) pp.552–56

moral rules of the form 'Always do. . . .' " The rules have to be interpreted as creating " 'a *strong obligation* to do. . . .' leaving [this] decision to individual judgment."[10] Whatever all that means exactly, it seems a far cry from branding inconsistency "a fatal defect, a mortal thrust." It suggests, more rightly in my view, that some inconsistencies are tolerable even as regards the governances we commonly employ in human affairs. And it follows that at least across some "maps" (of rocks and rivers?) a system of rules and principles that can give us some satisfaction in some cases should not collapse if in other cases it should prove not only incomplete, but in some circumstances virtually contradictory.

The Sisyphus Prescription

Even if there exists a single covering rule, plaguing possibilities are not eliminated. Consider the prescription "If one finds the bison safely on shore, one must place it in the river; conversely, if one comes upon the bison in the river, one must save it." This is called the Sisyphus Prescription[11] because it obliges one both to do a task and to undo it. The result is odd, but not illogical in the sense that "The bison is in the river and is not in the river" is illogical, that is, flat-out contradictory.

My interest here being in formal constructions, I am not concerned to analyze from what substantive moral viewpoint such a prescription might be derived or defended. If anything, it has the air of a navy work-rule designed to keep seamen busy and disciplined on long cruises. Moreover, as with the Orestes Quandary it is hard to see how this prescription could stand in a single-maximand system, for assuming either one state or the other, the bison-in-the-river or the bison-out-of-the-river, to be measurably superior, the act that produced the better state would be chosen. But once we move out from under the domination of a single maximand, we have a choice. We can guard against such bothersome prescriptions by introducing an axiom that mimics the traditional law of noncontradiction.[12] That is, we could hold that a system that otherwise produced interesting, suggestive directions for conduct, but also led to a few conclusions like the Sisyphus Prescription, would have to be rejected or revised. Or, we could refuse to adopt such a restriction in recognition that perhaps in some moral realms, the rules required to make sense of things generally will entail an occasional queer (and ultimately nondirective) edict. Whichever choice we make, to invoke an axiom of noncontradiction or not, we are contributing one more element to the plane's "logical character." And, as I intimated in response to the Orestes Quandary, it is conceivable we would exercise a different option depending on whether the moral governance with which we are concerned deals with Persons, remote persons, nonsentients, or other classes of entities.

Multiple-Choice Criteria

The Orestes and Sisyphus prescriptions may appear contrived. But when we advance to consider more typical dilemmas—situations in which both the facts and the applicable rules are more richly and realistically detailed—the problems presented are not more tractable. The most common difficulty arises from the presence of multiple-choice criteria:[13] in effect, there is more than one criterion for determining what is right, and the criteria potentially conflict.

The problem is not one peculiar to efforts, such as my own, to fit unconventional entities into moral discourse. It is a problem that pervades morals, both in everyday talk and academic analysis. For example, some maintain that there is more than one basic good that deserves to be pursued. We ought to act in such a way as to advance friendship, knowledge, the common good, life, justice, and community, all deemed to be "equally fundamental."[14] But this multiple-goods view masks a difficulty that receives very little systematic attention, perhaps because it is so formidable. What do we do when justice or knowledge pulls one way, friendship or the common good, another?*

*I have the impression that some of these conflicts are more fully, and certainly more interestingly, explored in literature than in philosophy.

To illustrate the ubiquity of the dilemma, consider allocation of advanced medical technology, such as renal dialysis units, when there are more patients dying of kidney failure than there are devices to go around. There are several morally appealing bases on which the limited devices might be allocated. Remember, here we are putting aside allocation on a single-maximand basis, which was examined in the last subsection. We are therefore disregarding as the sole principle for allocation both unconstrained utilitarianism, which would make the decision turn only on the relative utility to society of the various allocations of the machine, and unconstrained queuing ("first come, first served"), which would also produce a unique transitive ordering. Indeed, most of the commentators feel that actual cases and actual morals call for us somehow to blend a whole range of factors, a multiplicity of goods. But this plunges us into the problem of how to integrate different criteria, not all of which point in the same direction.

Based upon one proposal,[15] we might consider the following criteria in deciding who should get the dialysis unit.

1. *Progress of Science:* Of two applicants, Al and Barbara, Al will be favored if the scientific information gained from treating Al promises to be superior to that gained from treating Barbara.

2. *Prospect of Success:* Al will be favored over Barbara if the prospect of healing Al is more favorable.

3. *Potential Future Contributions:* Al will be favored over Barbara if the prospective service to the community of a healthy Al exceeds that of a healthy Barbara.

4. *Past Services Rendered:* Al will be favored over Barbara if society is under a greater obligation to Al for services Al has rendered.

5. *General Equitable Consideration:* Al will be favored over Barbara if Al had more reasonable expectations of receiving the device—if, for example, Al had reasonably relied upon assurances from the staff that he would be preferred over Barbara.

Suppose that there are four applicants, Al, Barbara, Charles, and Dot, whose claims to the one available device are to be determined under these criteria. Suppose further that we can unambiguously rank the strength of each one's claim under each criterion, from strongest (top) to weakest (bottom) as follows:

1	2	3	4	5
Scientific Progress	Probability of Success	Potential Contributions	Obligation for Past Services	General Equitable Consideration
Al	Barbara	Charles	Al	Barbara
Barbara	Al	Barbara	Charles	Al
Charles	Charles	Al	Barbara	Charles
Dot	Dot	Dot	Dot	Dot

Something comes of this: we can eliminate Dot, who ranks last under all criteria. But then what? If criteria 1, 2, and 3 are all deemed to express utilitarian considerations, we can collapse them into a single utilitarian ranking (U), leaving us with the following table:

	U	4	5
	Combined Utilitarian Ranking	Obligation for Past Services	General Equitable Consideration
Best	Al	Barbara	Charles
Middle	Barbara	Al	Barbara
Worst	Charles	Charles	Al

This leaves us with the question of how to combine the utilitarian ranking with the others, and the others, each with each, so as to yield a single right decision. Comparable combinatory problems crop up throughout practical ethical reasoning. Suppose we had illustrated with two animals in danger, only one of which could be saved. How ought we to account for their relative usefulness, rareness, beauty, humanlike qualities, and soon? It is a quandary that has to be faced by anyone proposing to combine unlike goods of any sort: utility with rights, friendship with knowledge, pleasure with justice. How do we *combine* such different things, when an advance in one is purchased by a retreat in another?

The point is not that multiple criteria are of no assistance. We saw that the recipient who ranks consistently last under each criteria, Dot, is eliminated. And it is conceivable that in some multiple-choice-criteria analyses, a single candidate might score best in every category. But in the great number of cases not so easily dispensed, what ought we to do?

First, we can devise and defend a system of weighted points, assigning to different criteria different multipliers according to their moral importance. Finishing first in Probability of Success could be made three times as important as finishing first in Obligation for Past Services. Such a system would extend the prospects of producing a single winner, but faces the obvious question of how to justify the weightings.

The second alternative is to accept a certain degree of ambiguity, that is, to renounce the aspirations of producing one right answer. A viewpoint may be regarded as a contribution to moral thought if it constrains, but does not eliminate, alternatives. Some viewpoints produce systems that can take us only so far in the sorting and eliminating of options. At that point, left with several possibilities to choose from, there are two broad alternatives. We might take the position that all remaining options are in fact equally good—or equally evil. Morally, we can be indifferent. On the other hand, it might be that one of the remaining possibilities is really better than the others, but it lies beyond the province of any formal, verbalizable method of determination. In the last analysis, facing a dilemma no identifiable rules or paradigms can mediate, we are left to our educated intuitions. Some people will regard such indeterminateness as fatal to any moral viewpoint that permits it and conclude that, like a faulty product, the whole framework has to be recalled for repair. Others, however, will accept a certain amount of openness in some spheres as a welcome condition of our moral lives— as an element of the freedom from which our moral character is to be built.

SINGLE, NONMAXIMAND PRESCRIPTIONS

There are nonmaximand systems that aim to avoid such difficulties that the Orestes, Sisyphus, and the multiple-choice-criteria dilemmas illustrate. Like classical utilitarianism, they offer a single overriding principle. But unlike utilitarianism, they make no pretense of maximizing anything. Some of these alternatives are rule oriented, such as Kant's Categorical Imperative, which enjoins us "never to act except in such a way that I can also will that my maxim should become a universal law." We can imagine that if Orestes had been a Kantian, faced with a choice between a rule 1 (avenge father, kill mother) and a rule 2 (fail to avenge father, protect mother), he would have asked which of them could be generalized into a maxim that he could resolve to apply to all mankind. (One wonders at his answer.) Other alternatives are less rule regarding than they are paradigm or person regarding. It is obvious that such approaches are problematical unless the maxim or paradigm addresses the case in the most unambiguous way. Less obvious is that even if the terms or paradigms are clear, attempts to substitute a nonmaximand for a maximand prescription give rise to some additional problems of their own.

Problems Latent in Intransitivity

Earlier I discussed how measurable properties such as "heavier than" and "warmer than" can yield a rank ordering across all the things being compared in respect to that property, in the general form:

$$A \; > \; B \; > \; C \; > \; D. \ldots$$

But not all properties yield such a clear ranking. Consider three basketball teams, T_A, T_B, and T_C. It is possible that team A, with its intimidating center, can beat team B (which lacks outside shooting ability); team B can beat team C; but team C (because its offense is strongest exactly where A has its one weak point) will be able to beat team A. Once more, when $A > C$ stands for "A dominates C":

A > B & B > C & C > A.

Graphically, the situation, which we will refer to as *cycling*, can be depicted as follows:

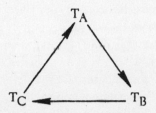

The potential for such an outcome is why the popular news service rankings of teams are curious. "Better than" is not "heavier than"; it is not "illogical" to find A ranked above C even if C had beaten A in their only meeting.

When a moral system renounces a single quantifiable maximand, cycling presents a comparable problem in moral analysis. Suppose I am a Kantian, committed to abide only by maxims that can be willed for all mankind. As such, I might judge it right to save the bison under a sympathy-for-all-living-creatures principle that I am prepared to generalize and prescribe for everyone similarly situated. However, I then consider the outcome that action will produce: to leave the bison to rampage on the land, hazarding humans. When I proceed to compare that result with shooting the bison, I might prefer the latter, under a special-sympathy-for-safety-of-humans maxim that I am equally prepared to universalize. But then, the cycle continues. I compare shooting the bison with pushing it into the river, letting nature thereafter "take its course." I find myself embracing that decision under a universalizable maxim based on the notion that humans ought not to stain themselves with the direct killing of a wild living creature. We are stuck.

Closely related to the problem of cycling is the problem of agenda dependency. To understand this concept, it serves to compare, once more, the lumps of coal with the basketball team. In determining which lump is "heavier than" all others, the order in which the various lumps of coal are paired makes no difference in the final outcome. That is, whether we first weigh lump A and lump B, "pitting" the heavier against lump C, or whether we begin with lump B and C, pitting the heavier against lump A, the heaviest lump will emerge the "winner" in any case. In other words, the correct identification is independent of the order of consideration, that is, the agenda. Note that this is not true of a relationship subject to endless cycling, as among basketball teams. Under the assumptions we made above, the order in which the teams meet in the qualifying round determines which team will win. If team A and team B meet in the qualifying round, the winner will be A, which, facing C in the finals, will lose. But if B draws C first, B will vanquish C, and A will take the tournament. That is why seedings are so significant in athletic tournaments: they have the potential to determine outcomes. In this lies a further problem with nontransitive moral systems. Some styles of moral reasoning, otherwise appealing, may turn out to have the complications of "better than" in basketball tournaments, to be agenda dependent.

Consider, for example, an intuitionist who seeks to generate general moral principles from intuitions about the rightness of outcomes by considering a series of separate thought-experiments. Assuming that intuitions are not transitive, it is hard to see how the rule or other decision that prevails can fail to be influenced by the order in which the hypotheticals are taken up for consideration. I do not know how an intuitionist would respond, because it is not, as far as I know, a question that many moral philosophers have recognized.

Problems of agenda dependency are not eliminated by replacing intuition and senses of fittingness with a system of rules, so long as the rules remain nontransitive. To illustrate, suppose that D, just deceased, had, prior to entering the hospital, signed an anatomical donor's card authorizing the hospital staff to remove his heart for transplant in the event of his death. The hospital ethics committee has adopted the following rule for organ transplants: "Transplant organs will be distributed to applicants in the order of their application, except that when two applicants are related by blood, the organ shall go to the younger."* The three claimants, Ann, Barb, and Cal, had applied to the hospital for a transplant in this order: first Ann, then Barb, then Cal. Ann is Barb's older sister by the same father; Cal is Barb's younger brother by the same mother; Ann and Cal are un-related by blood.

Note that if the hospital staff initiates its decision by examining the folders of Ann and Barb, Barb (the younger of that pair of siblings) will prevail over Ann; and when Barb's case is then compared with Cal's, Cal, the younger of the two, will be awarded the heart. On the other hand, if the staff begins by comparing Barb and Cal, Ann will be awarded the heart. And if consideration begins by comparing Ann and Cal, Barb will be awarded the heart.

The point is this. When we untie evaluative procedures from a sole maximand, we run the risk of cycling. One can imagine some general viewpoint from which one concludes that finding oil reserves is better than saving bowhead whales; saving whales emerges better than preserv-ing the Indian culture; and preserving the Indian culture dominates finding oil. Which alternative is to prevail? It seems arbitrary to let the whole thing depend upon the fortuities of agenda, of the order in which the alternatives just happen to be taken up for consideration. We could of course restrict the outcome by introducing some agenda rules. But there is still something arbitrary about the process, unless the rules establishing the agenda are themselves part of a morally defensible package. That is not to say that no such rules could be devised. It is to say that designing the rules to anticipate and deal with this problem is a further task for anyone determined to work through the details of a comprehensive ethical viewpoint. And—to reiterate the Pluralism theme—there is no reason to suppose that the agenda-constraining rules need to be identical, as we move from plane to plane.

*I will not try to articulate and defend whatever substantive basis might make this rule more appealing than rivals, although some will observe that I have combined a broadly appealing equitable principle, queuing—or, more plainly, "first come, first served"—with a consideration favoring, in any familial gene pool, the probability of that family's genes being represented in the next generation.

SUMMARY

First, let me be clear that to examine the "logic" of morals is not to evaluate right and wrong conduct, which comprises our ultimate interest, but to identify and clarify the rules which may structure how those evaluations are reached. Second, it has not been suggested that moral discourse, with all its far-reaching subtleties, can be girded on a system of postulates and axioms, all tidily expressed in pseudo-mathematical notation.

In this, as in much else, Aristotle's wisdom still holds:

> We must be content . . . in speaking of [ethics] . . . to indicate the truth roughly and in outline, and in speaking about things which are only for the most part true, and with premises of the same kind, to reach conclusions which are no better. In the same spirit, therefore, should each kind of statement be received, for it is the mark of an educated man to look for precision in each class of things just so far as the nature of the subject admits; it is evidently foolish to accept probable reasoning from a mathematician and to demand from a rhetorician scientific proofs.[16]

Nor, even, has it been suggested that such a "logic" (or "logics") as we can provide for morals explains or recreates the paths that our mind actually takes in the moral analyses of which we are capable. Logic is often less a guide than a check.

Nonetheless, in our common everyday reasoning, which is carried out largely unselfconscious of logical constraints, we benefit from testing ourselves against the demands of conventional logic before we reach final judgment. So, too, ordinary moral reasoning, which concededly was taking place long before anyone braved to formalize its groundrules, can benefit from intermittent testing against analogous, though quite likely less stern and ambitious, constraints of its own.

It does not therefore detract from the value of the "logical" inquiry that to a large extent our moral views may be arrived at not by derivation from first postulates in the style of geometry, but rather by a much less orderly shuffling about with paradigms and intuitions. The point is that by whatever paths our initial judgments in moral reasoning are arrived at, no one seriously doubts that it is appropriate to test them by recourse to what has become fashionable to call "thought experiments." It is at this stage, when our moral analysis turns rigorously inward upon itself, that such logic as we can enlist should be brought to bear, so that the notion of "thought experiment" evolves into something that is less metaphor, and more considered procedure. Indeed, the requirement that our tentative judgments be subjected to "logical" constraint is as old as the notion of universalization, the idea that before we judge an inclination "right" for ourselves, we try to generalize it across others similarly situated. It is in this spirit of locating logic-like pegs that I have asked what other formal scaffolding, in addition to some effort of universalization, might operate to shape moral discourse.

My principal motive for the inquiry, however, is much more specific to Pluralism. If for different domains there are different governances, then there is the question, of what differences might different governances be comprised? What are the variables?

With regard to prescriptions, no one doubts that the familiar "substantive" rules, principles, and so on, can constitute possible variables. But these rules considerably underdetermine the range of governance alternatives. Room for difference lies in the texture of the concepts (whether the morality speaks in terms of "equality" or "cruelty"), which introduces questions about how much vagueness, ambiguity, open texture, and so on, is to be condoned. Less obvious is the fact that even when a prescription is relatively unambiguous as far as state descriptions go—assume we know what p and q mean and that q is better than p—its application may remain open for further reasons of logical character. We have variations in the operator to consider—O, P, and !, and the relations among them. There seem to be systematic ambiguities in expressing contradictions. What, in moral thought, is the equivalent of a flat-out contradiction in ordinary logic, of saying "p and $-p$," and when are we guilty of it?

As we shift away from viewpoints dominated by a single maximand, we find the alternatives are underdetermined in further respects. We either have to rule out or to admit certain outcomes that are logically possible, but strange: the Orestes Quandary, the Sisyphus Prescription, cycling, the difficulties presented by multiple-choice criteria, and so on. How these variables are resolved determines whether we countenance a governance (or some governances) in which the aim of morals is to produce one right answer to every prescriptive quandary, or whether we settle for a governance in which the aim is to rule out some of the wrong alternatives, identifying a range of choices each of which may be equally acceptable.

Where does this leave us? Ethics seems an uncertain enough adventure when the debates merely revolve around contending substantive principles. Now it appears that it must deal with less well lighted elements of logical style as well, details that are commonly obscured or dismissed by too ready a referral to "thought experiments" constrained only by intuitions.

Yet, this richness of variables, demoralizing to a Monist, represents to a Pluralist opportunity. The richer the range of variables, the greater the potential to construct a flexible community of moral frameworks, each appropriate to its respective domain. In other words, regard for lakes may seem silly—or even unintelligible—if we feel committed to flesh it out by reference to the same governance that applies to Persons. But we are not limited to either treating lakes as indistinct from humans, and subject to the exact same rules (I am not even sure what this would look like), or cutting them off from regard completely. There is the prospect of a middle ground. Perhaps there is no way we can sensibly inject into our relationship with lakes prescriptions that carry the sense of what one must (!) affirmatively do, or what is morally impermissible ($-P$). But that would still not rule out developing intelligent things to say about one's moral obligations regarding lakes. Suppose that we have to choose between two lakes of equal utility to humans: need the choice be arbitrary? The decision may have to be expressed in terms of ought-making (O) prescriptions, perhaps even in the softest sense of what is morally welcome. Such judgments, in turn, could then be entered along with other elements into the package of considerations that bear on the ultimate, and ultimately complex, decisions regarding what course to take in a particular situation.

Many questions remain open: whether we can fashion coherent patterns from this governance material; whether any such pattern can be defended as appropriate for certain domains; whether, indeed, this is a defensible way to go about ethics. These are matters to which I shall return after a closer examination of another activity: how Nonpersons may have a niche in the appraisal of character and in other moral grading.

14

Character and Other Attributes

"Seal Killers Aren't Evil, but Seal Killing Is"
—headline in the *Los Angeles Times*

Most of the contemporary literature in moral philosophy is preoccupied with choice of action:[1] What is the right thing for someone to do in a particular situation? Hence, the emphasis on prescriptions in the previous chapter. One almost forgets that the nearly one-sided emphasis on "quandary ethics," as it has been called,[2] is of rather recent origin. In earlier traditions as diverse as Aristotle, the Church, and Chinese religion, ethics was thought also to involve something broader: "how to live," or "what is a 'good' or 'virtuous' character." The intuition that I now want to explore is that in the assessment of life and character a footing is provided for Nonpersons distinct from their footing in the evaluation of actions. In other words, put aside for a moment whether we are all under a general obligation to act in a certain way, to minister to an animal. The burden of this chapter is to show that a pattern of life which includes such ministration (e.g., the cleaning of oil-fouled sea gulls) may be independently laudable according to distinct governance; one may be the better person for it, or be leading the better life.

Now, certainly, an interest in acts does not preclude an interest in character. Much of what we mean by good character involves a propensity to do good acts. There are, however, three distinct views of the role that character might play.

On the first view, the emphasis remains where it was with prescriptions, that is, on solving a quandary. Should the passerby rescue the bison? The right choice being hard to identify, one may employ a character-oriented maxim as a guide: "Act in situation S in the way X (an actual historical or ideal exemplary character) would have done." Weighing whether to rescue the bison, the passerby might consider the life of St. Francis of Assisi (who would, we presume, have gone to the rescue). But the focus of attention is not on being a good person, but on doing the right thing. Here, concentrating on St. Francis is simply a means to discovering what to do.

On a second view, the focus remains on doing the right thing, but in deciding which choice is right some allowance is made for traits of character, either generally desirable traits or special qualities of the particular actor. The fact that one person ought to rescue the bison does not necessarily mean that everyone ought to do so.

On a third view, the interest in character is primary. Good character is conceived not as a means to identify or assess the goodness of actions, but as itself an intrinsic good, that is, something to be pursued for its own sake.

To illustrate the contrast between these three positions, consider a provocative hypothetical that Bernard Williams uses in a critique of utilitarianism. We are asked to imagine a botanist, Jim, who, marching through a remote, isolated South American town, comes across a group of soldiers who are about to kill twenty Indians, randomly selected, as part of a program to stanch anti-government protest.[3] When Jim objects, the captain offers Jim a "guest's privilege" of killing one of the Indians himself. If Jim accepts the grisly honor, the captain will immediately release the other nineteen. In Williams's view, a utilitarian is committed to Jim's accepting the offer as *"obviously"* the right response: better one innocent person dead than twenty. And this, to Williams, shows us one of utilitarianism's flaws: that it makes a difficult dilemma appear easy. It achieves the illusory appearance of simplicity by excluding a particular kind of valid consideration, "the idea . . . very simply put . . . that each of us is specially responsible for what *he* does, rather than for what other people do. This is an idea closely connected with the value of integrity."[4]

Now, the issue Williams is raising through his concern for integrity is the place of character. But character, as I have suggested, can enter our moral thinking in at least three distinct ways. On the first view of character, Jim, to reach his decision, might consider character attributes such as integrity; but what matters is his choice, and Jim would ultimately be judged good or bad by implication from whether that final choice was right or wrong. On the second view, before we judged what Jim ought to do, we would consider his character. We might conclude that what was right for Jim, in the light of his character, would not necessarily be right for someone else, in the light of hers. On the third view, which conceives character as an intrinsic good, what we are principally concerned to evaluate are not Jim's actions, what he ought to do, but (something else) Jim's character, what he ought *to be.* The act analysis and character analysis travel along distinct, although often parallel, lines.

Because these three views are not well sorted out in the literature, let me expand upon each of them, in turn.

1. CHARACTER AS A DEPENDENT VARIABLE

On the first view, the principal interest of ethics remains where it was in chapter 13, on right conduct. To identify what choice is right, there are various guides. These include rules and perhaps customs and conventions. But these alone are inadequate. Not all contingencies can be foreseen in detail, the language in which rules and moral maxims are cast is imprecise and open to interpretation, and so on. Therefore, something less literal and more internalized, "character," is enlisted as further insurance that people will find the right way.

Certainly, as a description of how character supplements other conduct-guiding devices, I suspect that this view has considerable support among sociologists. The development from primitive to industrial urban societies is marked by some overlaying or even substitution of rules for customs, and of generalized notions of good character for rules, each as a means to ensure the same ends: the performance of good acts. In some respects the internalization of virtue may be a superior means, particularly in societies that are in a state of rapid change. David Riesman emphasized such a shift toward reliance on character during the industrial revolution.[5] One can find suggestion of the same process in biblical literature. The Old Covenant placed reliance on specific rules, e.g., the Ten Commandments, and the detailed injunctions of Deuteronomy and Leviticus. By the time of Jeremiah, there is talk of a Second Covenant in which law will be engraved, with more effect, it is hoped, not on tablets, but on people's "inward parts . . . their hearts" (Jer. 31:31–34). And there are interesting parallels in the Confucians' opposition to the reduction of a criminal code to writing. Better to rely on and cultivate righteousness *(i)*, just usage *(li)*, good faith *(hsin)*, and benevolence *(jen)*.[6]

On the other hand, our principal interest is not here descriptive, with how cultures develop, but normative, with how one ought to act and be and judge. As with any other heuristic device, character can be of only so much help; it can misguide. In determining whether to rescue the bison, the selection of St. Francis as an exemplar may have been misleading. For example, regarding Williams's Jim, I presume a utilitarian would rejoin that his qualms about doing the right thing—for the utilitarian, shooting the one native so as to save the nineteen others— are *wrong.* With adequate moral training and reflection, Jim's character could be, and should be, modified.*

2. CHARACTER AS AN INDEPENDENT VARIABLE

In the above view, character operates in diverse ways to supplement, or even to substitute for, reliance on rules and unarticulated conventions

---

*The same theme, that good character is instrumental, can be developed from sociobiology. The sort of moral character that we generally consider "good," including traits of loyalty, devotion, and courage, are often traits that preserve the gene pool.

as a device for ensuring right conduct. The ingraining of various character traits may be a better or worse ensurer of good conduct, but in no way will it alter our judgment as to what conduct is good. On the second view, by contrast, character descriptions are admissible in conduct evaluations.

Character can enter into our evaluation of actions in two ways. First, someone might maintain that there are some traits which (1) are universally good in themselves, that all people ought to possess, and (2) are more valuable than achieving otherwise good consequences in particular circumstances. This is what I take to be Williams's point about "integrity" in his hypothetical. Integrity is a good. Everyone should have it. Killing a man conflicts with it. (For Williams to flesh out his argument, he has to show that this character attribute, "integrity," warranted the death of nineteen innocent people.) Such a list would presumably include—in addition to integrity—loyalty, trustworthiness, frugality, incorruptibility, courtesy, and the like.[7]

A second way in which character could bear on actions is more akin to the way in which we admit roles, that is, as special pleadings in evaluations of conduct. Just as someone's office affects our judgment of her actions ("Remember, she was a policewoman"), so might our judgment depend upon traits of the actor's personal beliefs or life plans, that neither she nor we would necessarily enjoin on everyone. This is not the conventionally accepted view. Most traditional moral analysis, while routinely prepared to account for differences in situation and social role in evaluating actions, considers it improper, within special limited exceptions, to make allowances for the agent's personal history, personal beliefs, values, ambitions, life plan, and so on.

Part of the reluctance, I suspect, is that a general rule of the form "What is right for me must be right for anyone" is troublesome enough to apply across situational variations. (Isn't there always something justifyingly "special" I can put forward about my own situation?) Allowing for variations in character is all the more problematic. If there are, for example, privileges right for me, *considering my character,* but not necessarily right for you, *considering your character,* then much of morals appears to rely on open-ended descriptions of the most invitingly subjective and potentially self-serving sort. Could a Hitler claim that his crimes against humanity were "right for me" because they flowed from his character and fitted—is not *Mein Kampf* the evidence?—into his life plan?

Such considerations support the predominant view that particularly where variations in character are concerned, one's good actions establish one's character—not the other way around. Yet, having indicated some of the difficulties, let me give an example where I think such an accounting of character is plausible. Consider once more the struggling bison in the river. Let us imagine (1) that the bison cannot be rescued without some hazard to the would-be rescuer and (2) that the only rope strong and handy enough to do the job lies in an unlocked truck, the owner of which has wandered off. Thus, to rescue the bison will require not only a personal risk, but a nonpermitted opening up of the truck door and "borrowing" of the rope, a form of trespass I will assume to constitute a prima facie, if minor, moral wrong.

Now let us imagine that of two onlookers, one (but not the other) is someone whose whole life has been dedicated to and organized around conservation, wilderness, and the protection of living creatures, particularly wild ones. He frequently lectures on the need for environmental protection and makes himself available to testify on its behalf before legislative committees. I am inclined to argue that for this person it would be "right," at least in the sense of *permissible,* and perhaps of *ought,* to rescue the bison, notwithstanding the personal risk and minor trespass it would involve. Yet, for the other passerby, particularly considering the personal risks of a rescue, the same conduct appears (at most) permissible; we would be less inclined to say he is obligated or mandated to snatch the rope and rescue the bison.

3. CHARACTER AS AN INTRINSIC GOOD

Both the conceptions above regard "good character" as instrumental. On both views, what is valued are good acts, the goodness of character being conceived alternatively as wholly dependent on the goodness of the actor's choice (the first view), or as one additional variable in evaluating the choice's goodness (the second view). Both views can be assimilated with prescriptions, the logical character of which was examined in Chapter 13. But there is a third, more radical employment to which character might be put: one not in the service of action evaluations, but as a good in itself. This is the view on which I want to focus in this chapter, since it involves a distinct enough moral activity, built upon sufficiently distinct texture, as might warrant consignment to what I have called a separate plane or planes.

Let me grant, at the start, that the difference between character-as-means and character-as-intrinsic-good can be presented as a mere difference in emphasis. It is hard to imagine an evaluation of good character that disregards a conception of good acts. But even should some connection be inevitable, the link could be of two sorts.

On the one hand, the linkage could be conceived as strong, but with character regarded as dominant. That is, rather than evaluate the agent's character depending on his actions, we could evaluate the actions depending upon antecedent judgments of good character. The distinction is like maintaining that Creation was good because God did it, rather than that God did it because to do so was good. Good acts are whatever a good person does. Presumably, someone who argued for the primacy of character would point out that even among those whose avowed focus is on actions, their analysis is typically dominated by an implicit valuation of character, e.g., that the preference- or pleasure-satisfying character is a human ideal.

On the other hand, it does not take so complete a reversal to account for character as an independent good of independent interest. We could pursue the tack that evaluations of actions and evaluations of character proceed independently. There is a suggestion of this in the fact that there are some predicates we characteristically apply to acts and not to persons, and vice versa. While many more predicates are common to both acts and character (e.g., " 'good' act" and " 'good' person"), the rules that govern their use, while assuredly related, need not be identical.

It seems to me therefore plausible to suppose that of the several planes on which moral discourse is conducted, some are drawn to accent what is required for actions; others, for character. Although there are enough common considerations to assure some loose linkage or mimicry between the endeavors, by detaching our consideration, differences that now lie latent and obscure can be identified and developed. Specifically, a plane that, regarding the two as being of independent, detachable interest, accented character would account for and expand upon the following differences:

1. In evaluating character, we bring to bear more data regarding the agent's history, ambitions, and so on, than is ordinarily deemed relevant (or appropriate) in the evaluation of actions. Indeed, character evaluations are commonly in the form of whole-life evaluations.

2. Conceivably, not only more, but different, sorts of information are relevant. On at least some theories of conduct evaluation, all that counts is the outcome. But in judging character we always consider the intent, motive, and attitude with which something is done. For example, the consequences are the same whether a person kills a bison accidentally, in self-defense, or from malice toward nature. A pure consequentialist, absorbed in outcomes, has a hard time—indeed, has no evident interest in—distinguishing the one act from the other. But no one would be indifferent to the actor's intention in evaluating character. In like vein, my guess is that someone utilitarian in his act evaluations who saw nothing useful about the salvation of some endangered species (and who found no redeeming general welfare value in fostering characters so inclined to fritter their time) might yet find such a character "admirable."

3. In evaluating character, a given action may be placed in a different light than when we are evaluating the action itself. Acts neither good nor bad in themselves may, in the aggregate and in light of a pattern, provide probative evidence of the actor's character because of the way the conduct disappointingly conflicts with or marvelously reinforces the life the person has selected for himself within permissible boundaries. It seems possible to speak without irony of "noble Brutus,"

the more noble for having joined the conspirators, without approving of Caesar's assassination.

4. The evaluation of conduct involves some amount of generalization. If act *a* is good, it is because acts of a class A are good. But with character, there is more tolerance, even appreciation for, qualities that may be uniquely good about the particular person being evaluated.*

To illustrate, let me return to Williams's hypothetical Jim. My interest here is not to adjudicate Jim's difficult dilemma. No handling of such a "lesser evil" quandary is satisfactory. Rather, I want to take the hypothetical in another direction, to gather up the intuitive material of which our repugnance to Jim's killing is made, and develop it more directly and naturally into assessment of character. The separable concern regards not how Jim ought to act in an isolated situation, but how we will judge Jim over a longer time horizon.

I do not mean that the evaluation of Jim's character is a foregone conclusion, or even easier than the choice of action. But in character judgments, we are not forced into the same dichotomies that we face in the analysis of acts, for example, that yes or no, the killing of the one Indian is permissible or impermissible, mandatory or not mandatory, within whatever permutations of O, P, !, and their negations are admissible. With character, there is a broader range of possibilities, with finer nuances of label. If Jim elects to accept the offer, we might say he was "wrong" (in that) but "pragmatic," or "decisive," or "resolute." These judgments of his character would be made with some reference to his conduct, and his announced attitudes toward a good life. For example, if Jim had been a pacifist, we might judge him differently than if he had spent most of his life in the military. Moreover, in the interplay between planes, one of the significant uses of character is to imply further actions that are required, consistent with personal variations, but responsive also to a sort of balance-sheet accounting. If Jim does elect to shoot the

*"In fact a man's character is likely to exhibit itself in his making obligatory for himself what he would not hold others obliged to do. A man does not attain moral stature by what he demands of others but by what he demands of himself; and that he demands more of himself than [of] others is not something in itself admirable, but is what is to be expected if he is to have a distinct moral character." (Edmund Pincoffs, "Quandary Ethics," *Mind* 81 (1971): 553.

sacrificial native, he might be expected to make amends in the future (e.g., to pay homage at the grave, to explain and apologize to the family) to show that he is not cold-blooded. There are parallels in Japanese Buddhist culture: the killing of certain animals is allowed—of oysters, to take pearls—but it is done with sober ceremony, including prayers for the departed souls of the oysters.

THE "LOGIC" OF EVALUATIVE PREDICATES

My inclination to afford separate systematic treatment gains further impetus from the fact that the logical style of character assessment and other gradings appears to differ from that of prescriptions. Most significantly, the basic element in a prescription is a transition in states of affairs. By contrast, when character assessment is elevated to an independent interest, we are concerned not with transformations in states of affairs but with special descriptions of the agents, namely, Jim is of some quality, heroic or wicked.* Such a discourse is girded on the resolution of two variables: (1) what moral-grading descriptions (good, evil, licentious) will apply to (2) what range of entities (persons, children, institutions, nations)? I will proceed to concentrate on evaluative predications of character. But we should keep in mind that in terms of (loosely) logical properties, the analysis of good overall character is comparable to an analysis of any allegedly intrinsically good quality (e.g., beauty or integrity) or intrinsically good thing (e.g., a lake) or intrinsically good way of life. Any of these, recall, could form the basis of a moral viewpoint that provides a coherent account of the moral considerateness of Nonpersons.†

*To underscore the contrast, consider the following: Deontic (prescriptive) logic is built around the term T for "transition"; where p represents the state of affairs "The bison is in the river," a typical expression is of the form $O(pT-p)$, which can be read, "One ought to transfer the state 'the bison in the river', to the state 'the bison out of the river'"; or, less ponderously, "The bison ought to be rescued." The basic element of descriptions is of the form Gx, that is, we predicate of a particular x that it has the general property G, "x is good."

†See chapter 9. Of course, the grading question "Is a lake [a] 'good'?" is closely tied to the prescriptive question "Is it 'good' (right, permissible, mandatory) to pollute the lake?" But they are not the same inquiries.

As I noted above, when we are prescribing conduct, the rules of discourse demand some generalization. To maintain that it was right to do some act, to save a particular animal in distress, takes the form "It was a case of an animal in distress, and generally one ought to save an animal in those circumstances." That is, a justifying reason is expected to indicate something about the generic nature of the act and its circumstances. Moreover, the nature of act evaluation exerts demands on the texture of rules and concepts, that they be fine-grained enough as to clarify choices in our conduct. The focus of interest is not on the application of a term, simpliciter, but on what to *do*, whatever we label it.

By contrast, in the course of grading someone, while there is some appeal to generality—some generality is inherent in any use of language—there is less universalizing. Moreover, a discourse of character, taking qualities as its object, and not being subject to the same pressures to *do* one thing or the other, allows for richer and looser, even overlapping, nuances. A person who did not go to the aid of the struggling bison might be callous, cruel, knavish, heartless, inconsiderate, heedless, or unfeeling. In light of the person's past history, we might add that he was hypocritical, insincere, deceitful, inconsistent, or unreliable—all without saying that he was obligated (O) to perform the rescue, much less that rescue was mandatory (!).

With such unruly nuances in play, is there any sense trying to yoke character discourse with constraints of "logic"? There is surely some. Consider the question whether to label "cruel" someone, perhaps an onlooker who did not join in the rescue of the bison. We can seek to structure our thinking along syllogistic lines such as this:

Major Premise:	Any person who without justification allows a sentient creature to die is cruel;
Minor Premise:	Jones unjustifiably allowed a sentient creature to die;
Conclusion:	Jones is "cruel."

To that extent, there is logic operative. But of course, the syllogism stands aloof from most of the controversy. The major premise requires a rather controversial demonstration. As to the minor premise, was failing to rescue the bison not perhaps justified, considering the risk? Perhaps Jones was not "cruel," merely callous. Or was he merely "steadfast" in his resolve not to interfere with nature? And, in all events, can a single act define one's character?

If any formal constraints on reasoning are to be found, where shall we look for them? Ethicists have traditionally tried to model their efforts upon mathematics and the sciences—and upon an oversimplified view of mathematics and the sciences, at that. In doing so they have undoubtedly been attracted by the rigor of the one and the tangible successes, the progress, of the other.

But my sense is that a search for any logical style or texture in ethics does best to turn away from math and the sciences and look toward aesthetics as a model. Generally, ethicists have sought to put a distance between their subject and aesthetics in order to avoid what might be considered a sullying alliance with a "soft" endeavor. By turning their backs on aesthetics, however, both fields have suffered. This is true throughout ethics, that is, of prescriptions as well as of gradings. But at least in the area of prescriptions, there are some contemporary philosophers, the social-choice theorists, for example, who have put forward rigorous analytic models that advance our understanding of the process. No one has come close to achieving the same standards of rigor and precision in the treatment of character. As a consequence, the neglect by ethics of the aesthetics literature is most grievous in this domain concerned with gradings—when we get involved with whether a lake is intrinsically "valuable" or a life "flourishing."

To locate the common grounds that ethics and aesthetics share, a mutual contrast with science is a useful start. Throughout much of science, we can lay down a fairly precise rule setting forth that if certain things are done, some result of interest to science will occur: if water is brought to such and such a temperature at such and such a pressure, it will boil. With aesthetic concepts, the place of such rules seems limited. We cannot specify what combination of colors and lines will bring a painting to the point of being "beautiful," "charming," or even "graceful." The same seems true of character assessments; what elements can we prescribe adding to a person's character, what particular action can she undertake, that will *assure* her "integrity"?

We must grant that part of the contrast is not one between ethics and aesthetics, on the one hand, and normal science, on the other.[8] It is in some sense the distinction between vagueness and precision, wherever they be found. Vagueness thwarts governance by formal rules, even to the point of paradox. Consider Mark Platts's "proof" that there can be no such thing as a "heap":

(1) One grain of sand is not a heap.

(2) If n grains of sand are not a heap, nor are $n + 1$ grains.

(3) Therefore no number of grains of sand is a heap.[9]

"Good" and "beautiful," one might say, are simply (and perilously) vague, like "heap." But with aesthetic and ethical predicates the affliction runs deeper and more rampant. With ordinary vague terms like "heap" or "bald" or "warm," we can at least specify that an increase in grains, a decrease in hair, and a raise in temperature all operate unambiguously *in the direction of* "heap," "bald," and "warm." With aesthetic concepts, that is often, perhaps characteristically, impossible. Again, can anyone specify *as a general rule* what one adds to make a painting more beautiful, or takes away to make it less garish?[10]

This does not mean that an aesthetic critic disdains or slides over the facts. There is in aesthetics, as there is in science, a commitment to provide reasons for our application of concepts, that is, to justify our judgments by supportive reference to specific, commonly accessible "facts." Consider the following passage from an Arlene Croce critique of a ballet performance:

> Makarova's slightly rigid head positions and the line from the nape to the extended instep in fourth position had an entrancing pathos.[11]

But no one can lay down rules which indicate how one gets from the level of positivist description accessible to any trained or well-guided eye (e.g., the dancer's line) to aesthetic judgments proper, that the position conveyed pathos. Much less can we specify what deems a performance worthy of an ultimate grading accolade, such as "superlative."

Consider another passage from Croce:

> Cynthia Gregory was steadfast about turning her points and then her flexed feet into the ground, and Makarova was steadfast about *not* doing it. But both gave fine performances.[12]

The parallels with ethical concepts (perhaps in varying degrees, whether they predicate actors or acts) are evident. Whether we are considering the ultimate accolades of ethics, "good" and "bad," or intermediate normative concepts such as "cruel" and "integrity," the problem is not just the obvious one, that they are vague or open textured in their application. Worse, it strains the power of rules to lay down in advance criteria capable of distinguishing even near opposites, such as "cruel" from "bold," or "conscientious" from "dilatory." One person does one thing and is good; another, something quite different, and is good, too. Can there be any consistent pattern to this?

The comparison with aesthetics does not mean that it is bootless to search out better and worse procedures for organizing thought, settling differences, garnering insights—better and worse "logical styles" in this loose sense. But it suggests that our methods will involve us in heavy reliance on narrative and example, on paradigms, and on the training of morality's equivalent to taste.* Learning the piano, for example, involves music theory, but also long sessions of listening to pianists. Someone with training *points out* certain features that make a performance whatever it was, good or bad—the timing, the phrasing, and so on. ("Just listen again.") It is similar with much of ethics, but particularly with moral grading. Much of what we learn, we learn through exemplary stories about good and bad persons. Our attention is drawn to the morally salient aspects of the story elements, to implications, parallels,

---

*Narrative is also employed to some degree in learning to evaluate acts. But with act education, I think there is more emphasis on abstracting criteria and constructing universal or general rules. In the evaluation of character, as in the evaluation of an artwork, credit is more liberally given for merits that are unique.

precedents, and to how implied ideas of virtue cohere with other related ideas. Up to some point there is pointing out, explaining; but beyond that, only pointing. Perhaps the region of *pointing* carries as far as it does because in ethics, as in aesthetics, there is a sense that some people have better-trained perception and "taste," persons whose opinions, therefore, carry an authority beyond what they can *tell* us. This emphasis on taste implies that some of the attention in moral training is turned inward, toward self-analysis and improvement of our own sensitivity and its use. What factors might be influencing our judgment of an opera or of a person? Which of those biases should count? And which should be discounted as illegitimate, as "personal prejudices?"

Throughout ethics there is an affinity with aesthetics, but particularly in this area of grading, where our ability to provide criteria wanes and trained intuition dominates. The implication for Nonpersons includes the fact that there is a separate set of questions quite aside from whether morality can provide prescriptions that it is, say, morally mandatory (!), or even morally welcome (O), not to disturb the floor of a remote forest. The separate enterprise is to draw a pattern of such conduct under the looser "rules" of the virtues, to hold the undisturbed forest floor to be a "good"—and to judge that the person who continuously disturbs it wantonly to be, if not "wicked," then perhaps "morally insensitive," or "of wrong character."

Such adverse judgments count against the person and may result in some alteration of social relations, such as, in extreme cases, ostracism. But that is not to say that the character is bad *because* it causes the actor social misfortunes or for any other effect. The character of someone who hectors animals is bad even if his contemporaries approve. Indeed, our judgment of the bully should be all the more severe if his demeanor is calculated to curry their favor.

Not only has grading to be detached from any consequences that the grading may have, but also from the familiar conduct-evaluative rubric of rights, duties, and so on. To say that a person who dedicates part of his life to saving sea gulls is a good person, leading a flourishing life, is not to say that the sea gulls have a right to be aided. Nor is it to say that the rescuer has a duty to minister to the birds, or that he has a right not to be interfered with, as against, say, society's determination to establish a restrictive zoning ordinance that prohibits bird-care centers in his neighborhood. All those other claims may be true, too, but they present separate questions fit for separate endeavors.

The rules of grading are, as I say, hardly clear—if they are "rules" at all. Aesthetics makes solid geometry child's play, and this aspect of ethics is no less complex. But whatever the nature and detail of the undertaking, I think it is quite intelligible to emerge with a judgment of the sort with which this chapter began: Perhaps "seal killers aren't evil, but seal killing is." The evaluations of act and of character are subject to separable governances. There is a niche for Nonpersons in each, in each's own way.

None of this settles the substantive questions: what are the virtues of human character and of the earth? What makes a person or a lake "good" or whatever else may be significant? Indeed, the analysis suggests that our final appeal may lie, unabashedly, in apprehension, rather than in anything like formal deduction from general principles. With right training we apprehend that a person who cares about nature is a better person, other things being equal, than one who does not. To so hold is no more mysterious or doubtful than our apprehension that, other things being equal, knowledge is better than ignorance, and that a simple explanation of natural phenomena is to be preferred to one that is complex.

MORAL PLURALISM: APPLICATION AND THEORY

We are now in a position to portray how the concepts of multiple maps and of variable governances can combine into the *moral planes* which form the basis of a Pluralist analysis. For purposes of illustration, I will return to the bowhead whale controversy introduced in Chapter 5.

Recall that the search for oil in the Beaufort Sea gives rise to several quandaries that induce us to sort out relations among different *sorts* of entities: contemporary persons, future generations, whales, Indian tribes, corporate bodies, species, habitats, and so on. How would the technique suggested advance our understanding of the oil drilling situation? What distinctive attack on a problem does a Pluralist make?

Pluralism holds, that we first have to decide which moral activities we are engaging in. In what immediately follows, I will put aside discourses aimed at the evaluation of character or at the alteration of underlying tastes. Instead, I will concentrate on prescriptive discourse, specifically, what ought the society, collectively, to do? I cannot, in this space, undertake to identify the right answer—if there is *a* right answer—to the question whether we ought to go ahead with Beaufort exploration, and, if so, under what conditions. But I can indicate some of the elements a Pluralist analysis would require and the direction it would take. To begin with, what does "mapping" involve in this instance?

THE EMPIRICAL MAPS

E1: Natural Features Map

The first map—the basic map upon which other maps will overlay —is an ordinary empirical map displaying natural features of the affected region. While evaluation of the Beaufort Sea development will be made from several moral perspectives, each perspective requires certain common geological and geographical information. Specifically, so far as risk to the whales enters into consideration (and it does to some degree, directly or indirectly, on all evaluative planes), one wants a display of the properties of which those risks are a function. These include the existing whale migration routes, the geophysical properties of the ocean floor and the structure being drilled, the tidal patterns, the water temperature, and physical properties of petroleum products likely to be discovered. All of these properties are mappable on conventional, if specialized, maps drawn to display all environmental features that might be disturbed by the development in such a manner as would put the whales in jeopardy.

E2: Action-Influence Maps

The function of the second map—or, more accurately, series of maps—is to reflect the fact that different levels of oil exploration activity are possible, ranging from no action to intensive accelerated development. For each of these plans, there are associated disturbances of the environment depicted in the first map (E1) and thus, for each plan, associated whale-related risks. For example, each area of proposed geophysical dynamiting presents a zone of risk, as does each proposed construction of a drilling island. Thus, for each plan of action, one should be able to produce a map that depicts as shadings across the topography the whale-hazarding zones of influence. I call these the action-influence maps because they aim to display the influence of proposed action.

Now, the data on these first two maps can be combined with biological analysis to display risk-to-whale probability configurations for each developmental plan of varying intensity and precaution. The highest risks will be where zones of maximum hazard overlay existing migration routes.

Note that what is involved thus far is, although highly speculative, in principle an empirical exercise. *Valuing* each level of risk involves, however, something more than gathering and presenting the dangers to various creatures of the various levels of projected risk. In valuing, we have to allow for the fundamental moral questions: what values are relevant, and in what way? At this point, we have to overlay upon the empirical maps what I will call Moral Reference Maps. They are maps in that they map natural features. But they vary in the features that they map, and each is associated with a distinctive governance: the rules, style, and texture of moral analysis fit for *those* salient features. It is their combinations, the natural properties and the governance, that I suggest we think of as *moral planes*. I will divide them into two broad groups. First, there are the planes dominated by utility considerations, which form the subject of Chapter 15. Then there are those founded on nonutility considerations, which are examined in the succeeding chapter.

The Utility Planes

U1: PERSON PREFERENCES

THE FIRST SET of Moral Reference Maps, the bases for the first set of planes, are all utility-oriented. Their analytical value depends upon the assumption that utility preferences as well as tastes are both fixed and determinative of the outcomes. The maps vary, however, in their assumptions about *whose* tastes and preferences are deemed to control. The first set of these maps (which can well be imagined as the first series of transparent overlays resting across the empirical maps) is drawn from the stance of all Persons. That is, the aim is to mark the terrain in such a way as to indicate the utility to contemporary humans of all things subject to influence under the alternative development plans. We would subtract from the expected social benefits of each plan the associated social costs. These costs account for resources that will be consumed to satisfy the utility of *those who count* (here, Persons).

Thus, the map has to indicate each thing (broadly understood to include even such *things* as the quality of light) in the area exposed to hazard that has utility significance to contemporary members of our human community. This significance will either be positive, as with endangered entities that are predominantly valued (such as edible fish), or negative, as with endangered entities that persons would pay to be without (such as mosquitoes). To present this material on maps, we can imagine the use of a particular color, say, green, to indicate those things of positive utility, with the greatest-intensity green indicating the things of highest value to collective welfare; another color, say, red, could indicate those things of negative value.* (Of course, ignorance of long-term consequences makes such an accounting hazardous; when future generations are considered, below, there may be a red-for-us and a green-for-them, or vice versa.)

To illustrate, how would whales be treated on this approach? Whales are, to begin with, *green,* in the above sense. Hence, the expected loss of every whale (but not *its* pain and suffering) has to be included in the calculation of costs, along with every other resource that is consumed and valued in the same way. That is, first there will be the question of true commercial price: what is the value the market would place on the bone, meat, and oil of each whale that will never reach market?[1] To this consumption price we may appropriately add some increment for a positive shadow price.[2] This accounts for those whose pleasure in the whales is not reflected in what they pay to see the whales in whale-watching boats, but who get pleasure from the thought that there are whales swimming freely about and will support the whales on much the same basis as they support public concerts they never attend.

In sum, the first evaluative view regards all things from the perspective of the satisfaction of personal preferences. In logical style, the operations performed with the mapped information, and which complete the plane, are those associated with maximizing a single objective function—utility or pleasure—as presented above. There are, indeed, logical-style variables remaining to be resolved. The question of the appropriate way to combine individual utility preferences is not uncontroversial, there being several rivals well debated in the literature. Moreover, does a finding that one state is welfare-superior mean that we must (!), ought to (O), or permissibly can (P) put it into effect? These, the governance variables, are matters to be worked out as fine tuning in the development of the U1 plane.

*For utility analyses, maps and colors are, strictly speaking, superfluous; graphs would serve because the governance is mathematical, with no impressionistic residue. I employ the color image here to make the treatment of the utility section consistent with the treatment of the planes that follow, for which ordinal representations seem less satisfying for the reasons suggested in the text; see pp. 139–40.

U2: EXTENDED UTILITARIANISM

We could appeal to a second utility plane that combined all sentient creatures—human and nonhuman alike—into a single extended utilitarian community, such as Bentham, in fact, envisioned.[3] Such a plane would embed two judgments: that animals are morally significant on their own account, and that, in principle, the way to account for them is through their pleasures and pains. It leaves room for significant debate over "fine tuning." Inter*personal* comparisons of utility are hard enough: how is my revulsion at whale slaughter to be integrated with your pleasure at watching your cat enjoy whale meat? In making interspecies comparisons, our problems are compounded by uncertainties both as to what sorts of things a whale finds pleasurable, and what the pleasures of a whale are like. But there is in all events a crucial difference of principle between this plane and U1, one that operates to the animals' advantage. On U1, the whales' pleasures/pains are accounted for indirectly, to the extent those pleasures/pains are the cause of pleasures/pains of persons. Hence, to the extent the harpooning of whales is a source of satisfaction to a human onlooker, H, that positive reaction counts in the moral evaluation of the harpooning toward making it good. That is true on U2 as well. The distinction introduced on U2 is that the whales' pleasures and pains (harpooning hurts) enter into the calculus *directly*. H's satisfaction is offset by the whale's own dissatisfaction. The whales continue to be regarded as potential items of commerce, a resource for the extended community, but they are now also elevated to the status of consumers whose own feelings are valued together with those of Persons. This has the advantage for the whales of assuring greater availability of something they like to nosh, for example, plankton, than would be warranted by calculations of human welfare only. On the other hand, from the perspective of protecting animals, a utility calculus is of limited advantage: If all morality boils down to utility, unsupplemented by any nonutility protection, the whales can be killed and eaten—it is indeed "right" that they be killed and eaten —if it serves the greatest good of the greatest number, even granting that the good we are talking about now is the good of an extended community of persons plus animals. The whales might be, as it were, outvoted.

Nonetheless, admitting animals on this basis would make a difference, and, quite arguably, a justified one. Working within such a framework, we would undoubtedly learn to develop compensation principles applicable to animals that would enable us to assimilate them into familiar welfare analyses. Primates, for example, cannot only communicate some of their preferences, but have been trained to do so in human-devised language. We have not yet reached this stage with whales. But, as I have already observed in Chapter 6, marine biologists certainly have some idea of what whales like, and this knowledge can form the basis of compensation principles administered through a trust fund.

U3/U4: THE TEMPORALLY AND SPATIALLY REMOTE

We can multiply utility perspectives by extending the moral community to include, alternatively, future humans, spatially remote humans, and all temporally (spatially) remote sentient creatures, human and nonhuman combined. Each of these planes presents separate special problems. Not knowing the tastes and alternatives of future generations, there is considerable guesswork, even an irreducible opacity, when we try to gauge what "resources," such as whales, they will value. There are the value-implicating complications of endogenous tastes: How much, and in what ways, are we prepared to affect their preferences, the sorts of creatures we are going to fate them to be? Many of these problems—and variables—have already been referred to.[4]

The relationship with the spatially remote deserves, however, a special word. Most of the literature on remote beings focuses upon future generations, i.e., those remote in (future) time.* There is, however, much in common between our moral position vis-à-vis persons

---

*There is also a considerable literature on obligations to those remote in past time, especially ancestors.

remote in time—the citizens of the twenty-second century—and persons remote in contemporary space—the starving millions in sub-Sahara Africa. I am not suggesting that the problems presented are exactly comparable. But in many respects our obligations to the remote of both time and space seem to stand on the same footing, and are subject to many of the same intuitions. Neither class is in a position either to reciprocate our good gestures or consent to our bad ones. Regarding future persons, this is true absolutely; regarding the spatially remote, it is true as a practical matter.*

That does not imply that we can, with impunity, irradiate either group with our nuclear wastes and effluents. In both cases, however, intuitive feelings of the others' considerateness appear to diminish with the "distances." Are these intuitions at all defensible? One must decide whether with spatial distance, no less than with the temporal and the biological, it is justifiable to introduce some principle that devalues those at far remove. Why and in what manner are high costs and benefits to persons *nearby* to be "corrected" for effects upon populations that are distant? To illustrate in the Beaufort drilling context, suppose that on balance Americans prefer to leave the whales undisturbed, rather than to increase the petroleum supplies. But a vote of the entire human population, including the energy-starved segments of the developing nations, would readily support trading the whales for the oil. Indeed, a worldwide vote would undoubtedly favor our relieving the energy situation by burning more dirty coal, even though it would be worse for us. In weighing, then, whether to drill, are we morally committed to treat the preferences of each spatially remote person equally with our own?

Peter Singer, arguing from the same utility foundation from which

*Obviously, it is a matter of degree how far removed persons have to be before they are considered outside the Persons community: Is a newborn child a part of our community? An aboriginal Australian? The principal determinant is whether the person can feasibly be drawn into reciprocal relations, either through personal contact, politics, or markets. This is a rough test, but precise boundaries are not required in evaluating most actions, particularly if we presume that the interests of marginal groups (1) are not likely to deviate significantly from those of the neighbor group (no one, near or far, likes to go hungry) and (2) will probably be swamped by the core neighbor interests, in all events, because of the dispersal of effects over distance.

he defends animals, asserts that degrees of need, not ties of citizenship
or proximity, should determine our global obligations: pleasures and
pains are the stuff of which moral relations are spun, and anyone who
wants to distinguish neighbor from foreigner (or one creature's pleasures from any other's) bears the burden of justification.[5]

There are at least two ways of responding to that burden. One way
is to accept the utilitarian orthodoxy, but to maintain that within some
limits, the practice of each person favoring one's kin, friends, and
community in his or her personal decisions works to the mutual advantage of everyone. No special discount or devaluation of the distant is
involved in the bias toward one's neighbors; in applying the utilitarian
principle, each calculator simply allows some credit for the strategic
value, to everyone, of a universal principle that neighbors "stick together." Another, more radical way to justify the bias begins by recalling
that there is nothing self-evident in identifying either pleasure or
human life as the exclusive foundational good. There are, as we saw,
several bases from which, either alone or in some supportive combination, a coherent moral viewpoint might be built. Among these is to treat
considerations of community, friendship, and so on, not simply as
instrumental to welfare, but as independent goods themselves.[6] Such
a viewpoint would legitimate some preferences for those with whom we
have, or at least have the prospect of having, the weave of a rich
communal relationship.

In other words, the injunction to treat each person equally has
obvious appeal, as a principle. But to treat the remote on the exact same
terms as one's neighbors is fraught with conceptual problems,[7] depreci-
ates community as an independent good, and sits poorly with the
requirement that a practical ethics be "livable." Of course, this does not
warrant our disregarding, much less our causing, the suffering of distant
others.

Morality might require a single principle at play that simply discounts for distance: The votes of ten Americans to save the whales that
pass through native waters outweigh the contrary preferences of one
hundred persons far away. Or it could require something more complex

and discontinuous, as is implied by the image of each group being in a distinct domain: one plane for spatially remote persons, another for the temporally remote, another for all remote sentient creatures, and so on. Among Persons, utility might yield judgments of what we must (!) do; whereas, as regards the remote, the judgment may be expressed in a softer operator, in terms of what we ought (O) to do. Or, the concept texture might vary: in sorting out our relations with the remote, we would rank only the most grossly characterized states of affairs, states of affairs that captured extremes of fortune—mass starvation and epidemics—but which did not discriminate between having more or less oil as a distinction of any moral significance.

The Nonutility Planes

To understand the next set of planes, we have to revert to the distinction raised earlier between one's utility preferences and one's morally corrected preferences.[1] We have just seen that the way in which we calculate utility may vary slightly, domain to domain. But that aside, much of moral theory supposes that there are certain things we ought or ought not to do even if the choice entails some sacrifice of (or, in a strong Kantian form, irrespective of) the general welfare. The point here is that as we pass across each of these same domains (of Persons, the temporally and spatially remote, etc.), there is a mirror governance for each, not anchored in utility at all. In each case, the nonutility governance may deviate from the utility-driven conclusion, forcing us to correct, constrain, or displace entirely the judgments we might arrive at on the utility planes.

N1: PERSONS

The first nonutility plane is mapped from roughly the same perspective as the first utility plane: only Persons are posited as inherently valuable. Nonhuman features are mapped as salient—say, a parcel of land or an animal—if they are the sorts of thing with respect to which a Person may have a claim. A claim here is thought to be governed by rules that express something other than pure utility. On N1, these things are, we might say, colored by some concept of rights, the right of the Person to or regarding the thing; for example, the person's so-called (by Locke) "natural right" to unowned goods, acorns or apples, gathered from the wild by his labors. Moreover, we can imagine each Person to be marked with a single shade of blue. That is, the *utility* of different individuals varies, so that on U1, Persons may be colored different shades of green (indicating different utility to their community). But if we regard all human beings in a common community as possessing some intrinsic value not reducible to utility—the basis of N1—everyone's intrinsic value is the same.

Several reasons warrant bringing Persons into a common, distinct grouping as one way to clarify and advance moral problems to resolution. First, our capacity to universalize and empathize ("How would you feel if you were . . .") is more informative when we let our minds run among Persons than when we attempt to reach across to other things, even to relatively "near" others such as spatially and temporally remote humans. Moreover, the fact that Persons are uniquely capable of arranging their relationships via a mutual capacity to consent and to exercise, waive, and forfeit claims affects the quality of rights and duties that prevail among us.

In terms of the Beaufort illustration, one such claim would be asserted by the Indians, presumably the right that their traditional hunting grounds and practices, their right to hunt whales, not be infringed.[2] On what basis can the Indians demonstrate moral claims of such strength that the society would be constrained to write them into law? How insurmountable are the Indians' claims in the face of conflicting claims—of the general welfare, or of competing rights of non-Indians? Under what circumstances would rights and duties relating to the Indians, some of which originated at the time of the original European conquest, be deemed to have lapsed or been waived? For example, suppose that the Inupiat should take to hunting in gasoline-powered snowmobiles and motorboats and fire at the whales with dynamite-tipped spears. At what point of assimilation would we be warranted to say that they have relinquished individualized claims based upon preserving their culture?[3]

There are many different approaches to these questions, and thus different ways to flesh out a rights-based or duties-based discourse. Indeed, this nonutility thinking enjoys, if not a clear answer, the most extensive attention in the literature. Therefore, here, in what is principally a suggestive survey of the scope and relationship among analytic approaches, I will not presume to engage those efforts, point by point, beyond what I have already said. Let me proceed, instead, to the less orthodox, less examined relationships, those that may obtain the further we move beyond the ordinary Persons realm.

N2: PERSONS REMOTE IN TIME AND SPACE

When our attention shifts from contemporary to remote persons, the focus remains upon *humans;* in establishing moral filament, there thus remains considerable play for principles based upon universalization and empathy. The question "How would you feel if you lived in the twenty-second century and could never see a whale?" does not permit a confident answer. Nor, however, can it be dismissed as clearly irrelevant. This suggests that many elements of familiar Persons governance are not inappropriate. But there is this difference, at least. Any claims that remote humans have, like any that animals may have, cannot be modified by transactions. Our relations with them have to be formed by our choices entirely. In my view, this makes it more appropriate to invoke a discourse based upon *our duties,* rather than to build upon *their rights.*

Even if we choose to work with duties, the fabric of duties has to be sensitive to the fact that incorrectly distributed obligations cannot be righted in the familiar ways in political and commercial arenas. Moreover, the earning and forfeiting of duty-based obligations, so important in affairs among Persons, have no place in regard to the remote.* All this makes it questionable whether we have the duty to treat

*The remarks in the text may not apply to the dead, toward whom our relations are complicated by the possible presence of obligations that they, unlike future persons, may have earned. On the general subject, might we have unearned obligations respecting the dead? Joel

each remote person exactly as we do ourselves. To be skeptical about a "same rule for everyone" morality is far from condoning complacency. More livable, more conscience-arresting, principles may be devisable along agapeistic lines, that is, based on principles of love and sharing which are not, however, of the indiscriminately one-man, one-vote variety. At the same time, a plane respecting our duties toward the remote may be informed by "floors" to conduct. In this, there is a useful, albeit imperfect, analogy between the remote and prisoners. We are not morally obligated to treat prisoners in all regards the same as everyone else. Yet there is some floor beneath which our treatment of them cannot fall. While the boundary is hard to define, we may say it involves some abrogation of "basic human values," or a failure to respect their "personhood."[4]

To illustrate using the Beaufort context, with regard to future persons we can probably say with some confidence that if we were they and had their tastes, we would probably *prefer* to be left a world with whales than one without. But from this forecasted preference we need not derive anything close to a duty (!) to sacrifice our preferences for theirs, to weigh their preferences equally with our own, or even to wrestle within a familiar utility framework at all, even one that introduces a future discount. Indeed, efforts to assimilate future generations by shuttling preferences into a utility framework are so fraught with problems and paradoxes[5] that to establish moral relations we may have to step outside utility entirely.

The following might be a defensible position. Except perhaps for future Inupiat, whales are not likely to play a critical role in the physical or spiritual subsistence of future persons. Without whales, future persons would still be *persons.* This is not to say that we are free to destroy the whales. We may (I believe we do) have duties that originate on a whale-respecting basis, a life-respecting basis, even a basis that accounts for the utility of the whales to future persons (U3). It is just to say that

Feinberg suggests that it would be a wrong to hold vilifying untrue beliefs about Nero even assuming that there would be no harm in any conventional sense. See Joel Feinberg, "Legal Moralism and Free-Floating Evils, *Pacific Philosophical Quarterly* 61 (1980): 122, 132.

so far as the killing of whales goes, little independent weight appears to be added on a respect-for-future-persons basis.

The point can be clarified if we contrast the killing of whales with other contemporary actions. Consider, for example, the massive ocean dumping of untreated radioactive and other toxic wastes, which would set in motion a chain of events forcing future inhabitants—those who survived—to live on a practically unrecognizable planet in practically unrecognizable ways. Can we not imagine a scenario of this sort that would condemn our descendants to live a life worse than that in any acceptable prison, to reduce them to something inferior to the minimum attributes of personhood? And this would be their fate without a breath of consent or, as with the prisoners, trace of blame. While we are not obliged to treat them as we do our neighbors, surely they deserve better than this.

N3: NONHUMAN ANIMALS

When we turn from persons to other living things, the enterprise of fashioning the appropriate plane is subject to opposing tugs. On the one hand, there are strong intuitions that this kingdom has to be divided internally. That is, one can argue that no single nonutility plane works to intuitive satisfaction across all nonhumans lives, from dolphins to dormice to daisies. Our capacity for empathy fades by degrees, and the attractiveness of certain principled arguments falls away, as, in descending through the kingdoms of living things, we pass through variations in intelligence, emotions, and so on. On the other hand, there is a growing literature that questions the moral salience of many such distinctions, and argues for combining different species, particularly vertebrates, on the same planes with humans. That is the essence of Peter Singer's challenge, that flatly to say, "I have a right to x because I'm human, and 'you' don't because you're an animal," is no more defensible than racism or sexism.[6]

Of course, a human who claims that humans are preferred is not likely to rest it on the grounds that he is human, period, but is almost certain to claim justifiable differences. That is a claim which is inadmissible *if* one accepts the view that there is only one morally relevant feature: the capacity to experience pleasure and pain. That appears to be Singer's exclusive dividing line. But other philosophers maintain other exclusive dividing lines, for example, with Taylor, not sentience, but life.

All this insistence on an exclusive dividing line is, of course, one face of Monism. The cutoff for considerateness is either sentience or life or the capacity to frame intentions—or something else. On this view, everything that possesses the one vital property is considerate—according to the same rules and in the same way—and everything else, every entity which fails the test, is out in the cold. The capacity to experience pain provides a good example. Those who adopt pain as a cutoff may accept an extended utilitarianism, so that man and animal are dealt with indistinctly, all thrown together into one large utility calculus. Or, a pain principle may crop up in a nonutility ("rights"-type) rubric such as Tom Regan espouses. Rights, rather than utility, perform the central analytic function. But then there is the question, who or what is entitled to be a rights holder? For many, the key is the capacity to feel pain. The consequence is that all pain feelers must be respected equally, as rights holders; non-feelers of pain, the rightless, do not count at all.

On the other hand, as I already illustrated in the context of animal experimentation (Chapter 12), there is no compelling reason to accept the either-or position that animals either have the same status (such as rights) as humans enjoy, or else are considerate, at best, only derivatively. Surely there is little support for, and I am not certain much cogency in, holding our conduct toward, say, krill and plankton answerable to the same principles as we apply among persons. They are only by the largest stretch subjects of a life. But this need not imply that our actions regarding "lower" animals and "higher" plants is beyond the province of morals, that we are faced with an either-or choice. We might make allowance for salient differences by recognizing a distinct texture of the concepts that apply. In regard to lower animals and plants it is not the individual organism but larger units that are characteristically, and I think rightly, championed as considerate: the school, the species, perhaps the habitat. In the case of insects we attach value to the hive or colony that we do not attach to the individual; the larger entity, the community, has an organic perfection, a brain, even a "personality" that the individuals lack.

Even beyond some such allowance for "sizing," the moral significance of each group may play out according to its own rules. There may be no general obligation of the mood (! or O) to rescue a school of krill from hazard; if the hazard they find themselves in is "nature's doing" (if, say, they are being pursued by a whale), to rescue them may even be impermissible. But if their hazard, say, a toxic spill, is directly man-made, then there is intuitive appeal to work out rules which sustain the rescue—undoing the intervention—as being permissible or even mandatory.

When we advance toward the so-called upper end of the animal kingdom, the most common question shifts, as I have said, from whether any moral considerateness is appropriate at all to whether we are entitled to treat them any differently from humans.

My own inclination is to relegate higher animals to a plane separate from humans, not because they are animals, but because they are different in morally salient ways. In effect, while I am open to argument, I doubt we can carry through an analysis of our relations regarding even higher animals without reference to relevant differences, differences that no single principle can capture.

Our bowhead whales, along with all cetaceans, present an especially interesting test case. Cetaceans are not merely humanlike in terms of their capacity for pain, but as possessors of a whole host of human capacities (including intelligence, sociability, and evidence of an emotional life) may come as close to approximating humans as any other creatures. Yet, they are not moral agents, that is, they cannot choose on moral grounds. We do not rely upon their commitments. I doubt that they have any sense that to favor one whale over another is "unfair" (although we might canvass whale trainers for their impressions).

From what has been presented above, it is clear that such differences do not excuse us from all moral claims respecting them. On the other hand, it does suggest there are aspects of the moral governance touching whales that have to vary from the governance that touches Persons. For one, any claims we recognize in our relations with them have to be of a sort that cannot be volitionally waived, traded, or forfeited. Hence, as between rights and duties, it seems more appropriate to fabricate our relations with them out of our duties rather than out of their rights.

This leaves it open for someone to respond as follows: Let's say that the discourse is to be girded upon duties. Do we not then have a duty to avoid inflicting pain upon whales on exactly the same terms as we have a duty not to inflict pain upon persons? The trouble lies with "exactly the same terms." The ineradicable differences between whales and persons so permeate any moral quandary which may arise that I doubt the terms on which our respective relations build are interchangeable. Consider the obligation to avoid inflicting pain. It never arises in the abstract, but only in a specific context, such as "in self-defense when attacked." If a person attacks us before we inflict pain upon the attacker, there are certain moral and legal rules about warning (such as the "duty to retreat") that derive from, and are indeed inseparable from, human capacities. I am not saying in regard to the repulse of an attacking whale that the excuse for abridging our prima facie duty not to injure or kill it requires *less* circumspection than in fending off an attacking human. That the whale is blameless might cut in the opposite direction, amplifying the human's duty to retreat.* It does suggest, however, that if we want to work through our relations with humans and animals, each in detail, our endeavor would benefit from the separate attention that the separation of planes promotes.

Moreover, I am assuming that the way we employ morally signifi-

*There is an interesting analogy in the question of whether explorers who come across natives utterly unacquainted with civilization have a duty to retreat, even not to defend themselves if ambushed. See David Price, "Overtures to the Nambiquara," *Natural History*, 93, no. 4 (Oct. 1984): 30, 33–34. Price recounts how an early twentieth-century Brazilian explorer ordered his men, on moral grounds and at considerable personal risk, not to respond to hostilities by Indians who had had absolutely no prior contact with outsiders.

cant words embeds cues to right conduct (which is not to say that linguistic conventions can settle moral debates). Some such terms, although applicable to our treatment of persons, do not typically apply to our treatment of animals. And even in the case of terms applicable across species there may be systematic differences in the concepts underlying them. Dispossessing a family from its homestead of one hundred years is indignifying and cruel. If there is a wrong to the whales in dispossessing them from their traditional route, it does not rest on our *indignifying* them. Offhand, I cannot say what the correct vocabulary is. But the project of fashioning it benefits from the concentrated attention that assigning animals to independent planes encourages. I grant there is a risk that important similarities will be ignored, but there is a gain if it encourages us the better to see whales as they really are, rather than through some idealized and perhaps inappropriate bundle of human preconceptions.

Let me reiterate, too, that assigning persons and animals to separate planes, and subjecting them to slightly different governances, does not, in and of itself, waive considerateness for animals. The partitioning leaves open whether they are to receive much the same considerateness as is owed humans, or even, in some circumstances because of their limited capacities, more. In our illustration, I have no doubt that however the status of the whales is analyzed—on a separate higher-animal plane subject to independent governance, or combined on a plane that governs them by the same principles that govern humans (with allowances for how those "same" principles apply)—simply killing a whale is prima facie wrong: one is obligated in a fairly strong sense not to do so. Does an analysis of the threat this duty poses to the Inupiat—not, after all, to the *lives* of various Indians, but only to their traditional but independently eroded life-style—present anything to rebut this?

N4: PREFERENCELESS AND NONSENTIENT ENTITIES

When we turn our attention to the most preference-lacking, even nonsentient, things, such as the so-called lower forms of life or even the ocean, the ocean bed, and patterns of current, certain considerations drop out, and certain thought experiments come to a quick end, as we have seen. Once we get past debating their utility to humans, what is there for morality to say?

Start with plants. Most people, when they first hear the idea, think that talk of "plants' rights" or (as I would prefer) "plants' considerateness" is about as silly as you can get. They suppose that the only function of assigning claims to plants is to foil a countervailing human desire, which strikes the skeptic as inconceivable. How could a plant be placed before a human? But that limited conception of "plants' rights" is a little misleading. Let us return to the framework of the Beaufort exploration to illustrate. Suppose that the oil crew, in an emergency, has to dispose of some drilling chemicals without regard for the prevailing land management procedures. Unless they are willing to endanger their own lives, they must dump the chemicals on the tundra on one of two adjacent sites. Deposit on one site is destined to smother a few wildflowers (which, as perennials, will pop up again next year); deposit on the other would eliminate a colony of arctic lichen. To put homocentric concerns out of the way, let us suppose that neither choice makes any measurable difference to humankind, present or future.

Now ask yourself the following question: Under that assumption, is the choice of deposit sites purely arbitrary, so that the crew might as well toss a coin? Or may one course of action be morally better than the other? My sense is that the choice is not arbitrary, that moral conversation is possible, that it would lead us to select smothering this year's last remaining wildflowers, if doing so were the only way to preserve the lichen colony.

Such an intuition is not irrational. Our relations with persons are dominated by the fact that persons have a wide latitude for self-transformation: to frame and select from among various goals and intentions. Our relations with animals (at least with animals that lack the self-transformative capacities) are dominated by the fact that they experience pains and, in some cases, something beyond: suffering. With plants, there is life, which substantiates respect for a natural unfolding. I imagine a moral conversation regarding the choice of sites would go something like this. The interference with the lichen—its elimination in a place uncongenial to its reestablishment—is a worse interference with life than the early closing down of the wildflowers for the remainder of this season. In a word, life is an intrinsic good, and life (rather than aims and pains) here dominating, the lichen colony merits more considerateness than the early lapse of the perennial flowers.

Thus, to talk about the considerateness of plants, to posit such a plane, is intelligible, and indeed required, unless such plant-versus-plant choices are to be regarded (where we are utility indifferent) as wholly arbitrary.

But might the considerateness of plants carry even further, so as to influence our judgment when the claim on behalf of the plant is opposed not to another plant's claim, but to the claims of a person? Suppose that one of the oil workers discovers a small arctic flower coming through the gravel. The flower is located where no one else will see it. Indeed, with winter closing in, it will die before anyone else could possibly gain any pleasure from its beauty. The human interest is this: there is at least one person who wants to crush it. (He just does.) The plant has no countervailing "interest" in the human sense. Ought he to desist? Does morality have anything to add?

There is, at the start, at least an intuition that the contemplated act is in some mood or meaning wrong. That is not to say that the crushing of a flower is as wrong as the crushing of a child. But it is equally wrong to suppose that the worker's inclination lies beyond the correction of moral conversation. The conversation cannot appeal to the plant's pleasures, pains, or preferences. But the guiding counterpart can include *natural unfolding* and *ecosystem stability*. Not only could we say that both contemplated plant-damaging acts are wrong, at least in the softest sense of "morally unwelcome." We could perform a ranking, that is, demonstrate that the elimination of the lichen colony is a worse act than the plucking of the flower (which will return next year).

But both the flower and the lichen are living. Is there any comparable method, or even foundation, for morally assessing our impact on the nonliving parts of the planet? Suppose the issue is whether we should compel the drilling company (at some human cost) to reduce the hazard to the ocean of oil spillage through seepage or blowouts.

One approach is to emphasize the pervasive interdependence between the living and nonliving. If there is oil seepage, *some* life is going to be affected somehow. One is tempted to say therefore that life provides an adequate foundation for protecting the environment and we need not worry about the sea as such.

But valuing life and valuing the sea are not the same. Imagine a spill that puts a slick on the water, with the consequence that oil-devouring bacteria assemble, more than compensating for any losses in other life, whether expressed in terms either of tonnage or diversity. If there is anything to be said against the spill, it would appear to lie in making the sea itself considerate. But is this intelligible?

One route is suggested by the "Gaian hypothesis," the suggestion that life not only adapts to (is in some sense "controlled by") the nonliving environment, but that the living environment also controls the nonliving.[7] The atmosphere may be inert, but its composition is heavily determined by the activities of plants. Even movements of the polar caps may be triggered by life processes acting via changes in ocean temperatures. Contending along these lines, the whole earth can be presented as a sort of superorganism: Gaia, after the Greek goddess of earth. This superorganic view, in turn, could serve as the foundational basis of an action-informing moral viewpoint.

Whether the planet can appropriately be viewed as an organism, as that term is familiarly understood, is controversial. But it is a controversy on which we need not take a side. Certainly the relationship among the earth's parts is more organized and interconnected than grains in a pile of sand. On the other hand, the relationship among the parts is far less preordaining, economical, and fragile than the relationships among the parts of a bird. Cut away a bird's heart, or even break its beak, and it will not unfold within its preordained limits. But the capacity of the planet to bounce back in a life-sustaining manner after cataclysmic shocks from without and within is simply fabulous. Two billion years ago, when contemporary life was thriving on an atmosphere that was predominantly ammonia, a subversive population of aerobic photosynthesizers led to a massive buildup in the air of (gasp!) oxygen. We could stand it today in L.A. At the time, however, it was a calamity. As J. E. Lovelock quips, "It must have been the worst atmospheric pollution incident that this planet has ever known."[8] But the earth rallied back with oxygen breathers and an environment congenial to them. On several subsequent occasions other changes, perhaps the result of collision with meteorites, led to radical revisions in life as it was then known, but did not prevent its replacement with life in an altered form.

What is the lesson? Suppose that this looseness does not disqualify the planetary whole from being considered something of an organism, that it only makes the globe a more marvelous and respect-worthy entity. Suppose further that respect for this organism can form the foundational basis for a plane, which might have as its categorical imperative "Do not deliver the planetary whole a mortal wound," where "mortal" is understood as including deletion of its ability to sustain life. The problem is that considering this history, considering what the earth has already gone through, mankind's capacity to disrupt it appears relatively meager. Probably not even an all-out nuclear war, ensued by a nuclear winter, can eliminate the earth's capacity to readjust to some life. Not to say that such a war would be moral; but its immorality would have to be based on a principle other than a planetary life-terminating one. Perhaps a Gaian viewpoint is best framed on a less tolerant impera- tive than an injunction not to wound *mortally*. After all, from respect for persons we derive the morality not to injure (and not merely, not to *kill*). On a parity of reasoning, the Gaian viewpoint might enjoin us to avoid less than cataclysmically life-fatal damage to the biosphere, the lithosphere, and so on.

Such a principle would give support for some measures on the human agenda. For example, it supplements ordinary homocentric rea- sons to limit nuclear weapons testing in the atmosphere. But in fact most human actions, such as the more mundane options that face our hypothetical Beaufort Sea drillers, do not hazard our surprisingly durable planet in the Gaian, superorganic sense. The worst oil blowout in history is something that the earth would barely feel.

If there is any moral guidance regarding options on this level, we have to appeal elsewhere than to Gaia, perhaps to a notion of the biotic community (Chapter 9). The community viewpoint is distinct from the Gaian in that it is biased toward existing relationships and is accordingly less flexible, and more directive. This bias may seem odd, but consider for a moment a human community in which everyone is courteous, friendly, and considerate. A member who is boorish and selfish can hardly rejoin that he *does* value *community,* that it is only *their community* he is undermining—that all he is doing is to bring about a new set of relations, one that just happens to be rude and aggressive, to replace the present one.

The selfish boor's rejoinder does not work, because to respect community is to give some preference for the well-working communal relationships in which we find ourselves. And similarly, to respect the biotic community is not to respect *any* set of animate-inanimate relations. It is to give some preference for existent biotic relations. It is true that in some sense this view makes its defense of the nonliving thing, the sea, symbiotic upon life; the foundational basis involves a claim that the boundaries between life and nonlife blur. But notice that on this view the sea's considerateness is not compromised by showing that a spill would lead (as it might) to more life, more valuable life, or even more diversified life. On the biotic community viewpoint, the sea as it is, is valued because it is presumed to be integral to the earth as we know it.

There still remains the intriguing prospect of a plane constructed on principles that in no way lean on life, and that might inform actions whose impact on life was really negligible. Suppose that there is a way to conduct the development, such as by staining the water with drilling mud dyed a striking shade of purple and firing a continuous stream of fireworks from the derricks, that would make the region more fun for the oil workers to look at. No harm would be done to life. Would it be wrong to so "beautify" the region?

Obviously, this is the toughest sort of case. As I have already stressed, if we are compelled to bring the sea under the same rules as Persons, it appears impossible to condemn the action. Still, I would pursue the thought that a moral defense is called for, because to a sensitive conscience, which I take as my standard of pleading, something like a prima facie wrong is threatened. The intuition that staining the water is wrong need not be founded exclusively in the considerateness (innate good) of the things being affected. The claim could draw upon ideal character, an ideal way of life, or the transcendent-self viewpoint (Chapter 9), each of which can be fleshed out into a plane, perhaps in some mutually supportive combination.

Note that rules of universalization would not be out of place in such frameworks, although they will be limited to universalizing of the "no one ought to" rather than the "swapping places" sort. That is, working within the governance of the preceding nonutility planes, one can reason that I ought not to do *that* to X (a remote person or higher animal), because if I were X, I would not want that done to me. By contrast, on Thing-regarding planes, I cannot meaningfully "trade places" with the object, a flower or sea, in the same way (although I suppose that poets and mystics have so aspired). Nonetheless, I can still put to myself the question "Am I able to will that all of mankind, if they were similarly situated, ought to crush the wildflower, stain the sea?" Quite possibly we should look for answers to such questions not in terms of what is morally impermissible, of duties toward a wildflower, but what is, less rigidly, morally unwelcome, or blemishing of character.

N5: MEMBERSHIP ENTITIES

Another plane (or series of related planes) is oriented to claims regarding what I call Membership Entities, things such as species, nations, corporations, and cultures. In some sense these entities are abstractions, mere intellectual constructs through which the actual flesh-and-blood beings, the entity members, are related. Pluralism does not reject the significance of the physical individuals. It holds, however, that Membership Entities are also independent focuses of moral interest. That is to say, the claims we set up on behalf of, or the moral interest in regard to, the species (whale) or the nation (Japan) may not be governed by the identical considerations that govern our relations with the individual whales or Japanese.

Of course, there are significant differences among these various Membership Entities. Private clubs and associations have purely conventional origins, and individual membership is voluntary. Other Membership Entities, such as species, exist naturally. There were whales before we had a name for them, and whales cannot choose to be warthogs. People are born into nations, but they can elect out. Culture is somewhat distinct as well. One cannot elect out from one's culture as freely as from one's club. Moreover, cultures lack the formal governmental structure, the bylaws and so on, of corporations. That is why I doubt that any single uniform plane could contain all Membership Entities satisfactorily. Nonetheless, for purposes of understanding their common features, it is worth considering them together as a class.

An illustration of the Inupiat Indians considered as a *tribe* or *nation*, * rather than as an aggregate of individuals, will clarify what I am driving at: how an argument that focuses moral regard on the Membership Entity enlists distinct considerations and takes different turns than arguments that focus on the sum of the entity's individual members.

*Early in the white settlers' (or, as the Indians might say, the invaders') history on this continent, the Indian tribes were recognized as independent nations with whom other nations concluded treaties and fought wars. The terms of many Indian treaties signed during the late colonial period, when the conflicts among France, England, and the colonists forced each side to curry the military favors of the Indians, testify to how literally this status was recognized. However, when the colonists had secured their independence and marked, in a series of successful military campaigns, their clear ascendency on the battlefield, the strength of the Indians' bargaining hand declined. With the deline in bargaining power there followed—continues to follow—a gradual erosion of their status as independent nations. For example, the Seneca could not today, as they did in 1764, conclude a separate treaty with the British Crown. They enjoy (if that is the word) the status of "domestic dependent nations," a term coined by Chief Justice Marshall to denote an ill-defined and shifting relationship that produces a body of distinctive and complex Indian law. Strictly speaking, the Inupiat (unlike the Cherokee and the Navajo) were never recognized as a nation, but in the loose sense of the term required for purposes of illustration in the text, it is useful and not misleading to think of them as such.

Take the question of whether we are warranted in putting limits on the Inupiat's traditional bowhead hunt. One way to attack the question is to posit individuals as the morally salient entities (individual Indians, individual whales, individual non-Indian Americans) and hash it out within the classic utilitarian framework of U1. In that framework, we would decide what was right by aggregating welfares (or combining preferences) in some way that gave equal weight to each person's pleasures or desires. Essentially, U1 would aggregate the utility gains to all those who benefit from increases in oil reserves and diplomatic maneuverability (roughly 200 million Americans) and subtract the utility losses to the several thousand Indians and their supporters. Even if the benefits of oil development to each non-Indian are individually insignificant, their weight in the aggregate will easily dominate in the final analysis. The calculations would not change appreciably if we included future generations in the universe of affected people, as supposed by U2. By most plausible measures, the benefits to the present-plus-future beneficiaries would still swamp the losses to the considerably smaller universe of present-plus-future tribe members.

Of course, it is for just this reason—to resist such a swamping of their interests—that the Native American groups, in common with other minorities, characteristically avoid tying moral choices to aggregated utility calculations. The math will always favor the majority. The conventional alternative is to ground claims in an individual-rights discourse along the lines supposed by the N1 framework. Specifically, an Indian will assert that the moral claim each tribe member has to retaining his cultural heritage is vital enough to be elevated to the status of a right, and therefore exempt from the counterbalancing of utilities that characterizes the utility planes. In discussions of law, this position ordinarily emerges as an assertion of the rights of individual Indians under the First Amendment or the American Indian Religious Freedom Act. One problem with adopting that strategy, however, is that each Indian's claimed right is destined to be met by a countervailing claim of right by the other side: the "property right" the rest of us have to lease the public lands for public benefit, perhaps even our First Amendment right to travel, an interest furthered by plentiful supplies of gasoline. Hence, for the Indians, a battle conducted on N1, carried out in the language of individualized-rights discourse, may carry the day in some cases, but in others is likely to be inconclusive or unsuccessful.

Sequoyah v. *TVA*[9] is an interesting illustration in that it arose from the same controversy as gave rise to the snail darter litigation.[10] In *Sequoyah*, a suit to enjoin construction of the Tellico Dam was brought on behalf of "all those present or future Cherokee Indians who practice the traditional Cherokee religion." The complaint alleged that construction of the dam threatened to flood grounds sacred to the Cherokee religion, thereby infringing the plaintiffs' rights to free exercise of religion. Plaintiff Sequoyah, a medicine man, believed that with the loss of the land he would lose his knowledge of medicine. Unlike the snail darters, who had the backing of special congressional legislation (the Endangered Species Act), the Indians' claims, based largely on an individual-rights strategy, failed to carry the courts.

Is it possible that another strategy would have been more successful, one that drew attention to a plane that was predicated on the moral salience of Membership Entities? In the bowhead illustration, the idea would be to take an argument for nondevelopment of the Beaufort region based on claims of individual Indians, and supplement it by claims of independent duties owed to, or rights of, the Indian tribe or nation or culture. The coherence of such an argument depends upon identifying a value in groupness or community, and a way of talking about that value that transcends the interests of and toward the individuals.* With the conflict so cast, the claims would not be a mere "summing" of the claims of individual Indians, and hence would not fairly be met by a summing of individual claims from the other side. They would have to be met, if at all, on their own plane by claims of the appropriate kind and weight.

Unfortunately, this proposal is made in the face of a large body of

---

*The *tribal* claim, nonreduced, would appear to be strongest in instances where the actions complained of have as their intended object affecting the tribe (its cultural heritage, etc.) and repress individuals only incidentally. *See* New Rider v. Board of Education, 480 F. 2d 693 (10th Cir. 1973) (expulsion from school of Indian for wearing hair in allegedly traditional style); Dept. of Interior, Office of Indian Affairs, Circular No. 1665 (Apr. 21, 1921) (tribal sun dance declared Indian offense).

skeptical literature. The first objection to such membership planes is typically an ontological one. Whales, citizens, stockholders, and Indians, the critics will say, are real things. Species, nations, corporations, and tribes are mere intellectual constructs. The latter "exist" only in some queer sense to which serious thinkers should pay no mind. In the philosophy literature, this line of reasoning, termed reductionism, redescriptivism, or methodological individualism, holds that the corporation or nation or tribe is nothing but contractual or political arrangements among various persons. It—the Membership Entity—has no interests independent of the respective personal interests of the investors, managers, and citizens that the arrangement connects. When we say, for convenience's sake, that a corporation did thus and such (or that something was done to it) there are always, at bottom, some flesh-and-blood mortals who really acted or were acted upon. The individuals are therefore the only real objects to praise, blame, or otherwise consider. For this reason, the reductionist maintains, we can take any statement in which a Membership Entity appears and restate it exclusively in terms of real natural persons, for example, the chairman of the board or the tribal council.

This whole area is very complex. Certainly there are reasons to approach group and corporate responsibility with suspicion. Focusing on the group may mask personal responsibility in circumstances where some individual really should be blamed (or praised) for the group's actions. Perhaps worse, blaming or even punishing the group may unfairly stain the members who are morally blameless. But as we saw earlier, in a bureaucratic setting a blameworthy act can occur for which no individual is fairly blamable.[11] Are we at an impasse?

Not the Pluralist. To speak of the responsibilities of and duties toward individuals does not exclude an alternative, "corporate," discourse. The man in the street, no less than the lawyer and judge, speaks of "Ford's blame for the Pinto design," and "Germany's obligations to make reparations." I am not maintaining that we can derive from the linguistic conventions a moral verity (or to make any other leap from what is to what ought to be). But we have to recognize how commonly and comprehensibly there appear, in law, in morals, and in ordinary speech, references to corporate bodies as more than the sum of the persons they contain. When a historian says that England's consciousness and destiny have been shaped by the Channel, she does not mean the equivalent of "the consciousness and destiny of William the Conqueror and of Edward I and of . . . have been so shaped." Considering the ubiquity of the corporate terminology, we ought not lightly to dismiss it as a mere technique for the ease of conversational effort, or as merely a stand-in for persons in some peculiar and unstraightforward way.

Indeed, if one had to choose between a discourse built upon individuals *or* a discourse built upon corporate bodies, there would be points to be made both ways.[12] But there is no reason why we cannot employ both a corporate language and a separate-member language, much as we employ body language (biology) and a mental-event language (psychology) as separate discourses for "the same" event, such as being pricked by a pin. The biologist will describe the event in terms of publicly observable phenomena: of nerve endings, neurotransmitters, special chemicals, and cortex. The everyday psychological language, "It hurts," deals with the unmeasurable and irredeemably private side of the experience. Note that in the mind/body case, we recognize that there is a relationship between the two conceptual frameworks. When I say, using mental language, "I am in pain," we assume in principle that there has occurred some associated physical change in my body, one that lends itself to biological expression. But while the two languages are related, they can be and are quite intelligibly detached. (Indeed: the thus-far insuperable difficulty for science lies in divining the attachment, in translating pain and joy to molecules and fiber.)

The separateness of corporate and agent discourses is most easily discerned in connection with actions that pertain to the one but not to the other. That is to say, there are certain acts that people can do, which corporate bodies cannot: make love and swill beer, for example. It follows that while people can be licentious and inebriate, corporations cannot. Conversely, other acts, such as merging, dissolving, waging war, honoring treaties, and nationalizing, pertain to corporate bodies, but not to individuals.

Take the declaration of war. Obviously it is a step furthered and announced by humans: who else? But not any human's declaration of war operates to establish a state of war legally. For example, suppose that a Middle East terrorist declares war on the United States, perhaps even accompanying the declaration with a hostile act, such as a bombing. He would not thereby activate the special rules of international law, regarding national blockades and so on, that apply as between belligerent nations.

But even if one recognizes the validity of separate discourses, granting that it is meaningful to detach talk about the Membership Entity from talk about the membership, it does not necessarily follow that different moral rules apply. If not, then of course it is vacant to speak, as I have, of separate planes, each with its own governance. This is a controversy that has received the most attention in the area of international relations. There it takes the form of asking whether nation-states are governed by morality and, if so, whether the principles are the same principles that bind humans.

One view, that of the so-called realists, follows Hobbes in holding that sovereigns are unfettered by any moral principles at all. At the other extreme is the view that I would associate with Monism: that sovereigns are so bound, and that indeed the rules that bind them, and which provide the filament for international relations, are the identical rules that bind individual humans. That position is exemplified by R. W. Mowat, who simply regards the Ten Commandments and the Golden Rule as "universal propositions without reservations, without exceptions," that apply among kinsmen and kingdoms indistinguishably.[13] In between, there is a view that traces to Hume which supposes that governments are bound by the same rules that bind humans, but that against nations they hold with less force. "There is," Hume held, "a system of morals calculated for princes, much more free than that which ought to govern private persons."[14]

The view I am maintaining, Pluralism, represents a fourth outlook.

Pluralism rejects the Hobbesian view by holding that nations are bound by at least some moral principles. It also rejects Mowat's position that the governance is the same, as it rejects, too, the Humean variation on Mowat, that states are governed by the same rules, but in some special watered-down way. For a Pluralist, requirements on the international plane may "differ from the requirements of common morality, and constitute a special 'political' morality, or even a peculiarly 'international' one."*

Some of the factors that lend Pluralism credence in this area have already been alluded to. First, it is not clear how tightly the same rules can be fitted to person and nation alike, when the choices they face are not the same. A person has the choice whether to marry or join the resistance. A nation, whether to abrogate a treaty that "it" signed— meaning, signed perhaps centuries ago by its authorized representatives, none of whom is now living. Second, persons and nations have different interests. Many personal interests are fabricated out of feelings of pleasure and pain, psychological states that do not pertain to nations. On the other hand, nations have recognized sovereign interests, such as that their national air space not be invaded. "Nations react strongly to unauthorized overflights because it is illegal, not because they are inherently damaging or 'painful.'"[15]

International law recognizes such distinctions and is able to deal with them intelligibly. The celebrated *Trail Smelter* case of 1949 provides a nice illustration. There, the United States took up against Canada the claims of private citizens in the state of Washington whose farmlands and woodlands were being damaged by pollution wafting south across the border. (It is no point of national pride to observe that we have since reversed the balance of bad-air trade.) The international arbitrator granted that no nation "has the right to use or permit the use

*Marshall Cohen, "Moral Skepticism and International Relations," *Philosophy and Public Affairs* 13 (1984): 299. Cohen suggests that some writers have held this position, but cites no examples (p. 301). The view is one with which I would associate. Cohen's own conclusion, however, sounds distinctly Monist, viz., that international conduct is open to moral assessment which rests "on principles that govern every domain of human conduct and govern them all with equal rigor" (p. 302).

of its territory in such a manner as to cause injury by fumes [how about nuclear radiation from Chernobyl'?] in or to the territory of another."[16] But there were several obstacles that prevented recovery. These included the fact that claims pressed on the international plane have to be the claims of nations, not of individuals. If the United States were really to press a state-to-state claim, "the measure of damages would be more difficult to compute . . . since the injury would then be to the sovereignty of the United States, rather than the particularized damage to the individuals in the state of Washington."[17]

When we pass from law to morals, we continue to find elements of ordinary individual analysis applied to nation-states in distinctive ways. Just as individuals have intentions and patterns of behavior which matter in our evaluations of them, so too do nations. Even as individual presidents and rulers come and go, countries establish and maintain regulations as peace-loving or belligerent members of the world community. Moreover, human morality is created with an eye toward human relationships and woven of human ideals, such as the attributes and possibilities of personhood. What is moral and just among nations derives from conceptions of a just and fair world order. The filaments of international morality include customs among nations, the balance of power, and equilibrium politics. While the concept of a just world order surely has to account for a conception of the good human life, I seriously doubt that the one can be translated into the other with any more success than if we attempt to derive the laws of political science from those of microbiology. Witness in this regard how the rights of nations are not merely the rights of persons at large. National rights include such rights as those to territorial sovereignty and sovereign immunities, rights that simply do not apply to persons.

Unsurprisingly, many familiar moral notions undergo a distortion of meaning when they are applied to nation-states, if they apply to them at all. In ordinary dealings among persons (in both law and morals), we recognize the nonmorality of coerced promises by annulling their force. American consumers have come to be protected against coercion of the frailest sort. Yet, peace treaties have not uncommonly originated with the most blatantly coerced promises: they are signed with a gun, indeed, many thousands of them, held to one party's head. The Indians did not for the most part repair to their reservations willingly. But on the international plane different moral rules appear to obtain, with the result that persons and nations are subject to distinct evaluative procedures.

Such a Pluralist outlook was expressed by Alexander Hamilton during an early and dramatic episode in our nation's history. George Washington's neutrality proclamation had the effect of annulling a provision of the United States' 1778 Treaty of Alliance with France. Many Americans opposed the action as inconsistent with the gratitude owed France for its assistance in the War of Independence. Hamilton came to Washington's defense with an essay in which he declared that "Faith and Justice between nations are virtues of a nature sacred and unequivocal," but that "the same cannot be said of gratitude."

> The rule of morality is [in] this respect not exactly the same between Natio[ns] as between individuals. The duty of making [its] own welfare the guide of its action[s] is much stronger upon the former than upon the latter; in proportion to the greater magnitude and importance of national compared with individual happiness, to the greater permanency of the effects of national than of individual conduct. Existing Millions and for the most part future generations ar[e] concerned in the present measures of a government: While the consequences of the private actions of [an] individual, for the most part, terminate with himself or are circumscribed within a narrow compass.
>
> Whence it follows, that an individual may on numerous occasions meritoriously indulge the emotions of generosity and benevolence; not only without an eye to, but even at the expence of his own interest. But a Nation can rarely be justified in pursuing [a similar] course; and when it does so out to confine itself within much stricter bounds.[18]

Now, what I am suggesting is the validity of, and not merely recognizing the convention of, moral discourses that "map" Membership Entities and consider them according to their own governance. By "validity" I mean that such discourses are capable of adding to, rather than, as reductionism has it, distracting from, the insight and direction which our moral lives require. Granted, any governance we devise cannot intelligibly ascribe to these entities utility, pleasure, or pain. Abstract entities are Nonpersons, indeed Things, and cannot be "harmed" in the way that persons are harmed. But this does not rule out the possibility of a discourse regarding them, even claims being set up in consideration of them, on the basis of one of the ideal-regarding theories to which we have already alluded.[19]

Turning from the general to the specifics of the bowhead illustration, to conduct an analysis on this plane one would introduce into moral evidence any existing treaties between the Inupiat and the United States, and all legislation that recognizes tribal jurisdiction in the matter of the whale hunting. Has there been, for example, warranted reliance by the tribe? Reliance by the tribe (as distinct from individual reliance) would be gauged by attributes of tribal existence, such as tribal rituals, customs, location, and laws. On this "nation" plane, there are also relevant obligations arising under treaties between the United States and other whaling nations. Treaties aside, sustained attention is owing to the whole history of dealings between the Indians and the white settlers. Does our nation, the United States, owe the Indian nations, on a balancing of past benefits and past wrongs, any special considerations regarding their continued whaling? In answering these questions, the moral paradigms and precedents one consults are drawn from the history and standards of international, not interpersonal, conduct.

Of course, I am not maintaining that the morality of whaling can be fully determined by examining the human Membership Entities (e.g., the nations) with no word for the whales. Analysis on the plane of nations has to be supplemented by analyses conducted on a number of planes, including one that maps species. But it is interesting to observe that in considering the governance of species, there is much to be learned by considering the other kinds of Membership Entities.

That is, while tribes, species, nations, and business corporations are each distinguishable, they often present common questions, and raise common insights. In regard to the moral considerateness both of tribes and of species, one faces common issues: (1) On what basis is considerateness owed to a transcendent Membership Entity? (2) How does one identify a Membership Entity that merits independent considerateness?[20] Why the bowhead, rather than cetaceans? Why the Inupiat, rather than "Alaskan Indians"? In both instances, to formulate an answer draws us into a consideration of uniqueness, intactness (purity), the age (lineage), number of members, the members' "sense" of themselves as a group (in species, as expressed by the boundaries of breeding), and the values that the entity may symbolize or give expression to, such as majesty, stoicism, independence, or self-sacrifice.

So far as we ground the claim of some species or tribe, say, the eagle or the Apache, on the symbolization of boldness and courage, the problem arises whether to discount the claim because there are alternative "objects" in the world that symbolize and spark consideration of the same qualities. Again, to implicate such planes—and such questions—is not to say how the final choice on either plane will resolve or even proceed. What I am maintaining is that by suspending any intuitive snap judgment, and partitioning our analysis into separate lines of thought, we advance our way to an ultimately more satisfactory—more "correct"—solution. My own sense is that when the Inupiats reach the point of trekking off in gasoline-powered snowmobiles to fire at the whales from motorboats with dynamite-tipped harpoons,[21] the tribal/ cultural claims, tracked through the appropriate matrix, will neither overcome the strong prima facie claim of individual whales to life, nor meet the claims to be made on behalf of the species. That is, even considered on its own terms, on its own home grounds, the tribe's "right" to kill bowheads appears to have been diluted. Their claims become questionable, somewhat like the claims on behalf of a species such as the red wolf, which has so interbred that it is presently unclear how cogently it can be regarded as a "natural kind."

N6: QUALITIES

Thus far, I have imagined planes that mapped various tangible and intangible *things*. But I would not rule out resort to planes that mapped *qualities*. In fact, I am not sure how (once we get committed to such an exercise) one can avoid doing so. For one thing, the distinction between things and qualities is always problematical, rooted all too tenuously in grammatical conventions. During an electrical storm is there a substantive thing, lightning, that flashes (making *lightning* the subject of an active verb), or does the sky take on, along with its other properties such as dark blueness, an additional quality, "marked-by-lightning-flashiness"? It seems as though the language we have adopted, by not having evolved a noncompound term for "lightning flashiness" (the quality) simply favors the subject-verb construction and leads us to suppose it "natural" that lightning is a thing. But that is a happenstance of linguistic convention, not a fact of nature. And even if we accept uncritically the conventional cleavage between things and qualities, the way in which we group things would appear to be secondary to, or entangled with, implicit judgments as to the significance of various qualities. For we can always ask, why should *these* things be grouped together and made subject to the same governance, except in virtue of some morally salient properties they share? One wonders, then, does it make a difference whether we imagine ourselves to be concentrating on a plane that is mapped from the dominating stance of life or courage (i.e., qualities), or on one that maps all living or all courageous things?

I cannot presently foresee how these various analyses are destined to work out. But I anticipate that (whichever is right) we would find thing-planes and quality-planes to display distinct logical textures. The Person planes, which take individual humans as the things that count, count their preferences equally (utilitarianism) or deem each to be of equal "intrinsic worth" (Kantianism). But the quality-dominated planes may be governed quite differently. Suppose that courage, communality, and beauty are valued qualities—valued either because they are intrinsically good, or good parasitically, as a prop for human virtues or for a flourishing life. On either account, objects symbolizing such qualities would warrant consideration.[22] But it seems more reasonable for the considerateness to attach to the *class* of all objects that conserve or carry forward the quality.

Such a foundation would not secure an argument that each member of each class is morally considerate, and that therefore no member of the class can be eliminated without some moral justification. Suppose first that the considerateness of the quality is based upon the position that the quality is intrinsically good. This would seem to support an argument making morally welcome the survival of one member of the class of things in which the quality was embodied; if *majesty*, we would have secured perhaps one majestic mountain or vista. But it is not as clear that such a basis would support preserving many embodiments of the quality. That depends on whether the quality is regarded as unitary and indivisible (beauty survives equally whether one beautiful thing survives or many) or in some way additive (there is "more beauty" in two beautiful things than in one).

One wonders, too, how strong an argument we can wring out of the derivative views, which do not value natural objects and so on as ends in themselves, but only as instruments to human virtue or worthy lives. Confined by that limited rationale, the preservationist's argument could not go beyond preserving enough members of the class to assure that the favored virtue or form of flourishing life will be a viable prospect for humanity. One might conclude that there ought to be enough Xs to go around, so that each person will have the opportunity to develop the right tastes and activities; but that is not the same as to conclude that each X has a right to endure, or even that the preservation of each X is morally welcome.

There is an instructive instance of this sort of thinking in the arguments for preserving species. Such arguments are typically not inconsistent with the taking of individual members, so long as the reduction does not threaten the optimal carrying capacity of a critical habitat. In like vein, those who value various qualities may find each of them embodied in a wide variety of objects. For example, bees are communal; but so are beavers. Hence, a conservationist's argument that is founded on some communality-advancing basis may marshal support for saving either bees or beavers. An argument that the elimination of both was morally unwelcome would have to come up with some independent foundational basis.

A Meta-ethical Unwinding

THROUGHOUT, I have deflected some of the toughest questions with repeated references to notions that will have to be "developed" and "filled in." A general theory of unconventional entities, legal and moral, does not compress easily into a single book. That is particularly true when what the general theory suggests is that the working out of individual problems requires a more particularized stratification, that there is no one particular theory in play. Certainly in some succeeding work—or works—any reader with the fortitude is entitled to be provided with some fuller development and filling in. How *are* our relations with animals composed? With plants? With rivers?

That has not been the primary goal, to provide full and final details on any one region of interest. The aim has been to show how those tasks should be approached in general, beginning with a renunciation of the commonly held Monist assumption that moral considerateness is a matter of either-or. It is not true that there is a single moral property, for example, intelligence, sentience, or life, such that entities are *either* morally relevant (in the same way, according to the same rules) *or* utterly inconsiderate, out in the cold. I have sought to demonstrate the prospect of a Pluralist middle way, and to give some sense of its direction and details and structure. But for the present, after so many pages largely dedicated to illustrating the Pluralist conception I am aiming at, let me close with some comments about it, about its own foundational assumptions, about where it suggests we head, and about the criticisms to which it will have to respond along the way.

AN EMPHASIS NOT ON PRINCIPLES
BUT ON FRAMEWORKS

Much, perhaps most, contemporary moral theory is engaged in seeking universal postulates, with the ambition of producing something roughly equivalent to an axiom system. Typical is the view that "an agent can only justify a particular judgment by referring to some universal rule from which it may be logically derived, and can only justify that rule in turn by deriving it from some more general rule or principle."[1] My position is not unmindful of postulates or principles, but aims to allay the single-minded stress on them. Substantive principles are only part of, and not necessarily the most determinative part of, larger frameworks or "planes." No one really accepts or rejects vegetarianism as the deductive application of a single abstract principle; one's judgment involves, and should involve, a commitment to a whole network of mutually supportive principles, theories, and attitudes toward consequences, that is, the sort of world that vegetarianism as a moral stand brings about.

We attain a better picture of moral analysis if we conceive of the planes as the fundamental units. The obvious analogy is to a view of science that gives principal emphasis to paradigms in science. Paradigms are conceptual frameworks that encompass not only the substantive working rules, the body of scientific laws to which one subscribes, but also "looser" elements: general theories, a common fund of received concepts, rules of "evidence," standards for confirmation and disconfirmation, a coherent tradition, and a shared sense of what the significant questions are, along with the accepted techniques for solving them.[2] It is the moral counterparts of paradigms, these planes, that ought to be the primary focus of investigation, that will give us the better platform on which to build our moral understanding.

NO SINGLE PLANE

Moreover, I would displace the quest for a single, all-encompassing framework, pretentious to govern all moral thought, with an effort to develop different planes that may be appropriate to separate moral activities and morally salient universes. Some planes are fashioned from special Nonperson-regarding viewpoints. Others lay as a foundation for more orthodox interpersonal analyses a fundamentally Kantian or utilitarian outlook, textured, in each instance, by suitable variables of logical style. By so partitioning moral analysis, we relieve the enterprise of a stricture nowhere justified, that every quandary has to be defined and attacked according to a single coherent set of rules. Pluralism nurtures the emergence of different frameworks for analysis, each capable of producing guidance that is less vague and general than if all problems had to answer to the same governance.

THE ROLE OF INTUITION

Now the question is, what makes a plane more or less appropriate? One determinant is intuition; but what do we mean by that? On one level, to speak of intuitions is to speak of a particular sort of emotion, a feeling of rightness or wrongness that we cannot derive from, nor even (more loosely) trace to, any particular principle. In this sense, we intuit that an act is wrong, or that an entity is worthy of some sort of moral heed, or that a plane is appropriate; but if pressed for justification, we have a hard time coming up with one. On another level, we can think of intuitions as the raw data of morals; the intuitionist believes that these hard-to-trace emotions stand to moral judgment in a relation exactly analogous to the relation between perceptual experience and scientific judgment.[3] The second view emphasizes emotions as the starting point or catalyst of rational analysis; the first view is broad enough to encompass the end point, the final feeling that the judgment to which the analysis has brought us is the right one.

Obviously, the intuitions cannot be offered as a certain guide in moral matters, since it is the very function of moral reasoning to submit our intuitions, particularly those presented in the form of initial responses, as "raw data," to more formal critical review. Hence, to emphasize intuition is not to imply that a planar viewpoint is expected to confirm our first reactions (in which case moral reasoning would have nothing to contribute). Rather, the plane must have moral perspicacity; the elements of a situation to which it turns our attention must "feel right." It must carry our thought along lines that feel right to a judgment that feels right—perhaps not so much right to each of us as individuals but (so far as we can grasp it) right to the collective conscience of mankind. I do not consider it paradoxical to suggest that the moral feelings should themselves feel right: consistent, coherent, rational, correct, satisfying. We should feel that each plane, and the system of planes as a whole, provides the capacity to recognize moral dilemmas where they exist, and in the right terms. And we should feel that the indicated treatment is such that our initial moral unease is quieted *rightly*.

To legitimate the role of intuition in this process is not to argue that our intuitions are fixed and complete. Like taste, which plays an analogous role in aesthetics, our moral intuitions are capable of education, of "improvement." Indeed, not all ethical discourse aims to evaluate something, to decide what to do or whom to blame. Some of it is more akin to gossip. Even when we are not seeking or cannot find "the right answer," moral discussion may clarify thought and intuition for another day, contributing to a community of perception and feeling, and developing what an earlier generation would have unembarrassedly called "the moral faculties." I do not see how we can get away from it.

THE ROLE OF IMAGINATION

It follows that Pluralism places large stock in the role of imagination in the development of ethical capacities, as well as in the making of particular ethical choices. It is a role not often emphasized; much of academic philosophy deems imagination as something outside itself—like the emotions, a potentially destabilizing influence and a threat to real rigor.[4]

Let me illustrate imagination's role with a less conventional approach, that of H. H. Price. Price asks us to suppose we are Englishmen living at the beginning of the sixteenth century, raised from earliest years sincerely to approve the principle "It is right to burn anyone who is a heretic," although never having seen an immolation.

> Then one day you leave your remote valley, go to London, and while . . . there . . . actually witness the burning of a heretic. . . . What you feel is the strongest disapproval, which could be expressed by saying "what is being done here is utterly abominable."
>
> That settles the question, at least for you. In this clash between a general moral principle and a particular moral experience here and now, it is the principle that must go. It has not been falsified (as "all crows are black" is by seeing a grey one). . . . But it has been nullified or put out of court by the particular moral experience you have had. [Y]ou will admit that in some sense you were making a mistake when you accepted it.
>
> What sort of mistake could it be? It was this. You did not fully "realize" what it was that you yourself were approving of when you said "it is right to burn anyone who is a heretic." You did not know what such an action would be like if it were actually done.[5]

What I am driving at is this. Moral thinking (and perhaps all vital and creative thinking) seeks an image, even to the point of conjuring the object of our *imag*ination as metaphor. Moral planes can be conceived, like novels, as providing a sort of "literature" for the development and play of this image-conjuring imagination. Some such sort of literature is particularly valuable when we are considering our relations with Nonpersons and Things.

To illustrate with a contrast, when we are evaluating our obligations to those most closely around us, Persons in our very presence, it does not take a great deal of imagination to identify the morally significant features of our relations. Surely in all cases *some* imagination helps. But a child drowning in front of us (like Price's heretic actually burning before us) is right there in our presence, testing our principled beliefs with the immediacy of its plight. The vast forest being leveled in Brazil —and the principles we formulate with respect to it—are abstracted from the feelings of immediacy, from real, if you will, existential choice. How do we make our relations with the forest, or the river, or the tribe less abstract? The answer is that the more we extend our concerns outward beyond Persons, the more a play of imagination is required. This is a play for which the moral planes provide the stages, conceptual stages on which thought experiments can be played out, dramatized in the mind, in richer detail of fact, principle, and texture than would otherwise be possible.

Note that in these dramatic experiments we are testing not merely the solutions—how the answer feels—but the stage, the moral plane itself. This is particularly important in working out our relations with Things and other Nonpersons. Familiar patterns, appropriate for Persons, just will not fit, and new ones are needed. Hence, we require all the more to concentrate sustained, imaginative attention on a particular plane, undistracted by a continuous demand to make the governance framework we bring to bear upon the one thing (say, the future human) "match" in all respects the frameworks we are developing to apply to the other (say, the river). The specialization improves the prospects that we will be really and rightly satisfied with, really and rightly committed to, the solutions we arrive at.

PLURALISM DISTINGUISHED FROM RANK RELATIVISM

Some readers will rejoin that all this accounting for diverse beliefs and multiple planes is destined to deteriorate into the rankest relativism. Ordinary relativism takes the position that there is one morality for you and another for me.[6] Is not the author's conception fraught with something worse, that there are several moralities for you and several for me?

The answer is, not necessarily. In and of itself, to subscribe to multiple planes involves no commitment as between moral relativism and (for want of a better term) moral reality.[7] That is, one can hold that there are really (and not relatively) universal right answers to moral quandaries, as immutable as the value of pi; but at the same time one can regard the planar analysis as providing us an ever-improving grasp of those really right answers, just as increasingly sophisticated calculations have gotten us closer and closer to the value, to a half-million decimal places now, of pi. For example, we have only to imagine a moral realist persuaded that the really right answers regarding our (all eternal mankind's) obligations to future generations are to be discovered through quite different considerations than those through which we discover our (all eternal mankind's) obligations to whales. Such a "realist" in regard to the validity of moral answers would be a Pluralist in regard to how those really right answers are discovered.

CONFLICTS

Although Pluralism is not equivalent to relativism, it faces similar objections. The relativist has to contend with the possibility of different communities dominated by different beliefs. One community holds genocide to be right; another, to be wrong. Lacking any independent critical perspective from which to arbitrate, relativism appears to be left with two irreconcilable moral truths. Someone will object that Pluralism only multiplies these possibilities. Prospective conflicts are raised not only among persons and communities, but even within any one individual. Working out a solution on one plane, we come to one conclusion; thinking it through on another plane, something else appears right. What does the Pluralist do about it?

To begin with, let us be clear that a moral viewpoint does not stand or fall on its capacity to induce consensus. But even assume that consensus counts as one desideratum among many (because there is some good in social harmony, for example, or because the consensus is some evidence of the judgment's validity). We should not be too quick to conclude that as we multiply planes we multiply the potential for conflict. Quite the opposite may be true; a priori, it is at least equally plausible that the prospects of consensus will advance, the more alternative schema there are to buy into.

To illustrate, imagine one person, A, who feels intuitive sympathy for an endangered species of whale. She also (1) considers herself a utilitarian, (2) supposes such a commitment to be one she has to carry throughout all moral thought, and (3) cannot find adequate utilitarian grounds for pulling whale meat off the market shelves. In those circumstances, A has no basis for agreement with B, who is prepared to build his pro-whale sympathies on an alternative nonutility basis, say, N3. I would think that the prospect of A and B agreeing would increase if we introduce them to the possibilities of some de-linking: A may come around to B's (N3) point of view regarding the whales, while still reserving utilitarianism as the exclusive arbiter in most domains. Perhaps B will agree.

On the other hand, as I observed, the ability to garner consensus is neither necessary nor sufficient for establishing what is right and wrong. For a nonrelativist the problem remains what to do about the conflicting directions that seem to be the price one pays for Pluralism. The fact is that Pluralism does not always lead to conflicts, or to conflicts that are fatally irreconcilable. Let us examine the alternatives more closely.

The Single-Plane Solution

The fact that there are several legitimate planes does not mean that each and every moral dilemma will require several analyses. It is conceivable that in some instances only one plane will be appropriate. Consider, for example, the good Samaritan dilemma in one of its conventional forms (Chapter 5); the decision whether to rescue the stranger is not compounded with implications for animals or the spatially remote or anything else. Or take the example of the oil worker who comes across the lone arctic wildflower, soon to wilt or freeze, whatever he does to it. If there are any claims touching his relations with the flower, I presume they will be drawn from a single plane, something on the order of my N4, alone.

Multiple Planes: Single Indication

There is a second possibility, that the contemplated action will admit of analyses on different planes, but that each analysis will validate the same action. This is an experience we all have in working through practical problems. We approach an answer from a series of angles, gaining confidence in the discovery that distinct mental paths each end in—confirm—the same conclusion. Certainly lawyers are not embarrassed to cast an appeal on plural grounds. Typically, an argument against the death penalty will be made from a utilitarian (deterrence) point of view and from a duty-oriented, neo-Kantian (personhood-respecting) point of view. If both lines of reasoning point in the same direction, so much the better.

Why then should an ordinary (extralegal) moral argument not be considered the more firmly secured because it is supported on two planes? It is easy to see how a vegetarian could argue her position both positing the moral considerateness of animals (U2 and/or N4) and that of humans alone (as per, say, U1 and/or N2). The contention would be that by eating animals the planet uses protein inefficiently, therefore reducing aggregate human welfare, even robbing humans—in particular, undernourished remote others—of a minimally human existence. One can anticipate our Monist labeling such a strategy as mere rhetoric, as a way of forming and changing beliefs. Ethics, he will say, should seek not *beliefs* as to what is true or valid, but what *is* true or valid. I have much sympathy for that position, when it is put this way (a view that I will expand upon below): that ethics is committed to seek moral truth, much as, in science, there is a commitment to find scientific truths. In both cases, the commitment is meaningful and worthy, even if we know, on another level, that our quarry is not merely elusive; we are not even sure what it looks like.

Still, from the commitment that truth is our quarry, what follows as to strictures on the method of its pursuit? In some pursuits, finding the wrong way to the right answer is surely unacceptable. If a scientist, calculating the earth's circumference, stumbles onto the correct answer because he applied bad math to the wrong data, and the various errors canceled out, we would feel that the truth had not been grasped. But in other circumstances we recognize that there are several equally valid ways to come up with the right answer. Consider how Vedic mathematicians have successfully performed complex calculations by recourse to apparently bizarre algorithms.

To some ethicists, Kantians, for example, finding the right answer in the right way may be far more important than finding the right answer. They would say that pulling the victim to safety or paying one's debts is not enough, if all it means is putting one's bones and muscles through the correct movements. To be truly moral an action must be the conscious expression of one's rightly determined duty. But I am not certain how restrictive we should be as to method. What if it turns out that the right answer, as an objective observer should construe it, is more likely to emerge if people are permitted (even encouraged) to pursue a solution through different paths? This is not farfetched. Stephen Toulmin, reflecting on his experience as a staff member of the National Commission for the Protection of Human Subjects of Biomedical and Behavioral Research (a congressionally appointed assortment of theologians, scientists, lawyers, and others), has observed how much more often this group was able to reach agreement on what was the right decision than on what were the right justificatory principles for that decision. Perhaps the solution they so variously discovered was the right one.[8]

We could, I suppose, restrict the incidence of such outcomes as Toulmin reports by restricting moral reasoning with a Monist fiat that people have to reach consensus on the right procedures and principles before they proceed any further toward the right answer. We would thereby purchase some converged consensus as to what was valid reasoning (expressed in a reduction in the number of planes), at the cost of producing more divergence in outcome. That is, if we start with a group of persons who agree on the evaluation of an action, albeit for different reasons, and force them to go back and agree on their technique before they proceed, we are creating the conditions for undoing the agreement. Perhaps under these constraints they will fail even to discover what is *wrong*. In any event, I think the burden lies on the person who presses for the restriction; unless that burden is met, I am not put off by the prospect that in many circumstances the same answer may be indicated on different planes.

Multiple Planes: Tractably Inconsistent Indications

We are in a more difficult position when, in considering a problem, we find that more than one plane is relevant; then, working out each plane's solution, we discover that the indicated actions are inconsistent. Analysis on one plane suggests that we save the bison; analysis on another plane indicates we should shoot it. We cannot do both, shoot and save. What, then?

The problem is of the same general sort as that which we examined under the heading Multiple-Choice Criteria.[9] One response, recall, is to try to construct a master rule. There is some appeal, for example, in weighing divergent judgments by reference to their respective firmness of mood. Such a conception is suggested by the prospect that at least some moral claims regarding animals should dominate at least some countervailing human claims. In the struggling bison illustration, suppose that on an analysis of interpersonal considerations, opening the truck door and borrowing the rope, the minor trespass, is something one ought not to do. Suppose further that analyzed on an appropriate animal-regarding plane, the outcome "save-the-bison" is supported in the mandatory (!) mood. Saving the bison would dominate.

Another alternative is to work toward some sort of lexical ordering of planes in accordance with general moral importance. Under such a rule, actions indicated on plane B would be suspended until actions indicated on plane A had been fulfilled up to some point. For example, our mandatory obligations to Persons might claim priority up to the point where all Persons had achieved a certain level of life-style, something above subsistence. But when that level of comfort has been reached, considerations of animals or of future generations, as per other planes, would be brought into play, as required by the priority rule.

One might respond that by legitimating an appeal to a master rule in certain cases, we are thereby endorsing a sort of Monism "after all." But it is an "after all" significant enough to keep Pluralism from collapsing into Monism. As guided by Pluralism, but not as guided by Monism, we defer attacking the question with a single coherent set of principles at the start. Each sort of problem is defined and dealt with according to separate, specially befitting principles. This has the advantage that it avoids launching the analysis with the wrong map in hand and deters premature closure on a mistaken course. If apparently irreconcilable judgments emerge, any master rule would be introduced solely on a contingency basis, and only after much of the work had already been done. The conclusion is not likely to be the same as if all of our problems had to be compressed into a single, all-encompassing framework from the start.

On the other hand, such tie-breaker rules as those of assigning different weights and of establishing lexical priorities are undeniably hard to establish and justify. In many cases, it may be that we are left to make those *a*-versus-*b* resolutions *as best we can*, creatively, and there is nothing more we can say. Indeed, does the continuing mystery of the human brain not lie precisely in this, that it has the power to create solutions not fully causally ordained by its antecedently pro-grammed "instructions"?

Put it this way. In some of the cases where we get down to the point of balancing off *a* and *b*, the "program" available for further processing may be too insubstantial, indeterminate, and unspecifiable to warrant speaking of an independent rule. It is in this sense that what we are left to is intuition. But the fact that we are so left hanging by methodolog-ical reasoning need not render the multiple-plane analysis a superfluous gesture. Having come to the conclusion *a* on A, and to *b* on B is something; for one thing, it is not *d*. Moreover, reflexive intuitive consideration of *a* and *b* may uncover a third alternative, *c*, one which would not have come to light, much less have been regarded as appropri-ate, if either A or B had been considered alone.

To illustrate, let us return to the bowhead. Assessing the Inupiat's whaling practices on either U3 (which posits the considerateness of all present and future sentient creatures) or N5 (which posits considerate-ness of the Inupiat as a tribe and the whales as a species), a plausible conclusion is that whales may be "harvested" down to the level where the species' biological carrying mass is threatened. Considering the matter on N3, however (which considers moral claims in regard to individual whales), any killing of a whale appears prima facie impermissible, unless perhaps the whale poses a distinct hazard, threatening to stave one's boat. Trying to put these irreconcilable "solutions" into some sort of equilibrium, a third alternative occurs to us (how, we cannot specify): to allow the tribe a limited number of harpoon "strikes" a year, whether the strike kills the stricken whale or not. It is just this sort of balance—for how can any single principle yield it?—that the Alaska Whaling Commission finally decided upon.[10] The Indians realize some of the cultural value of the hunt; the endangered species gets some breathing space; the sacrifice of individual whales is countenanced but minimized.

Multiple Planes: Intractably Inconsistent Indications

Let us continue to imagine quandaries for which analyses on several planes suggest support for inconsistent actions, *a* and *b*. Imagine now, however, that we not only lack a master rule to mediate the conflict, but that further intuitive reflection has no success revealing a third, best-of-all, satisfying alternative, *c*. What maneuver remains?

The question presents the interplanar counterpart of the intraplanar problems reviewed in Chapter 13. What do we do generally if and when the "logic" of our moral governance fails to determine a single answer? When friendship can be advanced only at the price of knowledge or of the general welfare? We may have to abandon the ambition to find the sought-for "one right answer" to every moral quandary, either because a single answer does not exist, or because our best analytical methods are not capable of finding it. The question, as Hilary Putnam puts it, is whether

given the desiderata that automatically arise once we undertake the enterprise of giving a justification of principles for living which will be of *general* appeal . . . will it turn out that these desiderata select a best morality or a group of moralities which have a significant measure of agreement on a number of significant questions.[11]

In some circumstances, areas of disagreement are ineradicable. If we can identify and eliminate the options that are morally unacceptable, we may well have reached as far as moral thought can reach. It may be that of the choices that remain, some strike us as equally good or equally evil or equally stumping.*

This does not imply that with regard to these open choices, one may be arbitrary—as though, from this point on, flipping a coin is as good as we can do. It is by the choices we affirm in this zone, no less than by our yielding to the dictates of a clear moral command, that we have our highest opportunity to exercise our freedom and define our character. Particularly if the considerateness of Nonpersons is legitimated, people who take morals seriously, who are committed to giving good reasons, will reach irreconcilably conflicting decisions on many questions. At what point of disparity in well-being ought we to share our resources with the remote poor, or with an endangered species? It should not surprise us that no moral structure, however ingenious, can dispel all legitimate differences of opinion in every context. But that is a far cry from accepting the skeptic's thrust, that in morals there are no answers. Moreover, in many cases of this unresolvable sort, collective coercive action is not required; that is, we do not all have to act together. The individual who concludes that it is better to share with the whales can follow his own conscience and give through a cetacean society. Those who conclude otherwise need not.

That does not mean that as a moral community we should not work toward a higher, even if ultimately imperfect, consensus on progressively better answers. The very process of working in that direction may itself be viewed as a valued element of a good society. But at any point in time, perhaps at all times, there will be some range of honest and rational differences.

---

*"It is certain that God sets greater store by a man than a lion; nevertheless it can hardly be said with certainty that God prefers a single man in all respects to the whole of lion-kind." Leibniz, *Theodicy*, §118, trans. E. M. Hoggard (New Haven: Yale University Press, 1952).

HOW DO WE SELECT PLANES?

Suppose that we acknowledge the validity of an indeterminate number of moral planes, of Pluralism in principle. How do we decide which planes to "buy into"? What *things* do we map as mere resources from whose (what's) point of view? Which of the many possible governance arrangements operates across which planes? And in the context of any decision, what are the right planes to bring to bear? These are the questions upon which the whole enterprise stands, and they are certainly the hardest to answer.

To start, we have to make a fundamental distinction between ordinary analyses that proceed *within* a plane and extraordinary analyses *about* planes, such as in selecting which plane to employ and in formulating procedures for disposing of inconsistent indications. On the ordinary, internal analysis, the aim is to arrive at the judgment indicated by reference to the outlook, the entities, the principles, and the logical texture embedded in the plane selected. But in the extraordinary tasks, when we are structuring each of several valid planes, and electing which plane to bring out on a particular occasion, the style of analysis and argument shift radically. Whether to embrace a utilitarianism that deems only Persons considerate, or one that extends to all contemporary sentient creatures, or yet another that extends considerateness to future creatures as well—that is a decision that lies external to the planes themselves. There is an obvious analogy in the selection of a geometry: within a Euclidean, Lobachevskian, or Riemannian system, analysis proceeds, rather tidily, according to the postulates.* But which geometry is "right" for which activities—which of them works for astronomy and which for architecture? Whatever else can be said on that score, it is clear that the answer is not to be found *within* geometry.

The same is true in morals. Fabricating and selecting the right moral plane cannot be disposed of by reference to the principles and other

---

*Euclid's geometry was built upon the assumption that parallel lines will never meet no matter how far extended. Lobachevsky and others constructed an alternate, but equally logical and consistent, geometry on the postulate that through a point not on a given line no line can be drawn that will intersect it. Riemann's postulate was that all lines intersect.

elements that endow a plane with its character, enabling us to carry out an internal analysis. Nor are these contests to be refereed by the familiar tests of truth such as we use to validate statements about the distance to the moon or the color of a car. No simple formula about truth is available when we ascend to the level of selecting a version of the world for scientific purposes, that is, in deciding whether and in what form to posit matter, space, energy, time, and their relationships.[12] All the more in morals should we expect truth to be supplemented with other, overlapping notions: from coherence, perspicacity, fittingness, and elegance, all the way to intuitions about fairness and justice. On some fundamental level, to embrace a framework that ontologizes lakes and declares that they count is no more problematical than to embrace one that ontologizes persons and declares that they count.

We do not have to dismiss as "intuitive" the way we handle issues like these, where intuition is regarded as a conversation stopper, the introduction of a barrier that further analysis cannot penetrate. It is just that these "big" questions lie outside the province of academic and legal philosophy, which are more at home working *within* or talking *about* planes. When we turn to the selection of planes—what things, as bundled in what governance, count?—we are removed to another jurisdiction in which our minds operate less by appeals to consistency than by provocations of irony and even humor. Here the dynamic involves the demonstration of buried contradictions in our lives, rather than of inconsistency among our ideas. Emotion has more legitimate rein (or reign); suppressed feeling and insight are released and mobilized. That is why the planar choices, those that go to the ground rules of each plane and the whole assembly of planes, are less under the sway of the stuff we academics do than of literature, folk songs, war, art, landscape, and poetry. I do not mean to suggest that they are therefore outside the province of intellect. Poetry and literature, obviously, are high forms of intellect; but, rather than to derive "truths," they make them manifest.

Consider one of the major "metaplanar" battles of recent history: racial equality. In the words of the great black essayist W. E. B. Du Bois, the older South was seized with "the sincere and passionate belief that somewhere between men and cattle, God created a tertium quid and called it a Negro."[13] In my terms, dealing with *them* took place on a separate plane of reference. What it took to combine black and white onto one plane, so far as that has been accomplished, has not been moral philosophy alone, although there has certainly been a tradition of principled debate going back to the abolitionists. Equally influential have been novels[14] and a war.[15] The most powerful statement I have ever read for vegetarianism—for a plane that makes animals considerate —was turned out not in philosophy, but in science fiction form.[16] Indeed, there is no reason why we should ignore the influence, even the right influence, of the most brute events: famines, plagues, and natural disasters.[17] Do they, too, not shape our planar commitments, enabling us to discern rights and wrongs that we were not able to see before?

ARE THERE REALLY MORAL ANSWERS? OR EVEN QUESTIONS?

The last issue some will suppose should have been, as it is logically, the first. We have assumed throughout that moral inquiry is worthwhile, that questions about right and wrong are meaningful. But are there any answers that are better than any others? Are there any that are "really right"? This whole book has been predicated upon the conviction that there are some affirmative responses. But is that so?

For my part the answer is yes and no. This is a rejoinder that will appear to be less of a lawyer's hedge if we return to the analogy of causality in science. In one sense causes do not exist in the world, independent of human mental effort. When we "find" that events of one sort are the cause of events of another sort, we are extending into the world a complex intellectual construct, one that implicates our views of physics, biology, or even common sense. We can regard that construct either as Kant did, to be a priori, that is, uncontrollably wired into our way of grasping the world's events. Or, we can regard causality as a product of conscious resolve. On the latter view, science, rational sequential thinking, is committed to causality, not because causes are believed to "exist" in some absolute, mind-independent sense. We commit to causes because science cannot exist without the search for them, without, if you will, rejecting the prospect that everything is haphazard and disconnected.

The same would appear to be true in morals. Either (by analogy to the first view) the search for moral truths is wired into us as a part of the human condition, on the first conception, *which* propositions are morally correct will always be controversial; but we believe there *are* moral truths to pursue for the same reason that our joints bend the way they do: because we are humans and humans are built that way. Or (by analogy to the second view) the search for moral truths is more of a meditated commitment. Probably both views are right, and possibly others as well. In all events, when I counsel searching for right answers regarding our treatment of trees and species, it is not because I believe that those right answers exist mind-independent. Then again, I do not believe that our ethical obligations toward humans have mind-independent validity either. In both cases, when we are committing to causes and to obligations, it is a way of life we are embracing. Those embracements, those ultimate choices, will define us and the planet we live upon.

A Final Prologue

DOGMATISM has no place, least of all in morals. We do not really know how much our judgments of what ought to be are constrained by imperatives of breeding and biology. We do not know the influence in moral development of natural catastrophes and war. We do not know how well we can shake the grip of our culture, even of our language. We are not even sure how hard we should try. All the years of mooting about rights have served only to expand the controversy over what rights are, whether people have them, and how conflicting rights combine with one another and with utility. Our understanding of duties and interests and the nature of "the Good" seems no more satisfactory. How, then, can we dismiss out of hand the suggestion that Nonpersons can be morally considerate, that they deserve some heed that does not immediately boil down to our own interests? That some of our actions toward them can be, if not mandatory or impermissible, at least morally welcome or unwelcome?

I am under no illusion that I have made out a case that will return a unanimous verdict for these unconventional moral clients, for Nonpersons and Things. (How "made out" is the case for our duties to one another?) What I have sought to do is get it past the pleadings. At the present margin of our agreement about and understanding of moral theory, I am not certain how much further it can be advanced. For if someone insists, "Show us your 'land ethic,' " a perfectly legitimate response is, "Tell me first: What is any ethic supposed to look like? How decisive need it be? On what foundation is it bound to rest?"

We are at the point where the enterprise cannot go forward without more thought given to the aims and constraints of moral reasoning in general. These are the questions that need to be faced by everyone with an interest in normative thinking, and not merely by what my human chauvinist friends refer to as the whale kooks and redwood nuts. Nor, of course, is it one for a lawyer to tackle alone. It is a challenge that merits the continued concerted efforts of ethicists, economists, biologists, aestheticians, and anyone who has ever just plain wondered at a river.

Source Notes

CHAPTER 1: A PERSONAL PREFACE

1. 45 So.Cal.L.Rev. 450 (1972). Reprinted in *Should Trees Have Standing?–Towards Legal Rights for Natural Objects* (Los Altos: William Kaufmann, 1974) (hereinafter, *Trees*); revised edition, New York: Avon Books, 1975.

2. Sierra Club v. Hickel, 433 F.2d 24, 32 (9th Cir. 1970).

3. Sierra Club v. Morton, 405 U.S. 727 (1972).

4. Some of the cases referred to are described more fully in the text. Readers interested in obtaining the official titles and citations of all these cases, together with a somewhat more technical treatment, are referred to my article, " 'Should Trees Have Standing?' Revisited: How Far Will Law and Morals Reach? A Pluralist Perspective," *U.S.C. Law Review* 59 (1985):1.

5. Subsequently, Walt Disney Enterprises, in the face of the court suit, and perhaps distracted by some intracorporate goings-on, withdrew its interest in the development project.

6. *See* Animal Welfare Institute v. Kreps, 7 Environmental Law Reporter 20,617 (D.C. Cir. 1977), reversing Animal Welfare Institute v. Richardson, 7 Environmental Law Reporter 20,073 (D.D.C. 1976). One of the principal post-*Morton* cases relied upon by the appeals court was United States v. Students Challenging Regulatory Agency Procedures (SCRAP), 412 U.S. 669 (1973), in which an unincorporated group of law students were granted standing, notwithstanding their tenuous interest, (and, indeed, the tenuousness of their whole position) to challenge freight rate increases that the Interstate Commerce Commission approved without requiring the carriers to file impact statements assessing the impact of the new rate structure on the environment. Although granted standing, the students ultimately lost on the merits.

7. Both the trial court and the court of appeals passed over the difficult issue of standing with the bland, untroubled conclusion that "plaintiffs have a clear right

to relief." American Cetacean Society v. Baldridge, 604 F.Supp. 1398, 1411 (D.D.C. 1985) and American Cetacean Society v. Baldridge, 768 F.2d 426, 444 (D.C. Cir. 1985). The United States Supreme Court reversed by a 5–4 vote, sub nom., Japanese Whaling Association v. American Cetacean Society, 106 Sup.Ct. 2860 (1986).

8. These include the Outer Continental Shelf Lands Act (OCSLA) and the Federal Water Pollution Control Act (FWPCA).

CHAPTER 2: MORALS MATTER

1. See Charles A. Walker, Leroy C. Gould, and Edward J. Woodhouse, *Too Hot to Handle? Social and Policy Issues in the Management of Radioactive Wastes* (New Haven: Yale University Press, 1983), p. 62.

CHAPTER 3: THE HISTORICAL LEGACY

1. The dichotomy presented here in the text between Persons and Nonpersons is essentially congruous with, but should be distinguished from, similar dichotomies enlisted by other writers. For example, Kant suggested a twofold division for the world between "rational beings," which he identified with persons, and things. Persons were beings whose nature marked them out as ends in themselves. Things were beings or objects that could only be instrumental to the well-being of persons. Immanuel Kant, *Groundwork of the Metaphysics of Morals*, 3d ed., trans. and ed. H. J. Paton (New York: Harper Torchbooks, 1964), p.68. Later in the text, my own division unfolds into a trichotomy consisting of Persons, Nonpersons, and Things. I introduce the term *Things* to designate the subclass of Nonpersons such as trees and rivers that have no interests or preferences, as opposed to "higher" Nonpersons such as *homo sapiens* of the remote future and chimpanzees.

2. Mullick v. Mullick, L.R. 52 Ind. App. 245 (Privy Council 1925).

3. Quoted in Edward Westermarck, *The Origins and Development of the Moral Ideas*, 2 vols., (London; New York: Macmillan, 1906–8), 1:51.

4. Act of June 16, 1980, ch. 182, 1980 Cal.Stat. 402, 403. The case was finally disposed of in Smith v. Avazino, No.225,698 (San Francisco Super. Ct. June 17, 1980).

5. See Tom Regan's excellent book, *The Case for Animal Rights*, (Berkeley: University of California Press, 1984), chap. 1.

CHAPTER 4: PRESSURES ON THE PERSONS FRAMEWORK

1. Protocol I Additional to the Geneva Convention of 1949, and Relating to the Protection of Victims of International Armed Conflicts Opened for Signature

on December 12, 1977, 16 *International Legal Materials* 1391 (1977), Article 35.3. Of course, some environmental devastation can be opposed because of the indirect effects on humans, not for the sake of the environment as such. But it appears that instrumental protection is covered separately under Article 55.1, which also mandates that "care shall be taken to protect the natural environment" which in that section specifically includes "such [environmental] damage" as would "prejudice the health or survival of the population." Attacks against the natural environment by way of reprisals are also prohibited under the provisions of Article 55.2. Both the United States and the Soviet Union are among the more than forty nations signatory to the related Environmental Modification Convention of 1977 (ENMOD). See Arthur H. Westing, ed., *Environmental Warfare* (London: Taylor & Francis, 1984).

2. If we liken an advanced A.I. to an immature child, then the imposition of liability on the manufacturer of the A.I. could conceivably raise constitutional objections. In 1971 the Georgia Supreme Court held unconstitutional a state statute imposing parental liability for the "wilful and wanton acts" of a minor.

3. The robot "murder" of the Michigan worker is reported in the *Wall Street Journal*, April 21, 1985, p. 1, col. 5; and more fully described in James W. Collins, Lee H. Sanderson, and James D. McGlothlin, "Death by Robot," *Business and Society Review* 54 (Summer 1985), pp. 56–59. A question of robot legal status has emerged in, of all places, the tax context. In response to a proposal that worker-replacing robots be required to pay federal income taxes, "[t]reasury points out that inanimate objects are not required to file income tax returns." Tax Notes, Oct. 1, 1984, p. 20 (reference doc. 84-6442).

4. I spell out some of these proposals in *Where the Law Ends* (New York: Harper & Row, 1975).

5. See Jeanne McDermott, "Biologists Begin Eavesdropping on 'Talking' Trees," *Smithsonian*, December 1984, p. 84.

6. Paul W. Taylor, *Respect For Nature: A Theory of Environmental Ethics* (Princeton: Princeton University Press, 1986).

CHAPTER 6: LEGAL CONSIDERATENESS

1. *See* Summerfield v. Superior Court of the State of Arizona, Supreme Court of Arizona, April 24, 1985. *And see* MacDonald v. Time, Inc., 554 F.Supp. 1053 (D.C. N.J. 1983) (libel suit not mooted by plaintiff's death).

2. See footnote, p. 45.

3. 456 F.Supp. 1327 (D.Puerto Rico 1978), *aff'd* 628 F.2d 652 (1st Cir. 1979).

4. 628 F.2d 652, at 674 (1st Cir.1979)

5. 437 U.S. 153 (1978).

6. See p. 10. Some of the legislation referred to there includes ceilings on recovery, damages being limited to $50 million per incident.

7. See Christopher D. Stone, "A Slap on the Wrist for the Kepone Mob," *Business and Society Review* 22 (Summer 1977): 4–11.

8. Committee for Humane Legislation v. Richardson, 540 F.2d 1141, 1151, n. 39 (C.A. D.C. 1976).

9. California Civil Code § 989(a)(3)(c). See footnote, p. 45.

CHAPTER 7: THE NONPERSON IN A POSITION OF LEGAL
DISADVANTAGE

1. See "Pampered Dog on Trial for His Life in Woman's Death," Los Angeles *Times*, January 17, 1985, pt. 1, p. 22, cols. 3–6; "Prize Dog Spared in Death of Woman, 87," Los Angeles *Times*, January 23, 1985, pt. 1, p. 4, cols. 1–3.

2. Los Angeles *Times*, Sept. 24, 1983, pt. 1, p. 10, col. 1.

3. *Laws* 9:873, as cited in Edward Westermarck, *Origins and Development of the Moral Ideas* 1:254.

4. Martinego-Cesaresco, *Essays in the Study of Folksongs*, quoted in Westermarck, *Origins and Development of the Moral Ideas* 1:254–55.

5. 43 U.S. (2 How.) 210 (1844).

6. Robert E. Conot, *Justice at Nuremberg* (New York: Harper & Row, 1983), p. 19. Conot reports defendant Von Papen as saying that Hitler should have been the chief defendant at Nuremberg, "even though he was dead" (p. 507). The prosecution's principal reservation was that naming Hitler "might generate rumours of his survival." Justice Jackson, the chief prosecutor, ultimately decided "there was no point in trying a dead man," dropped Hitler, and replaced him in the indictment with Papen (pp. 26–27).

7. Adam Smith, *The Theory of Moral Sentiments* (London; New York: Oxford University Press, 1976), p. 95.

CHAPTER 8: MORAL CONSIDERATENESS

1. P. S. Elder, "Legal Rights for Nature—The Wrong Answer to the Right(s) Question," *Osgood Hall Law Journal* 22 (1985): 285, 288.

2. See Arne Naess, "The Shallow and the Deep, Long-Range Ecology Movement: A Summary," *Inquiry* 16 (1973): 95; Bill Devall and George Sessions, *Deep Ecology: Living as if Nature Mattered* (Layton, Utah: Peregrine Smith Press, 1985).

3. Conceivably, the adjustment could be down as well as up. On moral reflection we might disvalue some object, deeming it worth less than people are willing to pay.

4. The agent-patient distinction is Tom Regan's in *The Case for Animal Rights*, pp. 151–56 and passim.

5. Joel Feinberg, "The Rights of Animals and Unborn Generations," in *Philosophy and Environmental Crisis*, ed. William T. Blackstone (Athens: University of Georgia Press, 1978), p. 51.

CHAPTER 9: UNORTHODOX MORAL VIEWPOINTS

1. See John Passmore, "Conservation," in *Responsibilities to Future Generations: Environmental Ethics*, ed. Ernest Partridge (Buffalo: Prometheus Books, 1981), pp. 49, 51. ("The uncertainty of the harms [to future generations] we are hoping to prevent would, in general, entitle us to ignore them.") Martin Golding, putting forward as a basis for moral relations the sharing of a common conception of the good, discounts the more remote on the grounds that we are increasingly less confident about "what we ought to desire for them." Golding, "Obligations to Future Generations," *ibid.*, pp. 61, 70.

2. See Talbot Page, "Intergeneration Justice as Opportunity" (California Institute of Technology Working Paper 389, June 1981), pp. 35–58; a version of this paper appears in *Energy and the Future*, ed. Douglas MacLean and Peter G. Brown (Totowa, N.J.: Rowman and Littlefield, 1983).

3. See Larry Tribe, "Ways Not to Think About Plastic Trees: New Foundations for Environmental Law," *Yale Law Journal* 83 (1974): 1315, 1327.

4. Brian Barry, "Circumstances of Justice and Future Generations," in *Responsibilities to Future Generations*, p. 243.

5. Feinberg, "The Rights of Animals and Unborn Generations," pp. 64–65.

6. It is interesting to consider how far from interhuman conduct the concept of "sin" may extend. See "Japan and the Sin Against Whales," *New York Times*, August 15, 1984, pt. 1, p. 22, col. 1 (arguing for reform in the whale treaties from consideration, I gather, of sinned-against whales).

7. See "Before You Squash that Bug, Be Sure It Isn't One We Need," *Wall Street Journal*, Oct. 5, 1983, p. 1, col. 4.

8. Joel Feinberg, "Legal Moralism and Free-Floating Evils," *Pacific Philosophical Quarterly* 61 (1980): 122, 135.

9. Immanuel Kant, *The Metaphysical Principles of Virtue*, trans. James W. Ellington (Indianapolis: Bobbs-Merrill, 1964), pp. 105–6.

10. John Finnis, *Natural Law and Natural Rights*, (Oxford: Clarendon Press, 1980).

11. *Ibid.*, pp. 68–69.

12. *Trees*, p. 43.

13. Paul W. Taylor, *Respect for Nature* (Princeton: Princeton University Press, 1986). Taylor would prefer "inherent" to "intrinsic."

14. This sort of pyramidal interdependency was to form the basis for the "land

ethic" Aldo Leopold suggested in *A Sand County Almanac*, (New York: Ballantine Books, 1970), p. 252.

15. The classic work situating these concerns in the intellectual tradition is Roderick Nash, *Wilderness and the American Mind*, 3d ed. (New Haven: Yale University Press, 1982). For the philosophic side, see Kenneth W. Goodpaster, "On Being Morally Considerable," *Journal of Philosophy* 75 (1978): 308; Goodpaster argues that having rationality and sentience are too narrow a basis for moral considerateness, and that the line should be drawn at being alive. W. Murray Hunt, "Are Mere Things Morally Considerable?" *Environmental Ethics* 2 (1980): 59, challenges Goodpaster on the basis that if having interests, etc., is an arbitrary stopping point, as Goodpaster maintains, then there is no reason to stop at being alive, rather than "the condition of *being in existence.*" Goodpaster rejoins in "On Stopping at Everything," *Environmental Ethics* 3 (1980): 281, that he has committed no *reductio ad absurdum*, that the considerateness of some inanimate objects is *"simply incoherent"* (his italics). I seek to make a place for some inanimates through a more expansive definition of the moral realm. I do this in part by including as moral some considerations that are at the borderline of what Goodpaster considers to be aesthetic. See also Andrew Brennan, "The Moral Standing of Natural Objects," *Environmental Ethics* 6 (1984): 35; Scott Lehmann, "Do Wildernesses Have Rights?" *Environmental Ethics* 3 (1981): 129; Dieter Birnbacher, "A Priority Rule for Environmental Ethics," *Environmental Ethics* 4 (1982): 3.

16. Donald H. Regan, "Duties of Preservation," in *The Preservation of Species*, ed. Bryan G. Norton and Henry Shue (Princeton: Princeton University Press, 1986).

17. E. H. Gombrich, *The Story of Art*, 13th ed. (Oxford: Phaidon Press, 1972), pp. 105–8.

18. The advance from prudence to altruism is examined in Tom Nagel, *The Possibility of Altruism* (Princeton: Princeton University Press, 1970), p. 79.

19. Albert Schweitzer, *Out of My Life and Thought: An Autobiography* (New York: Holt, Rinehart and Winston, 1961), pp. 158–59.

20. *Trees*, p. 105.

21. "Nakasone Apologizes for WW II," Los Angeles *Times*, October 24, 1985, pt. 1, p. 14, cols. 1–3.

22. Compare the analogous treatment of a Thing's legal essence in chap. 6.

23. *See* Feminist Women's Health Center, Inc., v. Philobosian, 157 Col. App.3d 1076, 203 Cal. Rptr. 918 (1984), *cert. denied* 105 S.Ct. 1752 (1985) (prohibiting, on grounds of unlawful establishment of religion, plans by the county district attorney to arrange religious burial services for fetal tissue scheduled for disposal).

24. See, for example, Regan, *The Case for Animal Rights*.

CHAPTER 10: MORAL MONISM

1. Richard B. Brandt, *Ethical Theory* (Englewood Cliffs, N.J.: Prentice-Hall, 1959), p. 5. Contrast David Wiggins, who, complaining about "the dragooning of the plurality of goods into the order of an axiom system," asks,

Why is an axiom system any better foundation for practice than, e.g., a long and incomplete or open-ended list of (always at the limit conflicting) *desiderata?* The claims of all *beliefs* (about how the world is) are reconcilable. Everything true must be consistent with everything else that is true. But not all the claims of all rational concerns or even all moral concerns (that the world *be* thus or so) need be reconcilable. There is no reason to expect they would be; and Aristotle gives at 1137b [of the *Nicomachean Ethics*] the reason why we cannot expect to lay down a decision procedure for adjudication in advance between claims, or for prior mediation. (Wiggins, "Deliberation and Practical Reason," in *Essays On Aristotle's Ethics*, ed. Amelie O. Rorty [Berkeley: University of California Press, 1980] p. 239, n. 8 [emphasis in original])

2. See J. C. Smart and Bernard P. Williams, *Utilitarianism, For and Against* (Cambridge: Cambridge University Press, 1973), which pits a utilitarian against a deontologist in just such a thoughtful exchange.

3. Historically, there have been occasional proponents of plural, possibly conflicting, goods, Isaiah Berlin believed a society's political structure, to be good, required a tolerant accounting for the citizenry's good-faith belief in conflicting moral goods. But Berlin did not directly examine the case that there might be plural goods in fact. His position seems to have been that social institutions ought to account for the diversity of beliefs. See Isaiah Berlin, *Two Concepts of Liberty* (Oxford: Clarendon Press, 1958). Mark Platts sketches the case for a pluralistic ethical intuitionism that he regards as "austerely realistic," and conformable to his general views on semantics and epistemology. Mark Platts, *Ways of Meaning* (London: Routledge & Kegan Paul, 1979), especially chap. 10. And there are sympathies for Pluralism in the Aristotelian tradition, as expounded by David Wiggins, "Deliberation and Practical Reason." Robert Nozick examined one facet of Pluralism early in his career; see "Moral Complications and Moral Structures," *Natural Law Forum* 13 (1966): 1. Michael Walzer, *Spheres of Justice: A Defense of Pluralism and Equality* (New York: Basic Books, 1983) advances a notably congenial Pluralism, but essentially limited to distributive justice among (in my usage) Persons. I do not doubt that others, more familiar with the philosophy literature than I, will think of further examples.

4. John Rawls, *A Theory of Justice* (Cambridge: Harvard University Press, 1971). Robert Nozick conjectures the possibility of "utilitarianism for animals,

Kantianism for people," but does not appear particularly inclined to pursue the implications. *Anarchy, State, and Utopia* (New York: Basic Books, 1974), pp. 39–40.

5. Williams, in Smart and Williams, *Utilitarianism*, pp. 135–36.

6. Contra Williams, whatever animated Bentham originally, and whatever was his main thrust, Bentham did advance utilitarianism as a principle of morality generally, and not of legislation alone, as the title *An Introduction to the Principles of Morals and Legislation* suggests.

7. Peter Singer, *Animal Liberation* (New York: Random House, 1975) represents the most prominent effort to bring animals into an extended, what he calls "preference," utilitarianism, reinforced with a concept of equality.

8. Tom Regan's nonutilitarian defense of animal rights aims to avoid just such limits as he claims to find in Singer's work. See Regan, *The Case for Animal Rights*.

9. A contractarian of a Rawlsian sort, although not technically trading places with someone else, has to place "himself" under such constraints of knowledge, etc., that the intellectual move he is obligated to perform comes close to the same thing.

CHAPTER 11: CALLING MORAL MONISM TO QUESTION

1. Thomas S. Kuhn, *The Copernican Revolution* (New York: Random House, 1957); *The Structure of Scientific Revolutions* (Chicago: University of Chicago Press, 1961).

2. "The Sentiment of Rationality," in *The Will to Believe and Other Essays*, ed. Henry Burkhardt (Cambridge: Harvard University Press, 1956), p. 65.

CHAPTER 12: FOUNDATIONS FOR MORAL PLURALISM

1. Otherwise, Rawls imagines, each person, as a rational egoist, will favor institutional arrangements favoring his own strengths and weaknesses. Rawls, *A Theory of Justice*, pp. 136–42.

2. "Most of the actions that we perform are neither right nor wrong, good nor bad. They fall, rather, within the zone of moral indifference." James S. Fishkin, *The Limits of Obligation*, 20 (New Haven: Yale University Press, 1982), p. 20.

3. Stephen Toulmin, "The Tyranny of Principles," *Hastings Report* 11 (1981): 30, 35.

4. Thomas Nagel, "What Is It Like to Be a Bat?" *Philosophical Review* 83 (1974): 435. Nagel concludes that what the experiences of a bat are *really* like lies beyond our ken, but that in the last analysis the same opacity affects our efforts to comprehend other humans' experiences in their subjective aspects.

5. The best treatment of this distinction is Birnbacher, "A Priority Rule for Environmental Ethics."

6. See Friedrich Waismann, "Language Strata" and "Verifiability," in *Logic and Language*, ed. Anthony Flew (New York: Anchor Books, 1965), pp. 226–47, 122–51.

7. See pp. 196–97.

8. Problems of open texture aside.

9. See p. 196.

10. Hilary Putnam, *Reason, Truth, and History* (Cambridge: Cambridge University Press, 1981), p. 130.

11. Ibid. Compare Nelson Goodman, *Ways of Worldmaking* (Indianapolis: Hackett Publishing, 1978), pp. 3, 120ff. Goodman holds "truth" to be neither necessary nor sufficient in selecting versions of the world. The idea has origins in Dewey, if not in even earlier pragmatists.

CHAPTER 13: THE LOGICS OF MORAL DISCOURSE: PRESCRIPTIONS

1. Jim Robbins, "Do Not Feed the Bears?" *Natural History*, January 1984, pp. 12, 14–16.

2. See Goodman, *Ways of Worldmaking*, pp. 7–17.

3. A richer notation can indicate whether the prescription applies universally, i.e., whether it enjoins all moral agents so to act, or applies to some indicated subset of actors, e.g., policemen only. To simplify the presentation in the text, the distinction is not specified.

4. Garrett Hardin, "Living on a Lifeboat," in *Religion for a New Generation*, 2d. ed., ed. Jacob Needleman, A. K. Bierman, and James A. Gould (New York: Macmillan, 1977).

5. See Bernard Williams' efforts to distinguish consequentialism "from anything else" in J. J. C. Smart & Bernard Williams, *Utilitarianism: For and Against*, (Cambridge: Cambridge University Press, 1973), pp. 82–93.

6. See "Reducing the Likelihood of Future Human Activities That Could Affect Geologic High-level Waste Repositories" (Battelle Memorial Inst., Human Interference Task Force, 1984).

7. Amitarya K. Sen, "Rights and Agency", *Philosophy and Public Affairs* 11 (1982): 3, 7–9.

8. Whether a utilitarian can extricate herself from such an unwelcome commitment by adopting rule utilitarianism, as Rawls once proposed, seems highly problematical. See Rawls, "Two Concepts of Rules," *Philosophy Review* 64 (1955): 3; John Mackie, *Ethics* (New York: Penguin, 1977), pp. 136–38.

9. Brandt, *Ethical Theory*, p. 173

10. Ibid., p. 18 (emphasis in original).

11. I adopt the term from Georg Henrik Von Wright, *Norm and Action* (London: Routledge & Kegan Paul, 1963), p. 147. Von Wright's work is the seminal effort to investigate the character of deontic logic.

12. See footnote, p. 162.

13. I adopt the term, and am indebted in some of the analysis that follows, to my colleague Matt Spitzer's seminal employment of social choice literature to attack problems involving the combining of *criteria* (desiderata), rather than, as in the conventional literature, the combining of *voters* (desirers). See Matthew L. Spitzer, "Multicriteria Choice Processes: An Application of Public Choice Theory to Bakke, the F.C.C., and the Courts," *Yale Law Journal* 88 (1979): 717.

14. See Finnis, *Natural Law and Natural Rights*, pp. 92–93.

15. See Nicholas Rescher, "The Allocation of Exotic Life-saving Therapy," *Ethics* 79 (1969): 173.

16. *Nicomachean Ethics*, 1094(b).

CHAPTER 14: CHARACTER AND OTHER ATTRIBUTES

1. Although not wholly; most notably, much of John Rawls's work—for example, *A Theory of Justice*—and much of the social choice literature, is concerned with evaluating institutional arrangements.

2. Edmund Pincoffs, "Quandary Ethics," *Mind* 81 (1971): 552.

3. See Williams, in Smart and Williams, *Utilitarianism;* pp. 98–99.

4. Ibid., p. 99.

5. David Riesman, *The Lonely Crowd* (New Haven: Yale University Press, 1961). pp. 13–25

6. See Joseph S. Needham, *Science and Civilization in China*, 2 vols. (Cambridge: Cambridge University Press, 1956), 2:521–22.

7. See Laurence G. Thompson, *Chinese Religion*, 3d ed. (Belmont, Cal.: Wadsworth, 1979), p. 15, regarding these attributes as aims of Chinese "concentration upon character building."

8. I use "normal science" in Kuhn's sense, that is, activity within an accepted paradigm. Thomas S. Kuhn, *The Structure of Scientific Revolutions* (Chicago: University of Chicago Press, 1962), pp. 23–34. In choosing between frameworks or paradigms the role of aesthetics in the broad sense—in favoring the more "elegant" solution—remains.

9. Platts, *Ways of Meaning*, p. 218.

10. Frank Sibley, "Aesthetic Concepts," in *Philosophy Looks at the Arts*, rev. ed., ed. Joseph Margolis (Philadelphia: Temple University Press, 1978), p. 68.

11. Arlene Croce, *Afterimages* (New York: Vintage, 1979), p. 76.

12. Ibid., p. 44.

CHAPTER 15: THE UTILITY PLANES

1. We put aside here the fact that under present treaties and law, the killing and commercial marketability of the bowhead is restricted.

2. See p. 78.

3. Jeremy Bentham, *Introduction to the Principles of Morals and Legislation*, 2 vols., (1789; rpt. London: E. Wilson, 1823), pp. 235–36.

4. See pp. 39–40, and 86–87.

5. See Peter Singer, *Practical Ethics*, (Cambridge: Cambridge University Press, 1979), pp. 264–73.

6. See Finnis, *Natural Law and Natural Rights*, chap. 6, in which Finnis advances concepts of Aristotle and Aquinas on the good of a community, understood independent of modern notions of utility.

7. See Brian Barry, "Humanity and Justice in Global Perspective", in *Ethics, Economics, and the Law*, vol. 24 of *Nomos*, ed. J. Roland Pennock and John W. Chapman, (New York: N.Y.U. Press 1982):219–52.

CHAPTER 16: THE NONUTILITY PLANES

1. See pp. 76–79.

2. The Inupiat, although in some ways culturally removed, are voting U.S. citizens within U.S. jurisdiction.

3. See Priit J. Visilind, "Hunters of the Lost Spirit," *National Geographic*, February 1983, pp. 150–51 (photograph); and p. 237 of this book.

4. For an effort to flesh out personhood as a guide to the treatment of inmates, see "Creatures, Persons, and Prisoners," *Southern California Law Review* 55 (1982): 1099, 1118–21, 1131. The student author, Samuel M. Pillsbury, draws some analogies to the law's recognition of obligations owed animals but not obligations of quite the strength of those owed humans.

5. See pp. 85–89.

6. Singer, *Animal Liberation*, pp. 3–7.

7. See J. E. Lovelock, *Gaia: A New Look at Life on Earth* (Oxford: Oxford University Press, 1979).

8. Ibid., p. 31.

9. 620 F.2d 1159 (6th Cir.), *cert. denied*, 449 U.S. 953 (1980).

10. See p. 54.

11. See p. 32.

12. Readers who wish to see a comparative analysis carried out in the criminal justice field might refer to the author's "A Comment on Criminal Responsibility in Government," in *Criminal Justice*, vol. 27 of *Nomos*, ed. Pennock and Chapman, pp. 241–56.

13. See Cohen, "Moral Skepticism and International Relations," *Philosophy and Public Affairs* 13 (1984):304.

14. Ibid., p. 330.

15. Louis Henkin, *How Nations Behave* (New York: Columbia University Press, 1979), p. 86.

16. *U.N. Reports of International Arbitral Awards* 3 (1949):1905, 1965.

17. K. B. Hoffman, "State Responsibility in International Law and Transboundary Pollution Injuries," *International and Comparative Law Quarterly* 25 (1976):- 509, 515–16.

18. See *Selected Writings and Speeches of Alexander Hamilton*, ed. Morton J. Frisch (Washington: American Enterprise for Public Policy Research, 1985), pp. 404–7

19. See chap. 9.

20. *See* Mashpee Tribe v. Town of Mashpee, 447 F.Supp. 940, 943, 950 (D. Mass. 1978), *aff'd sub nom.*, Mashpee Tribe v. New Seabury Corp., 592 F.2d 575 (1st Cir. 1979) (suit brought in tribal name to recover lands allegedly alienated in violation of Indian Nonintercourse Act; held: barred, in part of finding that Mashpee did not continuously exist as a tribe up to and including institution of action in 1976, because of the members' altered life-style and language); cf. Lilly-Marlene Russow, "Why Do Species Matter?" *Environmental Ethics* 3 (1981): 101, 104–5, in which Russow indicates the ambiguity and conventional basis of judgments as to what is a species.

21. They may not be far from it. See Visilind, "Hunters of the Lost Spirit," pp. 150–51 (note the photograph of the Eskimo whale hunter). Paul Ehrlich and Ann Ehrlich, *Extinction: The Causes and Consequences of the Disappearance of Species* (New York: Random House, 1981), pp. 188–89, point out how modern technology has amplified the natives' kill rate. They consider the long history of commercial whaling by the advanced nations as having been a more severe threat to the species, "from which the population apparently still has not recovered" (p. 189). Should the Indians pay for non-Indian sins? Moreover, if alteration in the tribe's patterns is to count against tribal claims on a "dilution" theory, is it appropriate to count changes that we *forced upon* the Indians, e.g., non-Indian language, schooling, and religion?

22. See pp. 89–98.

CHAPTER 17: A META-ETHICAL UNWINDING

1. Alasdair MacIntyre, *After Virtue* (Notre Dame, Ind.: Notre Dame University Press, 1981), pp. 19–20. The view is not MacIntyre's, but one that he identifies as having emerged in response to certain developments in modern philosophy.

2. Kuhn, *Structure of Scientific Revolutions*, pp. 10–11, 43–44. Note that Kuhn offers the paradigm, rather than rules, as the fundamental unit of science on the grounds that "paradigms can guide research even in the absence of rules" (p. 42). The same appears true of the planes.

3. See Michael S. Moore, "The Moral Worth of Retribution," in *New Dimensions in Responsibility*, ed. F. Schoenman (Cambridge: Cambridge University Press, 1987.

4. Of course, this is not universally true. R. M. Hare gives the imagination its due; see *Freedom and Reason* (New York: Oxford University Press, 1965), pp. 94, 126–28, 181–85; and Hilary Putnam has observed (in comments upon the place of literature) that "sensitive appreciation in the imagination of predicaments and perplexities must be essential to sensitive moral reasoning." Hilary Putnam, *Meaning and the Moral Sciences* (Boston: Routledge & Kegan Paul, 1978), p. 87.

5. H. H. Price, *Belief* (London: George Allen & Unwin 1969), pp. 401–2.

6. See pp. 132–33.

7. See generally Michael S. Moore, "Moral Reality," *Wisconsin Law Review* (1982): 1061, expanded in M. Moore, *The Semantics of Judging* (Oxford: Clarendon Press, 1987).

8. "The Tyranny of Principles," pp. 30, 31–32.

9. Chap. 13.

10. In 1979 the Indians were allowed either eighteen whales to be killed or twenty-seven to be struck. See Ehrlich and Ehrlich, *Extinction*, p. 189. In 1981, the number of strikes appears to have been reduced to five. Visilind, "Hunters of the Lost Spirit," pp. 150, 167.

11. Putnam, *Meaning and the Moral Sciences*, p. 84 (emphasis in original).

12. See Goodman, *Ways of Worldmaking*, pp. 3, 120–25.

13. W. E. B. Du Bois, *The Souls of Black Folk*, (Chicago: A. C. McClurg & Co., 1903), p. 89.

14. The first that comes to mind is *Uncle Tom's Cabin*, popular legend supposing Lincoln to have greeted Harriet Beecher Stowe as the little lady who started the big war. And the novel tradition continues with the writings of Richard Wright, Ralph Ellison, and James Baldwin, among others. Outside the novel, one of the most powerfully moving antislavery "arguments" that I ever read was presented by Charles Dickens in *American Notes* (New York: Charles Scribner's Sons, 1924). Its most effective portions proceed without any principled appeals at all, indeed, with only the sparsest interjections of the author. Dickens simply reprints an unrelieved torrent of excerpts from slavery-related newspaper stories, advertisements for runaway slaves, and "cash-for-negro" notices, until the reader is either numbed or horrified (see pp. 201–4).

15. The influence of the Civil War was not merely to have imposed upon the

world, by force, one moral view of the world. I am suggesting that what the war symbolized, so many deaths *for that cause,* integrated into social sensibility. Whatever the real mix of historical reasons, "equality" became the answer to the question "Why did so many fight and die?"

16. See Desmond Stewart, "The Limits of Trooghaft," in *Animal Rights and Human Obligations,* ed. Tom Regan and Peter Singer (Englewood Cliffs, N.J.: Prentice-Hall, 1976), p. 238. In a similar vein, I have observed elsewhere that Norman Mailer's *Executioner's Song* (New York: Warner Books, 1980) and the closing of Truman Capote's *In Cold Blood* (New York: Random House, 1965) more effectively fuel arguments against capital punishment than any of the academic literature I have seen. See Christopher D. Stone, "From a Language Perspective," in the "Yale Law Journal Symposium on Legal Education," *Yale Law Journal* 90 (1981): 1149, 1180.

17. It is H. G. Wells, in *Outline of History* (Garden City, N.Y.: Garden City Publishing Co., 1920), pp. 745–47, who credits the great plague with stimulating a reevaluation of social conventions through its impact on the labor market.

Index